Ha... Ch... '94

BRIDGE OF SIGHS

BRIDGE OF SIGHS
Chelsea's 1996 – 97 Season

STEVEN DOWNES

MAINSTREAM
PUBLISHING

EDINBURGH AND LONDON

First published in Great Britain in 1997 by
MAINSTREAM PUBLISHING COMPANY (EDINBURGH) LTD
7 Albany Street
Edinburgh EH1 3UG

ISBN 1 85158 940 6

A catalogue record for this book is available from the British Library

Typeset in Plantin Light
Printed and bound in Great Britain by Butler and Tanner Ltd, Frome

Acknowledgements

Researching this book has got to have been one of the best and most sought after assignments of any Chelsea-supporting sports journalist's career. I don't want to give the impression that writing a book about a season at Chelsea Football Club was in any way easy . . . (you should note, at this point, that typing with one's fingers crossed is a very tricky skill to acquire).

Along the way, I have been helped by a number of people, some of whom might not thank me for mentioning them here. So I won't – but they ought to know that I appreciate their help, advice and guidance. The reason they remain anonymous may become clear during the course of the book.

It would be wrong to give a false impression of Chelsea's chairman, Ken Bates, as some all-powerful, control-freak ogre. But Mr Bates does control Chelsea. I am reminded of a conversation with Neil Barnett at Chelsea's Harlington training ground early in the new year. Barnett has known me, if not by name then at least my face, from the numerous times that he has provided help and information at Stamford Bridge on matchdays when I have been covering Chelsea games, most usually for *The Sunday Times*. Barnett, as Chelsea matchday programme editor, author of many articles in Chelsea's members' newspaper *Onside*, and the Clubcall reporter, is frequently at the source of all things Chelsea. Indeed, Chelsea publications were frequently points of reference for me in writing the book.

On the staircase leading up to the dining room at Harlington, I buttonholed Barnett. 'I'm writing a book about Chelsea this season, Neil,' I said to him.

'Is it official?' he asked, seeming somewhat startled by the sheer audacity of the venture, or perhaps concerned that no one within the club had informed him.

'What do you mean?' I asked, intrigued by his reaction.

'Has Ken given his permission? Because if it hasn't got the official permission of the club, I can't have anything to do with it.' End of conversation. Barnett, as the press and media's point of reference with the club, wanted nothing to do with an unofficial book about Chelsea.

There were others at the club, though, who did try to help me in the course of compiling material to include between these covers: Graham Bell, Gwyn Williams, the staff in the front office who patiently humoured me while I was kept waiting one afternoon in Cup final week, and Mr Bates himself, who granted me a very important interview, was a polite host, gave up some of his valuable time, was entertaining in his own way, and very informative, both about the club and his own nature.

In conceiving the book, I should like to thank Catherine and Ian for their initial efforts and constant encouragements; Bill Campbell for being good enough to commission the book for Mainstream and John Beaton for patiently guiding me in my usual disorganised manner once more through the editorial process. For their contributions – above all in their patience in putting up with this neurotic seated alongside them throughout the season, but also for their careful checks and observations on the manuscript – thanks are also due to Paul Pope and Mike Boyle.

It is not giving anything away to say that the story the book tells ends in a victory. I was too young to see Chelsea win at Old Trafford in 1970, and my Dad certainly was not going to take me to Athens in 1971. By the time I was independent enough to pay my own way, Chelsea were already well into their gloom years, years that, by the time I saw them lose at Wembley in 1994, seemed as if they might last forever. So when, at last, in May this year, I saw a Chelsea captain lift a trophy for the first time, the success was sweet indeed to savour. Yet I was also reminded of my very first Chelsea match, against Southampton at the Bridge, at a time when football stands were still constructed of wood, which could be made to reverberate by the excited stamping of thousands of season-ticket holders.

Gill, our season ticket-holding downstairs neighbour in Waterloo, could not go that Saturday, so she let us have her tickets. It was not a great match – the only thing I remember is my hero, Ian Hutchinson, being kicked all round the pitch by some Southampton defender – but it was enough, it was a start. So thanks for this book are due, too, to my Dad for taking me that day. It was only many years later that I realised what a sacrifice he made that day, to save me from an even longer period of constant disappointment. My Dad, you see, is a lifelong Millwall fan.

Steven Downes
Croydon, July 1997

Prologue

The teenager was transfixed by what he saw. Looking down from the North Stand, the round-faced youth had already sensed that he was witnessing something very special when the young player out on the pitch had shown his passing skills and footballing vision earlier in the match, but now . . . now he was amazed. What he was seeing was unbelievable. Breath-taking, in the most literal sense: it took his breath away.

Although only 16, the young fan had been going to watch Chelsea games half his life. By now, it was probably the most important thing in his world. Like so many devoted supporters, the teenager knew his football, and he knew *his* Chelsea. And he knew that this fella he was watching was something *very* special.

The Boy Fan had never seen the like of this before. Maybe it was the effect of the floodlights in the half-light that early evening in the spring of 1970, but somehow the new player – immediately The Boy Fan's new hero – seemed to be bathed in the spotlight. Equally, the player seemed to relish the attention. The player was only a few years older than the lad in the stand, but he, too, had always been Chelsea. Now, he was wearing the blue shirt at the Bridge, something he had worked and grafted and fought for. The shirt seemed to glisten when it caught the light, as if touched by star dust, as he glided past first one, then a second opposition defender.

Somehow, the lad in the stands thought, the player was making his way through the defence and directly towards him. With every move that the Chelsea player made, it was as if the players from the other team were stepping aside, out of his way. With the ball at his feet, the player never seemed to have any doubt about the absolute control that he exercised over its path.

Inside the penalty area now, the goalkeeper started to charge towards the ball, as if in slow motion. Watching from the stand, The Boy Fan knew the keeper never stood a chance, he would never get to the ball. His player took barely a glance up, never broke his stride, chose his angle, and slid the ball past the keeper. Goooaaaallll!!!!!

More than a quarter of a century later, The Boy Fan had become a grown man, a husband and father, and a tremendously successful businessman. Chelsea, though, were still among the top three or four things that he took delight in. He still remembered that goal, and the player still had a place in his enthusiastic, boyish affections. Somehow, that goal had drawn the two men closer together, the fan because it had seemed to be special, scored just for him. It had been special for the player, Alan Hudson, too, because it had been the first goal he had scored for Chelsea at their home ground, Stamford Bridge.

Drawn closer together, maybe, but the distance between the professional footballer and his public was often far greater than the simple width of the old dog track which encircled the Stamford Bridge pitch in those days. For many youngsters, the players – their heroes – were untouchable, unreachable gods who trod the turf but whose feet never touched the ground. 'I never felt the need to meet Alan,' the fan recalled some years after seeing *his* goal. 'With that Chelsea shirt on his back I already knew him. He was part of my life, and that was that.

'The pleasure and the pain – Chelsea are both those things to me. It's hard to explain, but like any great love, I don't question it or ever feel tempted to stray. I just know that Chelsea and I were meant for each other.'

The words were Matthew Harding's, the goal recalled and written up for Hudson's autobiography just a few months before the helicopter crash in October 1996 which ended the life of Chelsea's millionaire vice-chairman. For many Chelsea fans, Harding's shocking death ended an expedition into Fantasy Football unlikely ever to be matched. While Harding was involved in the club, anything seemed possible. It probably did seem too good to be true, too good to last. For despite the vast wealth of this self-made man, Harding remained a *fan*, the same lad who had watched in awe from the North Stand all those years before. When Matthew Harding invested in Chelsea Football Club, he did so with no ulterior motive beyond wanting to see his team win, and win with style.

Surely, it was no coincidence that, with Harding's backing, Chelsea managed to progress to the FA Cup final in 1994, the first time they had made it thus far since the glorious days of Osgood, Cooke and Bonetti 24 years earlier, the same year that Harding had sighed and then roared when watching Hudson's first goal at the Bridge. It was Harding's finance and influence which led to the signing of Ruud Gullit from Sampdoria; to the high-profile recruitment of star players such as

Gianluca Vialli and Mark Hughes; and thus to the much-acclaimed style of play adopted in the 1996–97 season which was to win Chelsea friends, not a few matches, and the FA Cup. Chelsea's performances in the season '96–97, culminating in their Wembley triumph, would become the ultimate tribute to the man. Where the 1953 FA Cup final had become known as the 'Matthews Final' because of the role in Blackpool's epic victory of Stan Matthews, the 1997 final was dubbed 'Matthew's Final', in such affection was Harding held by the Chelsea fans.

Football, the sport which used to be known as the 'People's Game' had, by the 1990s, been touched by high finance, TV deals and sponsorship agreements until it seemed often to be little more than the Chairmen's Plaything. At some redeveloped stadiums, including Stamford Bridge, the working-class supporters' flat caps had been replaced by flats, along with penthouse suites and megastores, while the old fans' talk about the time of the goals had been replaced by chatter about time shares, ground shares and ordinary shares.

But for Matthew Harding, his priority was always exactly the same as every other true follower of Chelsea: the performance on the pitch, the result at 4.45 p.m. every Saturday.

Originally, this book was to trace the progress of Chelsea through the 1996–97 season. Because of the events on the evening of 22 October 1996, it is in fact an account of the progress of Matthew Harding's team in Matthew Harding's season.

For the first match after Harding's death, I watched from high at the back of the West Stand. Far down below on the pitch, one of Chelsea's new Italian signings, Roberto di Matteo, won a tackle and quickly passed to Dennis Wise. Something special was happening here, this fan could sense it. Wise passed the ball to The Man. The Man: powerfully built, perhaps not as quick off the mark as in his younger days, but still with a complete control of the ball, the like of which is rarely seen. 'Like watching an 18-year-old playing a game with a bunch of 12-year-olds,' one of his managers had described the way The Man's talents set him apart, dreadlocked head and shoulders above the others on the pitch. Here, The Man laid the ball back down the right to di Matteo and immediately set off himself for the Tottenham penalty area. Now everyone in the stand was on their feet – they, too, could sense that something special was about to happen.

An entire stadium – more than 28,000 people – shared the anticipation, shared the appreciation that something out of the ordinary was about to happen in front of them. They watched as the Italian midfielder took the ball deep into the Tottenham half. Di Matteo's cross was met by Hughes's powerful header, which rebounded off the foot of the post with some force. And there, in a swirl of dreadlocks as he spun around, was The Man to send the ball into the net. Goooaaaallll!!!!!

There were tears in my eyes when Ruud Gullit scored that goal on the Saturday after Matthew Harding's death. Some said that there were tears in Gullit's eyes, too, and that the tears remained there for most of that match. Certainly, there were other grown men around me that day who were in tears as they sang, or yelled, *Matthew Harding's Blue and White Army.* This book, like Gullit's goal, and the whole season, is for Matthew.

Chapter 1

Historians, when categorising periods of time, tend not to resort to using anything so simple as chronology. Mere dates are not enough in the continuum of history: there is a need for more than simply placing events in the order that they happened; the analysts seek causes for events and attempt to offer explanations. So it is that some modern historians regard the 19th Century as ending not on 31 December 1900, but with the outbreak of the First World War 14 years later. For the Great War truly marked the end of an era. The mood of the times, and the structure of society, would never be the same again.

In some respects, the assessment of fine wines often takes a similar approach. For while each vintage is known by the year it was produced, that batch of bottles harvested from one season is merely a reflection of many years' careful viticulture and nurturing of the vines to prepare them for a growing summer which will ultimately yield the precious, perfect fruit of the wine-grower's labours. So it is that the story of Chelsea's season cannot simply begin from the first blast of the referee's whistle on a sun-drenched, sleepy summer's Sunday afternoon in August, when the first game of the 1996–97 season got underway at Southampton. Instead, you need to look for cause and effect, action and reaction, for the time when the seeds were sown. For the genesis of the 1996–97 vintage Chelsea side – a team which would have even the sternest of connoisseurs slavering at their often intoxicating play – you need to look back to a cold, misty Sunday afternoon at the beginning of February 1996, in the middle of an earlier season.

If one can pinpoint an exact moment when one could see the shape of things to come for Chelsea in the 1996–97 season, then this was surely it. The moment was in the second half of a televised Premier League game against Middlesbrough at Stamford Bridge and, despite the cold of the day, every one of the 21,000 spectators there that afternoon was glowing warm inside. Even the 'Boro fans were awed. What they were watching was enough to warm the cockles of the hardest hearts, as Glenn

Hoddle's team produced an exhibition of total football the like of which has rarely been seen in these islands. But then, running the show on the pitch was *the* total footballer, the likes of whom these islands had never seen before: Ruud Gullit, the athletic, dreadlocked Dutchman who possesses unique, all-round football skills. Such skills saw Gullit likened by *FourFourTwo* magazine to having an ability to tackle like Bobby Moore, to pass like Hoddle, the control and dribbling skills of Johan Cruyff and an ability to head the ball like Denis Law.

Chelsea *v* Middlesbrough, 4 February 1996, 5–0. It was as good as it gets. Over the previous two decades, Chelsea, perhaps more than any other team in England, had cultured a reputation for being great under-achievers. In the handy, rent-a-phrase clichés of media commentators, the club from London SW6 might have been regarded as a 'sleeping giant', if only anyone had ever taken the club seriously. Instead, Chelsea were regarded more like dozing cavaliers: pundits would remark of Chelsea's 'flamboyance' when going forward, but this was always disastrously married with an inveterate lack of concentration or discipline in defence. One week, they would look like world-beaters, the next, they would be dumped out of the cup by a Wigan or Cardiff.

So often so much promise, so often so little silverware. If one discounts the Full Members' Cup – hardly the highlight of any other club's honours board – the last trophy Chelsea had won was the European Cup-winners' Cup in 1971. By 1996–97, only anyone aged over 50 could remember Chelsea's League Championship-winning side of 1954–55. By the 1990s, Chelsea fans' perpetual exasperation had turned their home ground, Stamford Bridge, into a Bridge of Sighs.

Yet on this February afternoon, for once, Chelsea produced a performance that had one scribe in the press box include in his next day's match report, 'At the moment, Chelsea could pass for prospective champions'. Chelsea – champions? Even the muttering of such words in close proximity would have normally produced a sharp rebuke and raise doubts about the utterer's sanity. But not here, not now. Chelsea had finally caught a moonbeam.

The warning signs for Middlesbrough were there from the start. Chelsea, marshalled by Gullit, were stringing together moves of ten and 11 passes at a time, the Dutch pass-master hitting the ball 40 and 50 yards up-field with unerring accuracy. Play back a video tape of the Sky TV coverage of the game (if you have not already worn out the tape by repeated re-viewing), and you can almost visualise the saliva running down commentator Andy Gray's chin as he drooled: 'Who said the long ball wasn't pretty?'

Player-coach Hoddle had said that all he wanted from his teams was for them to 'play to a pattern that will create time and space for us. I want my players to support the man on the ball, give him options. Time and space – why make these gifts your enemies?' Here, time and space were the enemies of Middlesbrough, as Gullit's control bought his team mates time, and Terry Phelan and Dan Petrescu – the flying wing-backs brought to the club by Hoddle – revelled in the space this created for them on the flanks. Soon, spaces were appearing in between Middlesbrough defenders wider than the Thames. 'Boro, bewildered, were trying vainly to stem a flood tide, as after half-an-hour's play, Gavin Peacock, John Spencer and then Peacock again breached their defences for goals.

Within ten minutes of the second half Chelsea were five up, Gullit hitting a 50-yard pass which set up Petrescu to make a shimmy into the area and hit a cross for Paul Furlong to score (the first of too few that the £2 million signing from Watford was to score at the Bridge). Then Spencer passed the ball nearly as far to set up Peacock for his hat-trick – the first by a Chelsea player in nearly six years.

During the second-half, Chelsea had strung together one sequence of 16 passes (each blue touch met with a resounding 'Olé!' from the crowd), and the confidence of the side was so overwhelmingly infectious that even Furlong, not a player noted for his deftness of touch, was inspired to try pull-backs and dummies. What's more, his tricks worked.

It was around this time in the match that someone, probably in the members' benches over by the West Stand, started an ironic chorus of 'Robson for England'. In the build-up to this match, it was clear that there would be more to it than just Chelsea v Middlesbrough. It was also Hoddle v Robson, a match between two of the top young managers in the English game, both being actively considered at that time as possible replacements for Terry Venables, the England coach who had announced that after that summer's European championships he was to give up his job with the national team in order to spend more time with his lawyers.

From the moment that 'Robson for England' chant went up from the West Stand benches, it seemed that, if Bryan Robson had any credible prospects of becoming the next England manager, then they were reduced to nothing. Perhaps, as per his public declarations, Robson did not want to take the step up from being Terry Venables' assistant to take on what has been called 'an impossible job'. But had the Middlesbrough boss harboured any secret ambitions of such a promotion, he must have known then that, in the recruitment process, on that afternoon at Stamford Bridge he had just failed the practical exam.

13

For Chelsea fans, full of the joys of such a magnificent performance, any greater significance of the outcome could be ignored. But in a head-to-head test of two of England's most promising young coaches, Chelsea's Glenn Hoddle had clearly emerged as the leading contender. This, of itself, contained an irony. Hoddle was once described as 'the most bounteously gifted footballer of his age'. After seeing the former Spurs player steer Monaco to the French title after just one season playing on the Côte d'Azur, Michel Platini expressed the opinion that if Hoddle had come from anywhere other than England, then he would have been among the greatest of international stars. As it was, Hoddle was born in Hayes, Middlesex.

Like any prophet in their own country, it was only after his playing career had come to an end that Hoddle's skills were truly appreciated in England. One magazine survey rated him the 14th best footballer in the world of all time, just behind Stanley Matthews and Tom Finney in the rankings, but ahead of, among others, Zico, Eusebio and Gazza. Perhaps Hoddle would have been rated higher still had he enjoyed a less fitful international career, which numbered just 52 more England caps in the nine years after he scored on his debut against Bulgaria in 1979. Bryan Robson, meanwhile, a midfield contemporary of Hoddle's who was never criticised for his lack of 'workrate', amassed 90 England caps, often as stalwart captain. Despite the yeoman service, the same magazine survey rated Robson 11 places below Hoddle.

'The manager was prepared to build a side around Bryan Robson and that style of play,' Hoddle was to say once he was seated in the uncomfortable chair reserved for England managers at Lancaster Gate. 'You can only really do what the manager wants you to do.' Hoddle, he of the deft passes and sublime distribution, was never going to be a hard-tackling, box-to-box sort of player like Bryan Robson. But fortunately for Chelsea fans, who had been dreaming of watching an entertaining side, once Hoddle became the manager of their team, he opted for a playing style in his image.

Perhaps it was the style of the victory over Robson's Middlesbrough that gave an extra element of satisfaction for Hoddle that day. As far as the England job was concerned, though, Hoddle was at pains to play down his claims. Mere speculation, he said. The day before the Middlesbrough match, Hoddle's club chairman, Ken Bates, had said, 'Glenn would be an absolute idiot if he were to take the England job.' It was a comment in typically forthright Bates style, though the comment carried an added significance since Bates, as a Football Association council member, would effectively become Hoddle's new employer at Lancaster Gate in a few months' time. If anyone knew what fate might await Hoddle in the England manager's job, then Bates did.

Perhaps Bates already knew, though, in his other role as Hoddle's employer at Chelsea, that his player-manager's time at the Bridge was running out. Certainly, the period of time left on Hoddle's contract at Chelsea was diminishing rapidly, and Bates – entangled in a bitter boardroom feud with his vice-chairman, Matthew Harding – seemed unable, or unwilling, to secure an extension.

With Middlesbrough beaten, and as he walked off the Stamford Bridge pitch that evening to the echoing cheers of the Chelsea faithful, Hoddle's mind was firmly on that day's game. Even he was forced to admit of his Chelsea side that day that 'We were fantastic'. After nearly three years in the job at Chelsea, with an FA Cup final appearance and European Cup-winners' Cup semi-final behind him, Hoddle had at last seen his footballing vision begun to be realised. 'That's the best we've played in the two-and-a-half years I've been at the club,' he said. 'Everything we've been working for is falling into place.'

For some of the older Chelsea fans at the game, who had perhaps brought their own small sons or daughters, their team's play that day had taken them fleetingly back to their own childhood, a time when Charlie Cooke, Peter Osgood and Alan Hudson – the 'Princes of the King's Road' – had made Stamford Bridge the most fashionable, the flashiest club in the Football League. It was a time when Chelsea were a draw to people who appreciated that a football has a greater purpose than merely being a bag of wind to be hoofed from one end of a field to another by various hefty pairs of Size Nines.

Yet even Hoddle, the arch-disciple of a technical, passing brand of football – the 'beautiful game' – had conceded, 'The most beautiful game is winning matches'.

To that end, it had been the arrival at Stamford Bridge six months earlier of Ruud Gullit which would move Hoddle's team closer to his ideal. Gullit's was probably the most significant transfer deal involving Chelsea Football Club since Jimmy Greaves had been sold off at a knock down price to Milan nearly 35 years earlier. For here, in Gullit's arrival from Italy, Chelsea had managed to secure the services of a soccer legend. Gullit was probably the world's second greatest footballer of the late 1980s, after Diego Maradona. In some people's notebooks, Gullit, more disciplined, more professional, more versatile, was even rated ahead of the little Argentinian.

Gullit was the midfield player for whom Milan had once broken all transfer records to sign, paying £6 million in 1987. He, in return, had helped to transform them into one of the greatest club sides in history.

When Milan sold Gullit – believing him to be over-the-hill following three career-threatening knee operations – their owner, Silvio Berlusconi, was forced to admit his club's error when he saw the Dutchman lead the line in Sampdoria's attack as a converted striker, netting 15 goals in the notoriously low-scoring Serie A and winning an Italian Cup-winners' medal.

Thus, in Gullit, here was a former world and (twice) European footballer of the year, someone who had lifted the European Cup and the European Nations' trophy. *And he had signed for Chelsea.*

While few Chelsea fans would openly criticise Hoddle's management, and most were grateful for the modicum of success (albeit near misses) and the style of play he had brought to the club, many were also unhappy with some of their young coach's signings of less obvious quality: Paul Furlong (not good enough), Mark Stein (injury prone), Andy Dow (not up to it) and David Rocastle (unfit) amounted to nearly £5 million-worth of bad business, without even calculating the wage bills these players would rack up while playing in the 'stiffs', unable to get a game in the first team. But Gullit, signed on a free, was more than enough to compensate. As Ross Fraser, the chairman of the Chelsea Independent Supporters' Association, said, 'On the day that the deal was done, every fan in the world had heard of Chelsea Football Club. They knew that that was the name of the club that Ruud Gullit had signed for.'

It was the manner of the deal, struck the previous summer, which was also instructive about the way in which a modern Premiership side such as Chelsea, is run. For the deal was agreed not by the manager, but by the managing director.

Originally, in May 1995, Hoddle had gone to Italy with Chelsea MD Colin Hutchinson to conduct inquiries into the availability of Paul Gascoigne, who was unsettled at Lazio. While there, they learned of the possibility that Gullit might be available as a free agent from Sampdoria. It was ten years since Hoddle had played in a Spurs side which had beaten Feyenoord in the UEFA Cup, but he had never forgotten the impressive performance of the young player the Dutch side had used at sweeper. With his own playing days numbered, Hoddle was searching for someone to play at Chelsea as a sweeper, and in Gullit he felt he had the perfect choice. The only problem was in trying to keep the approach to Gullit a secret from the press. So on the morning Hoddle and Hutchinson were due to fly from Rome to Milan on their 'secret' mission, they were horrified to see the headlines in an Italian newspaper announcing to the world that Gullit was to sign for Chelsea.

After trying to dodge the Milan press corps all afternoon by re-arranging their appointed meeting at hotels and agents' offices, Hoddle and Hutchinson eventually met with the man himself at the headquarters of AC Milan. Hutchinson recalls, 'I asked him, "Who are we negotiating with?" thinking that we would be talking to agents, and he said, "Just me".' Both Englishmen were taken aback: direct transfer dealings with players are virtually unheard of in football today. 'We spoke of nothing but football. Money was never discussed. He was interested in the football side rather than the money,' Hutchinson said.

It was only when they met for the first time in Milan that Hoddle discovered that Gullit, too, was seeking a new challenge, and that he liked the idea of a return to the sweeper's role. 'He asked for time to think it all over,' Hutchinson said, 'and a few days later rang Glenn saying he wanted to talk further, so we had another two-hour meeting in Milan when we discussed terms.'

The phone call that Hoddle and Hutchinson had been waiting on came just a few days later, during a bank holiday weekend as Hutchinson was settling down to watch the Reading–Bolton league promotion play-off game on television. 'By the time we finished talking, Reading were 2–0 up and Gullit had agreed to sign.'

By then, Hoddle was in mid-air above the Atlantic on his way to a family holiday in Florida. When Hoddle turned up to check in at his hotel, there was a message from Hutchinson awaiting him. It read simply: 'The man from Italy has said yes'. When Hoddle read the note – written in the style somewhere between Ian Fleming and the man from Del Monte – his feeling of excitement and anticipation was overwhelming.

There were a number of factors which swung the deal Chelsea's way, rather than seeing Gullit accept a £6 million deal to play in Japan for two years. Gullit, the master midfielder for Holland in the 1988 European championship who had then become a feared forward in Serie A, now saw a chance to round off his career as a defender. 'I can show my skills more there,' Gullit said. 'What gives me the biggest thrill is the successful functioning of the team – passing movements, one-twos, one-touch football in all positions.'

As well as the Japanese offer, Gullit turned down approaches from Galatasaray in Turkey, Bayern Munich, Tottenham, QPR and his old club, Feyenoord. 'The city of London appealed to me more than the port of Rotterdam,' Gullit was to explain. 'As soon as Chelsea turned up on my doorstep and I had met Glenn Hoddle, I knew I wanted to play at Stamford Bridge.'

And then there were the socks. Gullit's decision was also influenced by the socks: 'Chelsea play in white socks,' he said. 'I always win things in white socks.'

If Hoddle was the architect for change at Chelsea, drawing up the blueprint, then Gullit was to be his main contractor, the man who was to come in and build on the foundations. 'Glenn wanted to play a continental system,' chairman Bates observed of the period pre-Gullit, 'but we couldn't play the continental way with the players we had.'

The faltering performances in Hoddle's first season, which saw Chelsea in the Premiership relegation zone after only three League wins before Christmas 1993, was proof that the playing personnel had difficulties rising to the challenge of the new player-manager's favoured 3-5-2 formation (three defenders, five in midfield, and two out-and-out forwards), which utilised three centre-backs and saw the full-backs employed as utility wingers, or wing-backs as they have become known. With injuries and lack of match fitness limiting Hoddle's own availability to play in the crucial sweeper position, and with the club facing the calamity of relegation from the Premiership unless they started winning matches, in the New Year of 1994 he reverted to the more conventionally English formation of 4-4-2. It worked. Chelsea eventually finished safely in mid-table in the Premier League, and also reached their first FA Cup final for 24 years.

When Gullit's signing, on a reputed £16,000 per week wages, was formally presented to the public on 23 June 1995 at a spectacular press conference in Drakes, the club restaurant next to the new North Stand, Hutchinson then audaciously also made a surprise announcement, revealing that Mark Hughes, one of the finest strikers in British football, would be leaving Manchester United for Stamford Bridge for £1.5 million.

Of course the Welshman, at 31 was, like Gullit, at the tail-end of his career, but for Chelsea to sign a player who had so consistently led the line for Barcelona, Bayern Munich and Manchester United (in two spells), it marked a statement of intent. 'When you sign somebody like Ruud Gullit, it is sending out the right signals, to our supporters and his team mates,' Hoddle said. 'It says that the people here are trying to build something, that they are serious, that we want to win something. I've been here for three years and we've come close. But I'm not into transfer coups, I'm into trying to win trophies.'

It was Hoddle – one of Chelsea's 'Three Aitches' in Hoddle, Hughes and Gullit – whose presence in the manager's office had ensured that these top-quality players joined Chelsea. The price of Hoddle's success was the fact that he was soon to become England coach, a move which potentially left a vacuum at Stamford Bridge.

Hoddle's reign at Chelsea had begun with a home defeat to Blackburn, and was to end in the same manner on 5 May 1996, the end of an ultimately disappointing season in which Chelsea had again reached the

FA Cup semi-final but, despite taking a first-half lead against Manchester United (through a Gullit header from a Mark Hughes cross), they were beaten and had again failed to lift any silverware.

After a protracted courtship by the Football Association, Hoddle was pressed to make up his mind in the week before that final fixture of the league season against Blackburn. Hoddle had delayed signing a new contract at Chelsea, not only because of the possibility of managing England, but also because he felt unsettled at the on-going boardroom dispute between chairman Bates and the club's fanatical benefactor, Matthew Harding, the man who had put up much of the finance for Hoddle's player purchases and who had formed a close bond with the club manager.

Even until the last, Hoddle harboured reservations about taking the England job. He remembered how Bobby Robson, the England coach during his own playing career and the man who took the national side to the quarter-finals and semi-finals of successive World Cups, had been spat on by his own fans as he walked the Wembley touchline. As recently as the previous February, Hoddle himself had said of the England manager's job, 'I honestly think it's got to the stage where people are put off by everything that surrounds it.'

It was an early Monday evening, 29 April, when Hoddle received a phone call at his Ascot home from Jimmy Armfield, the FA's 'headhunter', offering firm terms of a £1.2 million contract over four years. Hoddle knew that his agent, Dennis Roach, was due to meet with Chelsea chairman Ken Bates in two days' time to discuss terms for him to stay at the club. The dilemma was obviously affecting him, and Hoddle took an hour out of his schedule to talk the whole thing through with his father. They parted with Hoddle junior still undecided: 'I don't know if I want this,' he told his father.

By the Wednesday morning, the news of the FA's offer to Hoddle was plastered over the tabloids, with Bates adding his own two penn'orth on Chelsea's Clubcall to protest at the way the FA had approached Hoddle before informing his club. 'It's very bad behaviour on their part,' Bates told anyone prepared to pay 49p per minute to listen, 'They are probably technically in breach of their own rules. But anarchy rules these days.'

Meanwhile, Hoddle had driven off to meet Harding at a discreet hotel 30 miles west of London in the Thames Valley. Their talks dragged on for nearly four hours, Harding attempting to assure Hoddle that further finance would be in place to buy new players, and offering the manager a deal believed to have been worth £1.4 million – slightly more than the England post.

But much of the talk between Harding and Hoddle revolved around the vice-chairman's future at the club. Hoddle was most unsettled about the dispute between Bates and Harding, When the two men eventually emerged in the early afternoon, all Harding would say was, 'It is important that he makes the right decisions.' The next morning, in another sign of the changing nature of the business of football, Chelsea Village plc made an announcement to the Stock Exchange that the football club's manager was leaving, 'to accept an offer of alternative employment' which left the unresolved matter of who would replace Hoddle at Stamford Bridge. On the Saturday, for the final game of the league season, as Hoddle bade the Stamford Bridge faithful farewell, the fans made their views plain. By that stage, it was thought that Bates favoured the appointment of a former Chelsea player and championship-winning manager, George Graham, as Hoddle's replacement.

At the time, Graham was serving out the final weeks of a one-year ban from the game after he had received illicit payments in transfer deals while at Arsenal. But that was only part of the reason that the home supporters began singing, 'You can stick George Graham up your arse!' during that Blackburn match. Arsenal under Graham may have been extraordinarily successful, winning twice as many trophies in his eight years at Highbury as Chelsea had won in their entire club's history, but Graham's sides were also notoriously defensive and negative, anathema to Chelsea fans who had already tasted the sweet nectar of Hoddle's brand of play.

Thus, Gullit was the popular choice as successor, even though the Dutchman had had no experience of management or coaching. Gullit himself had found the previous week difficult, ever since Hoddle had told the players at training on the Tuesday that he was considering taking the England job. Gullit was himself placed in the centre of speculation that he might join Hoddle as his assistant in the England set-up, something Bates robustly rejected: 'There is no way Ruud Gullit is leaving Chelsea.'

In an interview for Dutch television, Gullit, perhaps unwittingly, gave a strong indication that he knew exactly the direction he would like to see Chelsea take after Hoddle's departure. 'If Glenn Hoddle had not been Chelsea manager I might not be wearing a blue shirt now. It has been a marvellous year, one of the happiest in my career. But there is still a lot of work to be done. We need three top European players, and I have told the club several times which players want to play for Chelsea. I have a lot of contacts and I know a lot of the top players. Some of the biggest names in football have rung me and actually begged me to pass their name on.'

Within a week, those names in Ruud Gullit's little black book were in the in-tray in the office of the new player-manager at Stamford Bridge.

Chapter 2

It was almost a year to the day since he had sent the fateful fax to Glenn Hoddle's holiday hotel to inform the then Chelsea manager of the signing of Ruud Gullit. Now, Colin Hutchinson was delving into his Football Managers' Messages Codebook once again. Halfway through their own annual holiday in Cyprus, Hutchinson had left his wife, Linda, in order to tie up the final few loose ends of another transfer deal, and now, three days later, he was letting the new Chelsea boss know about another top player who had agreed to sign for the club.

Ruud Gullit, Chelsea's new player-manager, was holidaying in Mauritius when he was asked by a member of the hotel staff to leave the poolside because there was an important message waiting for him at reception. When Gullit read the single sentence on the sheet of paper, he did not need the Enigma code-breaking computer to know the full meaning: 'It is good news,' read the note, 'Yours, Colin'. Gullit, despite sunning himself in the Indian Ocean, had effectively just completed his first signing as Chelsea manager, and in so doing had secured the services of one of the biggest names in world football. Gianluca Vialli, the captain of Juventus, the new champions of Europe, had agreed to join Gullit's club. Chelsea fans would pinch themselves in disbelief.

At Stamford Bridge, as the baking sun of a drought-ridden English summer beat down, it was obvious that major reconstruction work was taking place where the old Shed terrace used to stand, as rising steadily out of deep foundations was a new stand, offices and hotel complex. But it was elsewhere in the ground where even more significant re-building for the future of Chelsea Football Club was being conducted. Gullit's appointment as player-manager had acted as a catalyst for more behind-the-scenes reorganisation in the offices at Stamford Bridge during a hectic and brief close season of 1996.

Gullit was concerned that his new job as manager of the side should not diminish his role on the pitch. After all, even at 33, he had just been voted runner-up to Eric Cantona as Player of the Year in the English

Premiership. So surely, injuries permitting, there ought to be another season or two of useful football left in Gullit. But the new responsibilities of management were something Gullit refused to underestimate. 'For the first time in my career I shall have to adapt to combined roles. That will take time,' he said. 'Playing football is still my main role and I don't want my performances on the pitch to suffer. The important thing for me is to make sure I can still perform on the pitch, so we will have to adapt slowly to a new structure and to ourselves.'

Just as the steel girders on the nearby building site would provide the support and framework for the new South complex's dual usage as a stand and hotel, so Gullit's new staffing arrangement was designed to provide the framework for him to perform in his new dual role. Colin Hutchinson, as MD, took a much more hands-on approach to the recruitment of players. Peter Shreeves, Hoddle's mentor in his playing days who became his assistant manager at Chelsea, left the club (his contract expired in the summer), to be replaced by Graham Rix, the former Arsenal and England midfielder who had been youth team coach under Hoddle, and who was promoted by Gullit to become first-team coach.

Ade Mafe, who at the age of 17 had raced alongside Carl Lewis in the 200 metres final at the 1984 Los Angeles Olympics, was recruited from a King's Road health club where he was working as a personal trainer, in order to look after the fitness programmes of all the players, while Gwyn Williams was put in charge of first-team administration matters. Gullit's thinking was that, if he could delegate enough responsibilites, then he would be able to concentrate on the overall direction of the team on the pitch, and continue to play at the highest level.

Alec Stock, a thoughtful and insightful manager from the 1960s and '70s, once described the role of the player-manager as 'violent physical exercise on top of a pile of worries'. Perhaps mindful of this idea, Gullit was cautious about the size of the task he was undertaking. 'I didn't want to manage the whole club,' Gullit said, 'that would be too difficult. You have to be on the phone, do a lot of paperwork and be in the office – and still Chelsea want me to be a player. The demands would have been too great, it would have been impossible.' Especially since the new coach had insisted on virtually doubling the players' training schedule.

Under Mafe's supervision, there would no longer be a morning's kick-about, followed by lunch and then an idling round of golf (to be followed by several other rounds at the 19th hole). After all, when Mafe was an *amateur* athlete, he had to dedicate himself in a fully professional manner, fitting in two training sessions each day to reach Olympic levels of fitness. Since Gullit, too, had been used in Italy to full-time footballers training full-time, the new routine seemed the sensible thing to do. 'Nine times out of ten a game is lost by players being tired and making errors. That's where I come in,' said Mafe, still looking young enough and fit enough that you would think that competing at the Sydney Olympic Games was a possibility.

'Two sessions a day and finishing at 4 p.m. – it's different to the way things were before I joined here. I can help them improve their speed over short distances, develop stamina and build upper body strength – make them stronger, fitter players, which can give an edge to their game. It's what I call professional training. I think the time of going down the pub is at an end for top-level players.'

Thus, the management team at Stamford Bridge was put in place along continental lines. In all of this, it is the role of Hutchinson which is pivotal. The days of managers going out and meeting in a local trattoria with a player from another club, accompanied by their agent, discussing deals worth millions of pounds and agreeing everything with a note on a serviette and a quick handshake over the cappuccino is a thing of the past. Perhaps the changes at Chelsea had been influenced by the tales from other London clubs of brown paper bags stuffed full of cash being exchanged under the tables of motorway service stations.

Certainly, there was a good deal more financial accountability about their new transfer arrangements when Arsenal had begun this trend. After George Graham's departure from Highbury as manager because of the bungs scandal, Arsenal set up a system where the team manager would draw up a 'shopping list' of players that he wanted to sign, with a rough valuation of their worth, and a club director (in Arsenal's case, David Dein) would conduct the transfer negotiations with the player and their club. At Arsenal, under Graham's successor Bruce Rioch – a manager steeped in the old-school manner of conducting football business – this arrangement created tensions between him and his board, particularly when a number of key signings fell through. But for Gullit, such a method of conducting transfer business was only what he had been used to throughout his playing career in Holland and Italy.

The other sea-change in the manner that transfer deals are done was created by what is known as the Bosman Ruling, resulting from a test case judgement by the European court involving a Belgian player who fought for the freedom to move to another club as a free agent once his contract had expired. If you think about it, it is all quiet reasonable. In no other profession would a change of job entitle your previous employers to a 'transfer' fee when you move on, as if you were one of their chattels or possessions. Certainly, once your contract with your employers had expired, in any other walk of life you would usually expect to be free to seek work elsewhere. Until the Bosman Ruling, however, in European football, players were still treated like some sort of latterday serfs, possessions for the club directors to sell on at their whim and fancy. Post-Bosman, and any player at the end of his contract was able to move to any club which offered him the best deal.

This was the situation in which Gianluca Vialli found himself during the first few months of the 1995–96 season. Vialli, bought by Juventus from Sampdoria in 1992 for a then world record fee of £12.5 million, was going to be released by Juve, his contract expired, for no fee. This was the same Vialli who had been voted the World Player of the Year for 1995, the same Vialli who had captained Juventus as they marched towards the final of the European Champions' Cup. That same Vialli *could now be signed for nothing.*

Vialli had got the message from Juventus that he was no longer really wanted when the club let him know that at the end of the season they would offer him only a one-year extension to his contract, with no extra pay. Vialli told Italian journalists as early as the previous October that he was considering a move to England. 'I thought Juventus might have asked me to stay, but there are ways to make a player feel unwanted,' he reflected later, speaking in his soft, precise diction, his thin, Errol Flynn-style pirate's beard emphasising a slight smile.

'My pride was a little bit hurt, but I was 32, they didn't want me any more, so I could try something else.' It was a bitter-sweet moment then, in front of nearly 70,000 roaring fans in Rome's Stadio Olympico, late into a sultry May evening, when Vialli lifted the European Champions' Cup so that it glinted under the floodlights on to his shaven pate. In this moment of success and celebration, Vialli knew that he had played his last game for Juventus. The following day, back home in his Turin apartment, and Vialli was signing the contract which would commit him to Chelsea.

Gullit, like most football managers in western Europe, had been well aware of Vialli's situation. Signing the Italian striker on a 'free' represented great business, but to lure Luca to London, Chelsea had needed to offer an outstanding deal. There may have been no transfer fee to pay to Juventus, but the club would still have to fund a competitive salary package to help to persuade Vialli to join. A year earlier, when he had joined Chelsea (also on a free), Gullit had become the club's best-paid player. It was in some ways ironic that when he was to make his first signing as the club manager, Gullit would have to shatter Chelsea's pay scales and see his new star signing leapfrog his own pay-band. 'I'm not interested in how much a player earns, even if it means paying them more than me.' Gullit said, 'as long as he can do a job for Chelsea.'

With offers coming in from Rangers in Glasgow, Japan and America, Vialli chose Chelsea. Or, perhaps more precisely, he chose London. 'London was always my dream,' Vialli said. 'It was a matter of image. I was a well-known player in Italy – I couldn't have simply taken off my black and white shirt and put on a different one. Footballers are professionals, but they are also expected to believe in their clubs, to love their supporters. Moving from one club to another is never easy.

'I said to myself: "If I am to change, it has to be a radical change". I got in touch with some English clubs, and then Rangers turned up offering me a lot of money. Living in Glasgow might have been fun, but I dreamt of London.' Vialli may have harboured hopes of being hired as a replacement for Jürgen Klinsmann at Tottenham, or being recruited by Arsenal. 'He wanted to play for Arsenal,' one close friend of Vialli suggested, 'but they didn't even make a phone call. They said he was too old.' One manager who did not think Vialli would be too old was his old Sampdoria team mate, Gullit. 'When Ruud became Chelsea's coach and phoned me up, he made my dream come true,' Vialli said.

In fact, the decision to get Vialli had been made in a meeting between Gullit and Hutchinson within an hour of Chelsea's final league match of the previous season, even before any formal announcement that the Dutchman was to succeed Glenn Hoddle. Gullit had been cheered to the rafters by the Chelsea fans and according to Hutchinson, 'even the unflappable Ruud was still slightly emotional by his reception and the "give him the job" chants'.

So it was that Vialli found himself moving temporarily into a Knightsbridge hotel, close to Harrod's, Harvey Nicks and Hyde Park, and convenient for the fashionable San Lorenzo Italian restaurant, where he quickly became a regular. 'It is better to live in a nice part of London,' Vialli said.

Vialli's three-year deal with Chelsea was worth a total of £4.2 million before tax to the Italian, a fact which obviously annoyed the rejected bidders from Glasgow. Rangers had offered a three-year deal worth £1 million more than Chelsea's gross, and they also offered to take care of the player's income tax bill as well. Obviously feeling a little miffed, Donald Finlay, Rangers's vice-chairman said, 'Those who turn down a club such as Rangers rarely prosper.' He could not have known quite how prophetic those words were to be.

Vialli explained his choice thus: 'I could have continued my career at Parma or Sampdoria or a number of other top clubs, but the adrenalin rush would not have been the same. When Gullit phoned me I knew immediately that Chelsea was the right choice to make.'

After he had carried out the necessary persuasion, Gullit left the detailed negotiations on the deal to Colin Hutchinson. In fact, when Vialli was signed, Gullit did not even know how much the player was to be paid – so much had been delegated to Chelsea's chief executive.

In his late 50s, grey haired, Colin Hutchinson hardly appears to be the epitome of the go-getting European dealer who brushes shoulders with the Armani-suited, cigar-smoking Continental agents as they schmooze out million-pound contracts in a style that they had carefully copied from studious and repeated viewings of Michael Douglas's performance in *Wall Street*. But Hutchinson's slightly foxed appearance belies a hard-bargainer. When seated at a desk, he sometimes comes over a little gruff, if not blunt, as one might expect of a Yorkshireman who does not suffer fools gladly. But he is not an 'in-your-face' type of wheeler-dealer: he sits with his shoulders slumped in an almost defensive posture. Therein may lie Hutchinson's success: according to one lawyer who was representing a player whom Hutchinson helped to sign, you immediately felt that you could trust what he said.

Hutchinson has spent all his working life dealing with the finances of sport, right from the time as a precocious 16-year-old schoolboy businessman when he brought some of Europe's top moto-cross riders to race at his home village of Boltby in Yorkshire. Back-room jobs in rugby league and at Carlisle (it was Hutchinson who sold Peter Beardsley to Vancouver Whitecaps in the moribund North American Soccer League when neither Newcastle nor Sunderland would pay the asking price) led Hutchinson to a post at Wimbledon in 1986, just as the club was promoted to the old First Division.

Ken Bates recruited Hutchinson to Chelsea to run the 'Save the Bridge' campaign, and he was promoted to chief executive and appointed as a director of the club in January 1989. The appointment as manager of first Glenn Hoddle, and then Gullit, saw Hutchinson's role expand. When vice-chairman Matthew Harding had his falling out with Bates, it meant that Hutchinson – rather than Harding, the man who had provided much of the finance – took on the job of negotiating players' transfers.

The signing of Vialli made tremendous financial sense for Chelsea. The season before the Italian's arrival, mini-buses began to appear at Stamford Bridge on matchdays, full of teenaged Dutch girls who had travelled over from Holland for the weekend and were eager to shriek out the name of their hero, Gullit. A year on, and the signing of Vialli, Roberto di Matteo and then Gianfranco Zola meant that between Fulham Broadway tube and the Bovril Gate, much of the pre-match babble was now Italiano. Vialli's arrival at the Bridge saw coach-loads of Italians swelling the numbers at the Bridge, so much so that sometimes it seemed as if season ticket-holders needed English-Italian phrasebooks to understand their conversation with the person sitting next to them in the posh seats in the East Stand.

With the building work going on at the old Shed end, the ground capacity was reduced to just over 28,000 for the 1996–97 season. Vialli's signing would ensure that every ticket would be sold for virtually every home game, with the 'Sold Out' sign effectively being put up outside the gates for some matches five months in advance. It represented an increase of more than 2,000 on the average gate from the previous season. With Chelsea's high seat prices this in turn meant that, in one respect at least, Vialli could be said to be earning his wages. There were other spin-offs, too. Vialli T-shirts, badges and other bric-à-brac became hot sellers in Chelsea Sportsland, the club shop just outside the ground on the Fulham Road. The Number 9 shirt had never been so popular since Peter Osgood and those heady, successful days of the early 1970s, a time when you did not need the name of your favourite player emblazoned across your shoulders to know his name and what position he played in.

Nor was Vialli's signing a one-off. During the summer, while the player-manager was wowing the BBC television audience with his erudite and witty comments and analysis of matches in Euro '96, Colin Hutchinson went out, armed with Gullit's 'shopping list', and bought the spine of the team which Vialli was to spearhead. From Strasbourg, Chelsea bought French international defender Frank Leboeuf for £2.5 million, while Rome's Lazio were paid a club record fee of £4.9 million for midfielder di Matteo. The deals certainly got the immediate approval of his chairman. 'He has bought the backbone of a full side for the price of a Shearer,' said Ken Bates.

Hutchinson, like a good Yorkshireman, ensured the best possible prices. 'I had spoken to Ruud about Frank Leboeuf, and he reckoned no more than £2.5 million,' Hutchinson said. 'I offered £2.25 million, knowing that Marseille had offered £2.2 million. Strasbourg said that they wanted £3 million, but they asked me over for talks.

'I know from experience that if someone asks you to come for talks, there is a chance of a deal. I took Graham Rix with me because of his knowledge of French football and the language.' The meeting was conducted right in the middle of the England-Holland match at Wembley during the European Championship. Hutchinson and Rix both had to struggle not to let their curiosity over the score distract them from the negotiations. 'During one of the breaks, I remember talking to Graham and he said he felt we might have to settle for £2.6 million or we would lose him. I told him that I thought they would take our offer.

'We went to £2.5 million and made it clear we would go no higher. They kept coming back to us, slightly lower each time. I kept saying no. Eventually, we got our man at the price we wanted.' An hour later, they also found out the final score from Wembley. All that remained to be done was another trip, this time to Wigan and France's Euro '96 training camp, where the player's signature was placed on the Chelsea contract.

Before his first season in charge, in appraising his purchases, and therefore the changes that would bring to his squad, Gullit referred back to the February afternoon six months earlier when he had personally orchestrated the 5-0 demolition of Middlesbrough. 'All the players said afterwards that it was too early for that to happen,' Gullit said. 'We made progress last season, and we've got to build on that this season.'

Gullit had always trusted Hutchinson to bring in the right players at the right price. After all, the big Dutchman had trusted Hutchinson with his own wages for long enough. For the first few months that Gullit was with the club, using much of his spare time searching for a new home, the Dutchman never bothered to pick up his pay cheques. When they began to mount up, Hutchinson felt obliged to point out to the club's star player that there was a significant value of money effectively sitting in the out-tray of his desk. 'I am not worried about that, Colin,' Gullit told Hutchinson. 'With you, it is as safe as in the bank.'

So, when Hutchinson returned from his continental shopping spree, Gullit was content. 'The players I have signed are like a skeleton,' Gullit said. 'When you have a spine, you build around it.'

As the BBC viewers discovered during the summer, Gullit is not afraid of mixing up his language to express his football views. 'A team is a car, and you can't start a car in fifth gear. You look at Manchester United: they start off in first gear, then they accelerate when they score, then they slow it down again, and then up again to score.

'The best teams win when they are not playing well: 1–0 and it's all over. At Chelsea, we often play for the performance, not the result. That's good, but that's not what we have to aim for. We have to get the results. But something is developing here, I can feel something starting.'

At least one thing was starting: Gullit as the football boss who ensured he got what he wanted. On arriving in England, Vialli was given just six weeks to learn English and find a house. The Italian was also banned from playing in an all-star game in New York in July: pre-season training at Chelsea came first.

It would not be long before such demanding high standards would create some tensions between Gullit and the players who, just a few months before, had been his team mates. When asked what difference it made in having Gullit as his boss, team captain Dennis Wise joked, 'We don't call him big nose anymore.' But the doubts and the questions about Gullit's management style were being put under scrutiny wherever and whenever Chelsea played. Even before a ball was kicked in anger, former Chelsea players, such as Ron Harris, 'Chopper', the old club captain who had led the great Chelsea side of the early 1970s to the FA Cup and European Cup-winners' Cup, were openly critical of his purchasing policy. 'Ruud's bringing in clapped-out Europeans not worth a toss,' Harris said.

But such publicly aired discontent was nothing when compared to the turmoil that already existed in the Chelsea boardroom in an on-going row between the club's chairman and its greatest benefactor.

Chapter 3

It was Sunday morning early in September 1993, the day after Chelsea had visited their happy hunting ground at White Hart Lane and come away once again without being beaten. At Matthew Harding's Sussex home, the phone rang. Harding picked up the receiver and was taken aback when the person at the other end of the line announced himself. 'I've been told you've got a lot more money than I have,' Ken Bates, the Chelsea chairman, told Harding in typically challenging style, 'so I thought I'd give you a ring and see if it's true.' The future of Chelsea Football Club was changed forever.

Stories vary about how Bates became aware of the existence of Harding, his fortune and his passion for Chelsea. One version has Bates being tipped off by a friend who had read an article in *Business Age* magazine about the 500 richest people in Britain and discovered that the man ranked in 78th position was a Chelsea supporter. Another version tells of one of Harding's regular visits to the Bridge, where he was among the club shop's best customers (when Ruud Gullit was signed by the club, legend has it that Harding was the first into the shop to order a team shirt with the number 4 on the back). On this occasion, Harding had gone to Stamford Bridge to buy shares for his family in Chelsea Pitch Owners', one of Bates's pet schemes for raising money. As he was leaving the CPO's Portakabin office, Harding is supposed to have turned and said, almost as an afterthought, 'You can tell Ken Bates that if he has a problem building the North Stand, then he should give me a ring,' handing over one of his calling cards.

A third version of this momentous meeting has Bates placing an advertisement in the *Financial Times* in the late summer of 1993, seeking backers for his grand schemes for the development of Chelsea Football Club. Harding, not yet 40 but with a fortune of more than £140 million made in the bear-pit of London's reinsurance markets, was keen to help the club which he had been supporting ever since his father had taken him to his first match at the age of eight, and accordingly, he responded to the ad. It hardly matters, in the end, how it was that the two men first came together. The basic facts of the matter are that Bates needed Harding's money. Within two years of Bates's call for help, Harding would pump more than £20 million into Stamford Bridge with a series of loans and investments, including buying £5 million of convertible loan stock in the Chelsea development company to pay towards the cost of the new North Stand, and providing a £5 million fund for team manager Glenn Hoddle to delve into the transfer market.

In modern-day, Premiership football, the amount of Harding's benevolence to Chelsea pales into insignificance alongside the £60 million which Sir John Hall's Newcastle spent to assemble their squad of players, or to the vast amounts which Jack Walker spent to redevelop Ewood Park and turn Blackburn into a championship-winning side after years in the doldrums of the lower divisions. But then, Sir John and 'Uncle' Jack both owned their clubs. Despite Harding's millions, Ken Bates continued to own Chelsea. It was a dichotomy which caused a feud in the Stamford Bridge boardroom that was to last more than a year, and which only ended with the death of one of the protagonists.

Without doubt, long before Harding had come along, Bates saved Chelsea from oblivion. When he first became involved in the club, he arrived with a reputation as something of a carpetbagger and a wheeler-dealer businessman, someone from humble beginnings who had dragged himself up by his boot laces. Born in December 1931 and raised on a council estate in Ealing, west London, by the time he was in his 30s, Bates had transformed his fortunes through a series of haulage and tipping businesses, and he enjoyed more success with quarrying and ready-mixed concrete concerns in the north-west of England. In those days, the Swinging '60s, it was the done thing for upwardly mobile businessmen to buy their way into the local town's football club, and Bates used his wealth to become chairman of Oldham Athletic in 1965.

As was to become Bates's hallmark, these were not uneventful times in the history of the club, which the chairman managed to propel into the national headlines when he took Oldham on a playing tour of Rhodesia, apparently oblivious to the political displeasure he created at home, since the tour was conducted in the midst of the UDI crisis, when strict sanctions were supposed to be applied to Ian Smith's breakaway, whites-only regime.

In 1968, Bates invested in property, buying Anegada in the British Virgin Isles, and set about developing it into an attractive tax haven. His interest in Oldham seemed to wane as he was distracted by making more money elsewhere, and he stepped down from the chairmanship in 1969. Around that time, while living in the Cayman Islands, Bates became involved in a variety of deals in southern Africa, including the development and management of a very successful hotel chain. Meanwhile Bates sold his majority share holding in the builders, Howarth of Burnley, not long before the firm went into liquidation after falling far short of its profit forecast. Bates also became embroiled in controversy as a director of the Irish Trust Bank, which was contentiously wound-up after four years, though he was later to win legal redress for malign practices against the bank. Bates did not forsake football entirely, though: in 1981, he also served briefly as a director of Wigan Athletic. But it was the experience and contacts which Bates built up during this period of his business career which he was to put to effect once he became involved in Chelsea – property development, building, construction and hotels, offshore investments, all would be brought to play as Bates gradually took firm hold of Stamford Bridge during the 1980s.

These were dark days indeed for football generally, with disputes over television deals, rampant hooliganism at many games, and gate receipts dwindling everywhere. Many clubs were in deep financial difficulty, often vulnerable to take-overs: it was around this time that Irving Scholar paid just £500,000 to take control of Spurs and Robert Maxwell rescued Oxford United with £120,000. In April 1982, Ken Bates bought Chelsea for £1. It was the bargain of the century.

The reason for the bargain basement price was clear: the team had been mid-table mediocrities in the old Second Division for nearly three seasons, with no prospect of money-spinning promotion. An independent valuation of the club's worth in 1980 had put it at £33,000. Two years later the club's debts were estimated to be £2 million. As part of the deal, Bates agreed to take on some of Chelsea's debts, but part of a complicated lease drawn up in consultation with Bates's own lawyers was a conditional option that he would also acquire a substantial asset – the famous old Stamford Bridge ground, a prime site for development on the Fulham Road, close by the London Underground system, and just 15 minutes from the West End.

Bates's brusque, no-nonsense manner soon placed him in conflict with the old Chelsea directors. This initial encounter made it clear to Bates that things must change. It was around the time Bates had bought the club, and the lorry driver's son from Ealing was invited to a pre-match luncheon by Charles Gerald Cadogan, the Viscount Chelsea, and his director colleague, Old Harrovian David Mears, whose family had established the football club in 1905. Now, 77 years later, along with nearly 20 other guests, Bates enjoyed a sumptuous four-course meal, two wines, liqueurs and cigars. Yet, on the very day that Bates had become chairman of Chelsea Football Club, a cheque for the players' wages had bounced. The distaste Bates felt for the situation was still evident years later when he said, 'I'd rather have a chat with a skinhead in The Shed than have dinner with some lord.'

From that one meal, it was easy for a hard-nosed businessman like Bates to see what needed changing. 'It was a freeloader's paradise,' he was to recall, 'and I stopped it.' One of his favourite tales of those times was about one of the old Chelsea directors. 'It was hopelessly insolvent, yet one director even had the nerve to claim expenses for attending away matches.'

While chairman Bates was busy stopping the freeloaders, his own plans were stopped in their tracks, too. As part of the deal in which he took on the club's liabilities, Bates felt he had an agreement from Mears and Viscount Chelsea that he would get first refusal on the purchase of the ground. According to David Mears, 'As far as I was concerned, Bates said to me and Lord Chelsea that he did not want to buy the ground. Had he wanted to, he could have had it at a very reasonable price.

'I remember, after the deal was done, Bates invited me to lunch, where he asked me to sell my shares in SB Property, the company which owned the ground. That was the first time I realised that Bates wanted control of the ground.' A price was agreed between Mears and Bates, but a deal was never completed. Eventually, property developers Marler Estates took over SB Property, with the football club given a lease to use the ground only until 1989. Marler made it clear that the only future that they saw for Stamford Bridge would be as the site for new luxury flats. Bates soon called an extraordinary general meeting of the club to oust Mears and Viscount Chelsea from the board, citing their disloyalty to the football club. It was just fortuitous, perhaps, that Bates's boardroom *putsch* also gained him some revenge for the way he was slighted over the property deal.

As he waged what seemed a one-man crusade to keep Chelsea at the Bridge, Bates, with his no-nonsense, man-of-the-people image, cultivated the approval of the Chelsea fans. As long as he was seen to be fighting to preserve the football club, Bates seemed to do no wrong. But Bates had not suddenly discovered a great empathy for Chelsea, shared with the fans. His motivation in working to save Stamford Bridge was far less one-dimensional, his dedication to the task – becoming a virtually full-time chief executive, spending five days a week at the Bridge without, at that time, drawing any salary – was surely the result of enlightened self-interest.

Bates's honeymoon with the fans would soon be over, in any case.

Hooliganism was rife in British football, and Chelsea fans had one of the more notorious reputations, one fan even being jailed for life, another for eight years, for their parts in incidents after a game against Manchester United. Bates's solution to the problem was to ban some journalists from the ground for reporting outbreaks of hooliganism, and to put up electrified fencing in front of The Shed. By now with business interests in farming, Bates could see no reason why the sort of fences he used on his herd of prize-winning dairy cows at his Beaconsfield farm could not be used to keep the crowd at Chelsea off the Stamford Bridge pitch. The Greater London Council ordered Bates to tear down his fences, refusing to grant a safety certificate, but not before Bates had called for the resignation of Neil Macfarlane, the minister for sport, when the politician had dared criticise the Chelsea chairman over his proposals.

As one of the revered 1970 Chelsea squad admitted privately, 'How can you believe in a bloke, have faith in the man running the club, when he turns round and says you're no better than cattle, and wants to stick you behind electric fences? I didn't want anything to do with the club after that.'

As Stamford Bridge remained a success-free zone, it was the off-the-pitch battles which became the more intriguing. Bates would spend much of the 1980s fighting to regain control of the Stamford Bridge ground. It would prove an effort well worth making. Bates needed all of his combative qualities as he saw off successive attempts to move the football club into various ground-sharing schemes in order to let the bulldozers move in. As the property boom took hold, the valuation of the ground soared from £4 million at the end of 1983, to Marler's sellers' price of £85 million in 1986 (compared to Bates's £15 million valuation). But after every boom, there is bust.

Whether Bates alone would have ever managed to win his struggle for control of the Bridge is a moot point. Circumstances eventually came to his aid from two quarters with which Bates may have never willingly allied himself. First, the local council fell into control of Labour – or the 'loony lefties' as Bates called them. The new Labour council made a policy decision to withdraw planning permission to turn the Stamford Bridge site into luxury apartments but to maintain the site as a football ground. The book value of the Stamford Bridge site plummeted. And then, charging to the rescue of Bates, the long-time property developer, came the unlikeliest knight on a white charger of all: the crash in the property market. Chelsea's landlords, Marler, were bought out in 1992 by Cabra. What followed is open to interpretation. With Cabra's assets – property – suddenly rendered virtually worthless by the collapse of property values, the company was doomed.

In the sale of Cabra's assets that followed, the Royal Bank of Scotland took over the lease of the Stamford Bridge ground. Under these more benevolent landlords, Bates had much longer to raise capital to buy the ground, and with the future more assured, redevelopment of the site could commence. Indeed, the terraces at Stamford Bridge needed a massive overhaul for the ground to comply with the recommendations of the Taylor Report, published in the wake of the 1989 disaster at Hillsborough, which demanded all-seater grounds in the Premiership.

But for Bates to carry forward his development plans for the ground, he needed capital investment. In Matthew Harding, he found a willing provider of that cash. Yet Harding was caught in a real fan's dilemma. Harding wanted, and enjoyed, doing all that he could for Chelsea. In some respects, when Bates invited him aboard Chelsea, he gave Harding the chance to play the ultimate game of Fantasy Football.

In an interview with *The Independent* newspaper at the beginning of the 1995 season, Harding expressed his philosophy behind becoming a director of a football club. Relations at the time between Harding and Bates were, superficially at least, cordial. Bates, after all, had accepted Harding's challenge during Chelsea's FA Cup run the previous season and, when the team reached the final, the grey-haired, sexagenarian gentleman farmer and football club chairman was as good as his word, arriving in the Royal Box at Wembley wearing an earring. But someone as worldly wise as Bates, on reading the interview, would have quickly detected that it amounted to only thinly veiled criticisms of the Chelsea chairman, his ambitious plans to develop Stamford Bridge and to stage a Stock Exchange flotation.

'I think there are two criteria to being on the board of a football club,' Harding told the newspaper. 'I think you have to be unequivocally wedded to that particular club, which is not always the case. There are a number of directors and chairmen who have been involved in more than one club. A committed football fan cannot understand that.

'This thing about me being a fan on the board – what are people doing on boards who are not fans? There is this amazing surprise that I get out of my seat when we score and wave my arms about – if that is a crime, football has gone mad. I do behave considerably better than the way I used to,' Harding added, 'but you can't just sit there.

'I also think you have to be able to afford what you have to do. People think that it is akin to running a business, but that is missing the point. Football club directors should not even be paid. Football clubs, as often as not, have been run as fiefdoms. I think you have to drag football from being run along Victorian lines to something more contemporary.'

That, however, did not necessarily mean that the club need be floated as a publicly quoted company. 'Once a football club becomes a plc two things happen which are potentially worrying. People can buy into the club without demonstrating they are wedded to it – which goes right against my beliefs.

'And you have to serve the interests of the shareholders who are not going to have an emotional attachment to the football club. They are going to expect capital growth in the share price and a dividend. I am all for running a club at a profit, but that profit should be reinvested in the club rather than paid out to shareholders.'

It was clear that even at this stage, if Harding was to sink any more of his personal fortune into Chelsea, it would not be unconditional. Matthew Harding had begun to demand answers from Ken Bates, the former chairman of Oldham and director of Wigan. Harding wanted answers from the club chairman who had appointed as a director the accountant Yvonne Todd, a woman who admitted she had never seen a live football match before she joined the Chelsea board, never mind supported the club. Harding sought answers from the Bentley-driving chairman of Chelsea who was paying himself £164,614 per year and still boasted that 'You can't get a good player for that, let alone a financial genius'. And Harding was asking for answers from the man who had spent more than a dozen years trying to win control of the real estate of Stamford Bridge.

The questions Harding were posing centred on the 'phoenix' operation which had seen Chelsea Football Club effectively wound-up as a business after 88 years in existence, to be replaced by a new company called Chelsea Village. If he was going to fund the continued development of the football team and the ground, Harding said, he wanted to know with whom he was doing business, yet the identity of the major shareholders of Chelsea Village remained a mystery, disguised by various offshore share holdings.

Until the day he died, Matthew Harding would not receive a full, satisfactory answer to his questions.

Chapter 4

Take a journey from the centre of London, heading west on the Thames Embankment. Along Millbank and Grosvenor Road, and just before you pass the elegance of Sir Christopher Wren's Royal Hospital, as it overlooks the lawns which run down towards the slow, grey old river, you take a right turn. Here, you will enter a district of the city that is like no other in the capital, and probably unlike any other area of Britain.

This district really begins with Sloane Square, a bustling fulcrum of traffic which in the 1980s lent its name to the 'Rangers' – the moneyed gadflies who drove Range Rovers around town ('Four-wheel drive is just so *essential* when loading the crates of Bolly outside the wine merchants, don't you find?'), wore Burberrys and green wellies in SW1, could be heard half-a-street away as they called to one another with 'Yah!' and 'Dahhhhling' at the top of their voices, and more often than not were named Caroline or Sebastian. Sloane Square is the heart of their natural territory, among the tall, cream-coloured Georgian terraced houses that run off to the left and right of the main thoroughfare. But it is the main road that runs west from Sloane Square which is synonymous with style, fashion and Chelsea – the King's Road.

Chelsea, the district, had always been fashionable with the In Crowd, from the 1760s right through to the 1960s. Chelsea, the football club, was less a fashion accessory, more often the butt of Music Hall jokes when it was first formed in Edwardian London. Having had comedian George Robey on the playing staff was never easy to shake off (for a modern day equivalent, imagine Eddie Izzard being on West Ham's books). But as the King's Road was a focus of Swinging London in the Swinging Sixties, so did Chelsea's football club manage to acquire a new reputation for glamour and flair on the pitch, as well as flares off it. The players were regarded as the princes of the King's Road.

As well as star players, Chelsea also attracted showbiz star supporters – the Bridge became the place to be seen on Saturday afternoons. Richard Attenborough, Vidal Sassoon, Honor Blackman, Laurence Olivier and Steve McQueen were among those to add celebrity glitz to the footballing glamour club. Actors Michael Crawford and Terence Stamp were friendly enough with the players that they often visited them in the Chelsea changing rooms to congratulate or commiserate with them after a game, before going off to their own West End dressing room for their own Saturday evening performances. One story at the time even suggested a romantic link between '60s sex icon Raquel Welch and one of the Chelsea players. For a while, it seemed that the world loved Chelsea.

By the 1980s, though, the heady days when the likes of Peter Osgood and Alan Hudson had swaggered along the King's Road, usually with a girl on each arm, taking in a meal before going on to a night club (as often as not on the night *before* a game as well as on the evening after a match), had become less than a distant memory, more a thing of folklore. The princes of King's Road had been transformed into paupers. In place of the artistry and skills of Ossie and Hudson had come the more prosaic talents of the likes of Alan Mayes and Doug Rougvie. Financially, the football club was near bankrupt, and the style of play on the pitch too often reflected that fact perfectly. The new, massive East Stand would be seen as the Mears's folly – a huge edifice which was rarely filled by paying supporters, so unedifying was the fare on offer on the pitch.

Commissioned shortly after the successes in 1970 and 1971, the building of the East Stand soon ran into delays and rapidly rising costs, so the club suddenly had no cash for transfers to rebuild the Cup-winning side. Chelsea's fortunes declined accordingly. When Gus Mears had first built the ground in the early 1900s, initially he had no team to play there. Now, three-quarters of a century on, it was said that Chelsea again had a ground but no team.

Things became deeply depressing for everyone connected with Chelsea. There came a point in the early '80s when Chelsea were so strapped for cash, the players even had to take their kit home to wash it themselves. For too many years, Chelsea wallowed in complacency and incompetence in their on-the-field performances.

While the downtrodden football club remained a success-free zone for a quarter of a century, it became something of an anachronism in the neighbourhood: Stamford Bridge anti-fashion in the heart of King's Road fashiondom. It would take a football stylist to get Chelsea back on the main street.

Ruud Gullit, the modern sophisticate – 'I am a citizen of the world' – was immediately at ease with the relaxed cosmopolitan atmosphere to be found so near to the ground, so much so that he bought himself a mews house off Sloane Street once he found something to suit. Likewise, Gianluca Vialli, the son of an Italian millionaire businessman and so already used to *la dolce vita*, moved in to an apartment in the exclusive Eaton Square. He must have felt at home when he saw the plaster busts of Roman emperors on sale outside *faux* antique shops just around the corner from Stamford Bridge. Chelsea's New Azzurri did not take long to adjust to the area's fashionable Italian restaurants and would have been reassured by the sight of the brightly-coloured sports cars which always cruise the neighbourhood with the soft top down. The sun, it sometimes seems, always shines on the King's Road.

But if Vialli, di Matteo or any of the other footballing newcomers had had to find their own way to Stamford Bridge after first signing for Chelsea, making their own way up from the King's Road to Fulham Road, they might have been confused by the signs as he approached the ground. Just beside a road bridge over the railway line that separates Stamford Bridge from the Brompton cemetery is a tall, dirty, red-bricked Victorian Mansion block. It has a huge sign fixed to the outside wall, clearly visible to everyone approaching from central London. 'Chelsea Village parking, 50 yards,' the sign reads. A hoarding across the road confirms this with a huge arrow. There is no mention on either of these signs of Chelsea Football Club or its historic Stamford Bridge ground: to a stranger arriving for the first time, they might not realise that, around the corner, is one of the top football clubs in the country. If the sign is their only guide, they might easily be confused into believing that the only thing on the site is a commodious corporate car park.

When Keith Burkinshaw walked out as manager of Tottenham Hotspur in the mid-1980s, he uttered a damningly memorable line: 'There used to be a football club here'. Burkinshaw, an effective and successful manager at Spurs who had led the side to win the UEFA Cup, left White Hart Lane a disillusioned man. He was fed up with the way that the club's footballing activities had been made subservient to the objectives of the accountants and men in suits who were trying to transform Tottenham into a 'sports and leisure' business empire. While Burkinshaw was told that money for new signings was unavailable, somehow the new business was able to expand by buying into companies that manufactured ladies' knitwear and bikinis, and setting up its own sportswear brand. All these concerns would eventually fail, losing Tottenham Hotspur plc millions.

Burkinshaw's remarks might have echoed with anyone who read those signs on the Fulham Road: after all, just what *is* Chelsea Village? Certainly that was a question which Chelsea's vice-chairman, Matthew Harding, was forced to ask repeatedly.

The one person to know the full story of Chelsea Village is Ken Bates, the chairman of Chelsea Football Club. That is the same Ken Bates who had, in May 1993, ended nearly 88 years of football history.

In a complicated series of commercial transactions involving three different business entities, over the space of nine months the company which had operated Chelsea Football Club since its formation in 1905 was wound up leaving substantial debts.

The end came out of the blue. In the last set of accounts ever filed by CFAC Ltd – the new name given to the original operating company – even the statement from the directors gave no real forewarning of impending doom. 'The directors consider that the result for the year is satisfactory but the position of the group at the end of the year remains unsatisfactory', read the statement from the directors of CFAC Ltd.

The Premier League was about to be formed, revolutionising income for the top echelon of the English game. While Chelsea desperately wanted to be part of the new competition, any financial uncertainty surrounding the club could have jeopardised its Premiership status. It was not widely known in football circles about the apparent financial difficulties which would see Chelsea's operating company wound-up within three months of those accounts being published. It was in the spring of 1993 – with the FA Premier League now up and running, and including Chelsea – that control of Chelsea Football Club passed to a new entity, called Chelsea Village.

As a result of the changes at Chelsea, in late 1993, the Official Receiver (a Department of Trade and Industry official), ordered an investigation into the actions of CFAC's directors. Simultaneously, the Football Association had asked its financial advisors, accountancy firm Touche Ross, to take a detailed look into the business affairs of CFAC.

Several areas of Chelsea's operations came in for scrutiny and some disapproval, from both the FA and DTI.

In July 1994 Touche Ross was removed as CFAC's liquidator, on the grounds of conflict of interest because of their involvement with the FA. 'Nothing untoward has happened at Chelsea. That was borne out by the High Court decision,' Bates announced. But in winning his High Court case, Bates's legal team also gave guarantees that all of CFAC's creditors would be paid in full.

It was into this situation at the Bridge which Matthew Harding found himself being courted to invest. Unease at the circumstances and ignorance of the identity of Chelsea Village's other shareholders forced Harding to be more circumspect. He knew that in funding the North Stand development by taking £5 million in convertible loan stock in Chelsea Village, he might have some leverage. Unless he chose to convert the stock, Harding knew that his £5 million loan would have to appear on the balance sheet of Chelsea Village every time that Bates sought further finance from the City. And Harding's condition every time that Bates asked him to convert the options into shares: 'tell me who really *owns* Chelsea Village'.

That, in itself, was enough to create a tension, an air of distrust, between Chelsea's two Bridge builders. Bates admitted frustration and annoyance at Harding's refusal to take up the shares. Their differences in politics – Bates an unreconstructed free-marketeer, drier than the Gobi desert; Harding, donor of £1 million to the Labour party – and their differences in philosophies over the running of the football club would not have drawn them any closer together.

But in April 1995, in one act of apparent benevolence for Chelsea Football Club, Harding used his enormous personal wealth to succeed where Bates had failed for more than a dozen years. If it was calculated as a sting, then it hurt, and it hurt deep.

Bates was cruising in the Caribbean at the time, oblivious to any behind-the-scenes machinations until he got a message to tell him that Harding had just bought the freehold to Stamford Bridge. Ever since he had been slighted by David Mears shortly after he had become chairman at Chelsea, Bates had worked tirelessly to gain possession of the ground. The title deeds to the broken-down old ground had become Bates's Holy Grail, the object of a 12-year crusade in which he had more often resembled Don Quixote than Richard the Lionheart, tilting at windmills. But finally, with the collapse of Cabra, Bates must have felt that he was coming close to the end of his quest, that ownership of Stamford Bridge was finally within his grasp. Imagine, then, the desperate feeling when he had discovered that Harding, through his own, new company, had paid £16.5 million to buy the freehold from the Royal Bank of Scotland, and that Chelsea chairman Bates would henceforward have to pay Harding £1.5 million a year in rent.

Before he did the deal, Harding had checked with Bates to discover exactly what the Chelsea chairman's greatest dream might be. Earlier that year, the two men were having lunch together at the Savoy. Between courses, in a lull in the animated conversation, Harding's chubby face wore a grin as he asked Bates, 'Ken, if a bit of stardust were to come down from above and all of a sudden we didn't have to buy the ground any more, how much then would we devote our energies to this development as opposed to the football club?'

Bates's answer convinced Harding that purchase of the ground would allow Chelsea to concentrate on winning football matches. Harding even based the name of the new company on his conversation with Bates: Stardust (Chelsea) Ltd were to become the new owners of Stamford Bridge.

'It's like swapping a hard-nosed landlord for a soft-nosed landlord,' Bates, putting on a brave face, remarked at the time. But the differences between him and Harding were by now irreconcilable, not least because Harding's refusal to take up his share options and his latest move seriously undermined Bates's plans for a stockmarket flotation of Chelsea Village.

David Mellor is the former Tory minister and prominent Chelsea fan who became notorious for appearing on the front page of *The Sun* after it was alleged that he had used his favourite team's football kit instead of pyjamas during one high-profile tryst. Mellor came to know Harding and Bates well, mixing with them in the Stamford Bridge boardroom and directors' box on match days. Mellor is, like Bates and Harding, a millionaire businessman, and he knew only too well that any power struggle at the Bridge would be long and bloody, with Bates stubbornly defending his fiefdom. 'Harding had not been with us when Bates battled through the 1980s at enormous personal cost and risk to stop the Bridge being flattened by property developers,' Mellor said. 'Now that battle was won, Bates was going to revel in his success, and not be marginalised just when things were starting to go well.'

Bates had planned the stock market flotation of Chelsea Village – offering shares in the company to the public through the Alternative Investment Market – as a means of raising another £30 million towards his redevelopment scheme for Stamford Bridge, a blueprint of a 45,000-seater new stadium that he had kept in his bottom drawer of his desk at Chelsea for nearly a decade. The millions of pounds which Premier League clubs were now receiving regularly from Sky TV, and the template for the off-the-field marketing of a football club as laid down by Manchester United, had inspired Bates towards believing that his dream of building a leisure and entertainment business empire at Stamford Bridge was finally attainable. The whole ethos of the football business in England had been changed. According to Rogan Taylor, the former Football Supporters' Association official, the course being taken by those, like Bates, driving the marketing and development of football into the 21st century was clear. 'Some people are trying to shape the game in such a way whereby the average couple from the Home Counties might say on a Saturday morning: "Well dear, where shall we go today, the golf club, the hypermarket, or the Arsenal?"'

But for Matthew Harding, Chelsea was more than simply another option in the leisure supermarket. He harboured deep doubts about Bates's plans for the Bridge, and in November 1995, just a few months before the proposed flotation of Chelsea Village, Harding threw another spanner in the works of Bates's scheme. Harding resigned as a director of Chelsea Village. While remaining on the board of the football club, and formally expressing his regret in taking this action, it was clear that Harding's resignation was a vote of no confidence in Bates. The simmering boardroom row between the two men now became a public battle for control of the club, played out on the back pages of *The Sun* and the *Daily Mirror*.

'If he wants to start taking over the club,' Bates told anyone who would listen, 'then he should start buying some shares. There are 36 million unissued shares as of today and a banker's draft for £18 million would do nicely.' It was known that Bates held 30 per cent of Chelsea Village shares, and that he spoke for the owners of most of the rest of the stock, but Harding could never discover who these mysterious, offshore nominee organisations were. 'I'd have had a minority stake in a private company whose shareholders I didn't know,' Harding said of his reasons for not buying shares in Chelsea Village.

Bates told reporters that he had been pressing Harding for almost 12 months to exercise this option, and that he did not believe he was going to get any further reply. 'Put it like this,' Bates said, 'it has taken a year not to get an answer. All we have is the fluff on the cappuccino.' On a table in his Stamford Bridge office, Bates had kept three framed cheques – one for £2.6 million, one for £1.6 million and another for £800,000 – all bearing the signature of Matthew Harding, all to pay for the signing of new players. This was Bates's 'fluff', and while Harding's investments in the club, which came to something like £26 million, may have amounted to the world's most expensive cappuccino, Bates was not overestimating the enormous value of what was at stake. 'Harding gave me those cheques,' Bates was to say, 'and I got rid of 'em.'

It was not only cash that Harding provided. Bates needed Harding's contacts, credibility and caché in the City. He also knew that if Harding really wanted to wrest control of Chelsea from his grip, it could cost him anything from £50 million up to £100 million to buy out the chairman's shares. Even for a Chelsea fanatic such as Harding, that represented a sizeable chunk of his fortune, much of which was tied up in his reinsurance business. Would Harding really sell-up at Benfields to give himself the money necessary to take over Chelsea? It was a gamble which Bates was prepared to take, probably because he knew, as Harding would have calculated, that even if the vice-chairman could release that capital to buy control of the club, it would leave him with precious little resources to continue any ground development or to help manager Hoddle build a winning team. Would Harding really want to give up the reinsurance business he had built up so successfully in order to take control of a half-built team in a half-finished stadium? In this millionaires' game of poker, Bates had effectively called Harding's hand by throwing the ownership of the club on to the table as the final stake.

According to Bates, Harding had approached him about taking over as chairman at Chelsea 12 months earlier. Bates, though, was not easily moved. 'We are just beginning to see the fruits of all the hard work that has been done here over the last 13 years. I am not about to walk away now,' Bates said. 'After what has gone on, what has been said, I cannot see how we can continue to work together.' What particularly irked Bates was that Harding, garrulous by nature but even more so when the topic of conversation was Chelsea, had openly consorted with journalists and aired his concerns and reservations to them. Harding's doubts about Bates and Chelsea Village had become football's worst-kept secret. 'He has been nice to my face,' Bates said, 'but said unpleasant things about me behind my back. I have made this club my life.' According to Bates, Harding was 'totally unfit to be chairman of this football club'.

'I haven't had one good reason why I should go. Anyway, I don't want to. Everything you see around Chelsea these days is growth. It's all part of the plan to make the club viable and financially independent of football. I have dedicated an awful lot of time to these plans and making sure we survived those difficult early times when the very existence of the club was in doubt. Now we have all this negative stuff and it does no good to anybody.

'It is for Matthew to consider his position, not for me to consider mine.'

Bates also said that he really did want Harding to succeed him as Chelsea chairman. 'I was hoping he would, because it was all part of the agreed succession. He'd have got his 17 per cent of the shares, then we'd have done a deal on how he'd have got to 51 per cent, then I'd have retired. The plan was that I'd like to finish the development. After all, it was my vision, my baby, it was something I said I'd do, and I'd like to finish it. Then I saw myself continuing as chairman for a few more years to enjoy the fruits of my labours. I actually said to him, "Then you take over".

'He's a young man in a hurry. He loved the adulation and it's gone to his head. The whole thing was there on a plate for him, but I didn't get any response. And to have a dialogue you need two people talking.'

When the storm broke, Harding was in the United States on a business trip. 'I'm surprised so much mayhem's gone on in my absence,' he said. 'I'm not looking for the hostility and war of words I'm led to believe Ken Bates is after. One of my life's ambitions is not to be chairman of Chelsea. In fact, I don't give a damn about being chairman. I've said all along that I'm only interested in the best for Chelsea FC, for the club to realise its potential. All I know is that at the moment we have the wrong chairman.'

Harding suggested that, were he to become chairman of the club, then he would make himself completely accountable to the fans every year by seeking re-election by the 25,000-or-so club season-ticket holders and members. 'I don't care who has shares or not. I believe that if someone cares enough about the club to pay his £25 or whatever a year, he or she should have a say in how it's run. Chelsea have more than 25,000 members, and they are the emotional shareholders of the club.' Harding even suggested that he would be willing to contest such an election against Bates, to resolve the differences. 'Let's say to the fans, "There's a ballot paper and a report of what we both stand for, you decide". If Ken gets 90 per cent of the vote, I'll leave the board and go back to sitting in the North Stand.'

Bates, the man who once said he would rather chat with a skinhead on The Shed than lunch with a lord, characterised this as Harding pandering to Chelsea's 'yob element'. When the Chelsea Independent Supporters' Association weighed in behind Harding, Bates called them 'jackals', and – without a hint of irony over his own position within Chelsea Village – accused them of being undemocratic and failing to publish a proper set of accounts. Meanwhile Bates, who had never subjected himself to any form of election, confirmed that he was not very fond of the concept of football club democracy: 'So what happens if he loses an election and someone with another set of policies comes in and then that person loses, too? Don't make me laugh.' When one newspaper ran a telephone poll to discover who the fans wanted at the helm at the Bridge, with 80 per cent in favour of Harding, Bates had an answer for that, too: 'So what? Ninety-nine per cent of Iraqis voted for Saddam Hussein.

'Those polls are a doddle to rig. I've done it myself. Got somebody to ring *The Sun*'s phone lines all day when they ran a poll about me sacking a manager. Screwed their poll right up. Load of nonsense.'

Populist as Harding's suggestion was to put the matter to a vote of Chelsea members, the idea of giving supporters a say in the running of football clubs was not just confined to Harding. When Lord Justice Taylor published his report on safety at football grounds after the Hillsborough disaster in 1989, his recommendations also advocated some form of supporters' representative at board level. Chelsea's London neighbours, Charlton, have had a supporters' representative on their board for some years, with success. In Harding, many Chelsea fans thought that they had achieved a similar representation, despite Ken Bates's best efforts.

What's more, Harding took the responsibility seriously, 'My job is to act as a custodian of the supporters' interests and to help the club in any way. It has always intrigued me that there are people on football boards who aren't football fans. That asks a few questions, doesn't it?

'I've been in love with Chelsea for 30 years. But it's a club that's won the championship once, and that was 40 years ago, won the Cup once and that was 25 years ago, had one success in Europe and that was 24 years ago. Outside of that, frankly, it's been a bit of a joke and yet it's got a great brand name and an underlying support both at home and abroad that I think deserves better.

'In recent years we would go out and beat the top side away and then get dumped out of the Cup at home to a Third Division side. We would kid ourselves that that is quite fun. It's not, it's hell.'

It was not enough to drive Harding to drink, although once hostilities with Bates had broken out, he stopped answering his phone with his usual, cheery, 'Chelsea dressing room', and instead he would say, 'Alcoholics Anonymous'. Bates, employing a favourite tactic whenever he has met with opposition, banned Harding from the boardroom and directors' box, even withdrawing Harding's car park pass. The ban was announced in a letter which the Chelsea chairman released to the press before Harding received it. 'It gives me no pleasure to do this,' Bates wrote in his best school-masterly tone. 'It will at least stop the embarrassment in the boardroom of the behaviour related to your heavy drinking both home and away.' Harding's response was simple: to decamp with his family and friends and watch matches from seats in the stand which he had paid for.

The showdown between the two men came at the club's regular monthly board meeting at Stamford Bridge on a Thursday evening in early December 1995. Board meetings at Chelsea are apparently rarely occasions for free and open discussion (although since Bates restricts the number of board members to less than a handful, accounts of the meetings are rare). Chris Lightbown, *The Sunday Times* football writer and one of very few soccer journalists whom Bates regards with anything more than disdain, has described the occasions as the equivalent of a one-party state congratulating its leader. Until Harding's appointment to the board, the chairman had headed up a *troika* with just managing director Colin Hutchinson and accountant Yvonne Todd also able to attend. Some suggested that as long as the chairman was there, the meeting always had a quorum.

The tension and animosity that had erupted between chairman and vice-chairman clearly had heightened suspicions. Bates had boasted in the press that he knew every move Harding was to make before he did it, and in the week before the board meeting, the Special Branch was called in to Harding's Fenchurch Street offices in London when a bugging device was discovered there. The implication was that Bates had had the device planted, though no evidence to support this was ever found. Later, Bates alleged that he, too, had been subject to close scrutiny, private detectives having been hired to look into his business affairs, both in Britain and in the Channel Islands.

By the time of the board meeting, though, Harding had at least one more shot left in his locker. Colin Hutchinson was ready to upset the meeting's equilibrium by presenting a report to the board which suggested that Bates's real priority lay not with the football club, but in the development of the ground. Hutchinson's report posed serious questions about the southern development, being built on the site of The Shed, where the size of the new stand had been reduced at the expense of the commercial projects behind it – hotel, megastore and offices.

Coming from such a loyal and respected Bates appointee as Hutchinson, this report could have been very damning for the chairman's plans. The point of the Hutchinson report seemed only to reinforce Harding's reservations: while in theory, Chelsea Village might well provide the football club with financial security, the fear was that, in practice, the commercial imperatives of any publicly quoted company – to secure the interests of the investors and pay them handsome dividends – would always override any more sentimental obligations towards a mere football team. That fear was compounded by the mystery surrounding the identity of the shareholders.

The Sunday Times described Hutchinson's report and its questioning of Bates's motives as the 'equivalent of a politburo member questioning Stalin at the height of the Cold War'. Come the meeting, and Bates rebutted the complaints about the reduced size of the South Stand by saying that planning consent would not allow him to alter the plans for the rest of the development, but the stand had to be made smaller when Glenn Hoddle asked for the size of the pitch to be extended, making Stamford Bridge 'the most overcrowded 12 acres in the world'. This did not stop Bates complaining about the size of the pitch again a year later, suggesting that the alterations to the pitch would cost Chelsea Village up to £20 million in lost revenues from the reduced sized stands.

When it came to the crunch, Bates always knew he would not be beaten by his own board. 'Two-two? If the directors split two-two, our rules say that the chairman gets the casting vote,' Bates said, suddenly discovering a new enthusiasm for a brand of democracy where he gets to vote twice. So it was that Hutchinson's report and Harding's opposition failed to oust Bates as Chelsea chairman. Later, Hutchinson and Harding resigned from the board of Chelsea Village, perhaps in the knowledge that Bates had put down his own, personal foundations so deep at Stamford Bridge that nothing could move him now. Despite it later emerging that the largest stake, 36 per cent, in Chelsea Village belonged to Hong Kong-based off-shore trust Rysaffe (later transferred to Swan Management, a company based in Guernsey), Harding would ultimately be foiled in his attempts to indentify the people behind these share-holdings. It would not be until June 1997, with a change in the Stock Exchange rules governing the Alternative Investment Market, that disclosure of the names of shareholders with more than £10,000-worth of stock would be required.

After the Chelsea board meeting, there was even a rapprochement, of sorts, with Harding, who got his director's car park pass back and was again seen as part of the 'management team' (if slightly semi-detached) as the new season approached. Bates attributes this change to his own skill in cornering his opponent. At a secret meeting in Drakes on 1 March 1996, Bates handed over a document to formally inform Harding that Chelsea Village would go public in 28 days' time. Harding had four weeks to take up his options, or lose out. Privately, Bates admitted that he was working to end Harding's influence at the club altogether.

Going into the 1996–97 season, optimists among the Chelsea faithful (which, if truth be told, is probably most of them – nothing less than complete and total optimism could sustain a Chelsea fan through thin and thin), reasoned that with Bates's abrasive determination, Harding's money and now with Gullit's genius applied to coaching, the coming season would be the one when, finally, the lean years would be ended. Perhaps they were right, though no one would have predicted the tragic and bitter circumstances under which those ends would be achieved.

Chapter 5

Thirty years of hurt, never stopped us dreaming . . . It was the song of the summer, the long, hot summer of 1996, when football was never far away, because, according to the song, it had come home. The 1996 European championships staged in England were acclaimed as a resounding success, on and off the pitch, managing to capture the attention not only of regular football watchers, but at times of the whole nation. The high-water marks included Spanish and Dutch fans joining in the choruses of the England song while seeing their teams lose at Wembley, Gascoigne's goal against Scotland, and lots of what Ruud Gullit called 'sexy football'.

And then there were those penalties, Gareth Southgate's especially. They say that that match, England *v* Germany in the semi-final, was watched by 25 million in Britain, one of the largest television audiences ever. After two hours of football, with the teams still level, half the country must have been silent as they watched Andi Möller step up to hit the ball past David Seaman. For just a moment, every one of those tearful viewers knew what it is like to be a Chelsea fan.

It had not quite been 30 years of hurt for Chelsea, but 25 trophy-less, success-starved seasons managed to replicate a similar amount of anguish. You would think, though, that after after a quarter of a century of unfulfilled promise, even the most faithful of Chelsea supporters would temper the seasonal optimism with a little bit of hard-earned experience. Not a bit of it: on the train out of Waterloo on a Friday evening in July, expectations were higher than ever.

'Yeah, I reckon that with Vialli and di Matteo, and Ruudi of course, we can win the title this season.'

'Nah, we'll be a cup team, definitely a cup team. It'll take a while to gel.' And so on as the train rattled through south London. There was a good scattering of passengers – or 'customers', as the new 'service provider' which had replaced British Rail Southern Region preferred to call us fellow travellers – who obviously were not regular commuters on the 5.15 to Norbiton. As the suits took their regular refuge behind the pages of the *Evening Standard,* unwilling to acknowledge the existence of others on the train, the football supporters could not contain their chatter. They were as excitable as children on Christmas eve. That they were Chelsea was a giveaway: such unbridled optimism, such cool disdain for reality.

It seemed odd, going to a game in the middle of summer, so soon after the end of the league season, so soon after Euro '96, but what had drawn most of the customers who got off at Norbiton station that evening was less an inability to stay away from football, and more the curiosity aroused by Chelsea's new signings. Vialli, Leboeuf and di Matteo, all were due to be paraded for the first time that night, as Chelsea's pre-season campaign got underway with a little friendly at Kingstonian, the non-league team's ground used for most of Chelsea's reserve games. Such was the anticipation for the display of these new signings that, as you left Norbiton station to cross the road to the ground, there came that cry so familiar for all sell-out sports events such as Wembley Cup finals, Wimbledon or the Lord's Test: 'Need any tickets? I'll buy any spares.'

Kingstonian's ground had never seen such a crowd. It is part of a local sports facility. To one side is an athletics track, and next door is the modest little football ground which most people driving into Kingston might barely notice, tucked away as it is behind some anonymous suburban houses and a sewage works. Entering the ground reinforces the feeling that you are going into your local sports centre to book a squash court. It all added to the sense of unreality: football in mid-summer? Chelsea, playing at such an unassuming venue? Here, the man who lifted the European Cup barely six weeks earlier now turning out wearing the blue of Chelsea? Surely some mistake?

The match against Kingstonian was effectively Chelsea's first sell-out of the season, all 4,000 tickets having been sold, the terracing packed far closer than is comfortable on such a muggy summer evening. In the bright daylight, with the players tanned and sporting new haircuts, as they warmed-up it took some staring to make out who was who. There is a minor panic among some of the crowd when one fan spots a big, shaven-headed black guy warming up, with a sadly familiar lack of ball control. 'For fuck's sake!' the fan yells above the general murmurings and banter, 'I thought we'd sold that useless bastard Furlong.' Indeed Chelsea had sold Paul Furlong: what an exchange, Vialli for Furlong on future team sheets, and £1.5 million from Birmingham City on the income side of the balance sheet. Furlong's time at the Bridge always seemed to be limited from the moment, playing against QPR the previous season, Gullit deftly put the striker through, with just the goalkeeper to beat, and Chelsea's then record signing managed to miskick the ball so thoroughly that he landed on his backside, the ball skidding past him harmlessly. Furlong should have scored a late winning goal, but instead he created a moment of high farce. Gullit's despair at such a wantonly missed chance and his withering look suggested then that Furlong was on borrowed time. 'If ever I'm in charge . . .' the glare from beneath the dreadlocks seemed to say. When the offer came to sell the player to Birmingham in the First Division, there was little hesitation by Chelsea's new player-manager.

In which case, who was this useless plank at Kingstonian showing himself to be just as incompetent on the ball even during the pre-game kickabout? Once he set off to sprint after one of his miskicks, the realisation struck home: it was in fact Ade Mafe, the new fitness adviser for the team. As word filtered out, there was a collective sigh of relief. This, though, was not any where near as palpable as the expressions of dismay when it was announced that none of the new signings would be playing.

In fact, Vialli could never play in such a low-key game. As is the manner for all players, Vialli was insured by the club when he signed for Chelsea, but the policy expressly forbid the star signing from being used in reserve games, for risk of a career-threatening injury by tripping over a loose turf. Or by a clumsy tackle from an opposition player either lacking the skill to keep up with the Italian, or simply narked at the idea that in Vialli, here was a player getting paid as much in a week as he might earn in six months. In any case, what would Vialli want with reserve team football? The Italian would never need such games to maintain his match fitness and sharpness. Would he?

'Is that him? Is it?' one supporter, wanting his first glimpse of Vialli, asked. Eventually, two of the new boys – Vialli and di Matteo – were introduced to the crowd, by which time no one in the crowd could see the players, as a throng of press photographers took their chances (better, ever, than Paul Furlong took his) to get as many close-up stock shots of the players, for use throughout the season to come.

In the end, it was a fairly unfamiliar Chelsea team that lined up for the game. But that a scratch Chelsea XI managed to beat their part-time hosts 7–0 did nothing to disperse the great expectations as the crowd dispersed afterwards. 'Leeds have done it, so have Blackburn. Why can't we win the title, then?' Long-suffering fans are like that: their degree of hopefulness seems to grow in inverse proportions to the club's actual achievements. For most Chelsea supporters, therefore, by the beginning of the 1996–97 season, with Gullit in charge of the New Azzurri, expectations had acquired Himalayan proportions.

There is a strong element of emotional investment at work here, too. Chelsea chairman Ken Bates had once written in his match programme notes that, 'We are not Mormons, we are not asking for ten per cent of your income,' as he implored the fans to pitch in with cash to help the club in one of its many hours of need. The pulpit message of sacrifice for the club's sake eventually got through. Bates's 'Save The Bridge' campaign saw Chelsea fans come to believe that by spending money on Chelsea, every little bit would help. It did not matter what their contribution might have been. The fans might decide to buy a season ticket, or they could visit the club shop to buy a club shirt from the notoriously naff Chelsea Collection. Perhaps they would buy a bingo card, or toss a coin into one of the blue buckets kept around the ground. There is an almost religious faithfulness about football fans and their club, and when they passed around the offerings plate after each week's service, Chelsea's congregation showed that they cared. Their belief was that their widow's mite would help not only to keep their Stamford Bridge home, but also to revive the team's fortunes. Such is blind faith.

Take Steve Thorn, for instance. At the start of the 1994–95 season, Steve, a loyal Chelsea fan, decided to keep an account of everything he spent on following Chelsea that season. Thorn embarked on an odyssey of every first-team game, plus friendlies, testimonials and reserve matches, and a couple of trips to Europe, too, as Chelsea progressed in that season's European Cup-winners' Cup. In a way, perhaps Thorn was 'lucky' that he did not spend more, as Chelsea failed to have much of a run in either of the domestic cup competitions that season.

Thorn's expenditure might not seem unduly extravagant, were he a single bloke with a good job and no responsibilities such as children or a mortgage to worry about. However, Thorn is a thirtysomething father of three, with a mortgage. Yet in 1994–95, he managed to spend £3,348.90 in order to follow Chelsea – more than one-quarter of his annual income. Thorn is not untypical of the sort of financial cost football fans are prepared to sustain in order to follow their favourites. Sure, they will moan and groan about the cost of tickets. But they will always pay.

Such a high price for loyalty sees some go to unusual lengths to see Chelsea. Tom Williams, for instance, got married in 1994, 'and we were going to use our savings to have a new kitchen put in to the house we were moving into,' he said, 'but once Chelsea were in Europe, I just had to get to every game. So I went to Bruges and Zaragoza. And we didn't get a new kitchen.'

According to Steve Thorn, the cost of following Chelsea has hit a high. 'Even allowing for inflation, I can never remember football swallowing up so much cash,' he said. 'What you also have to consider is money lost through not doing overtime on Saturdays, or from only working a half-day because you're playing Liverpool away in midweek.'

Thorn's football accounts did not include other optional extras, such as a pre-match pint and a sandwich, but the expense was never a deterrent. The true fan will always pay: 'I have never even entertained the idea of giving up football.' As a season-ticket holder in the most expensive seats in Stamford Bridge, the middle tier of the East Stand (price for 1997–98: £887), Thorn knew too well that he was trapped, a sort of *milchcow* that would contribute funds to Chelsea forever more, regardless of the cost. 'There is no way I'm ever going to give up my season ticket – it's the best seat in the house.'

While the fans underwent their pre-season limbering up to make sure their bank accounts were as fit as possible to withstand the pressures and demands of the coming months, so the players had also entered into a summer ritual of preparation. Less than a fortnight after the Germans had carried off the trophy from Euro '96, the Chelsea squad had reported to the club's training ground at Harlington. For the newcomers, it must have felt like familiar territory – having stepped off their aeroplane at Heathrow, they were now expected to train right under the flightpath of the world's busiest airport.

The Imperial College Sports Ground at Harlington is an unassuming facility – nothing more than a few football pitches on a broad sward of flat playing fields. There is no elaborate, state-of-the-art facilities for physiotherapy, no whirlpool or exercise machines. But then, Gullit did not need them. The essence of Gullit's plan was practice, practice and more practice, until the players had acquired the fitness and command of the skills which would allow them to draw sighs of delight from the Stamford Bridge crowds.

Being in the middle of the school summer holidays, the first few days of pre-season training always attract swathes of children, eager to get autographs. This was especially the case, with such high-profile players. The players were patient and obliging, carefully signing even the scrappiest scrap of paper, every letter of every 'Di Matteo' or 'Burley' clearly written, to be squirrelled away with the child's greatest treasures.

It is a football commentator's cliché, but it is true nonetheless – the great players always seem to have more time when they are on the ball. Their command of the basic skills is so complete, so absolute, their senses so alert, that they have an awareness that defies understanding by lesser gifted mortals. They can always cope with a bobbling ball, a turn, a swivel and then by-pass any on-rushing challenge. So it is with Gullit. Norman Mailer once wrote that in the humbling presence of Muhammad Ali, 'Men look *down*. They are reminded again of their lack of worth . . . so says the silence around his body when he is luminous'. So it is with Gullit, a man so altogether at ease with his own physicality.

Gullit embodies the idea of *presence*. He possesses that elusive 'extra time' that truly great sports stars have; he seems to have extra time even when he's just walking. It lends him a sense of extra poise, even grace. He strolls over, smiling beneath his dreads. Close up, he's more of a giant than he seems on the pitch. The smile is warm and disarming. Carefully, he ushers the children back behind a steel barrier, gentle touches of the shoulders enough to shepherd the group effectively. Gullit takes 20 minutes, signing everything offered to him. The smile continues throughout. The children ought to be in awe of the man, but perhaps fail to realise what it is they are encountering. Everyone else in his presence, though, is awed.

The press, meanwhile, hover in the background, also intent on getting small offerings from the manager and the players, by way of a brief pose for a photographer, or some exclusive *bon mot* for the journalists. As the training session winds down at lunchtime, they scuttle up some stairs and into a small hall for a formal press conference with Gullit.

The hall, with its moulded plastic seats and plastic mugs of strong tea, is quintessentially English. Utilitarian rooms, unpolished parquet flooring. Gullit takes his place behind a formica-topped table. It is a world away from the San Siro. When he was at AC Milan, Gullit would have been used to the manager sitting in front of a cluster of sponsors' logos, a small means of repaying some of these other companies' investments in the club. After all, whose money had helped pay for the £12 million-worth of new talent that had just been displayed on the training ground? But that was the San Siro. Here at Chelsea, the only signage behind Gullit is the honours boards for the Imperial College sports clubs, showing team captains at rugby and cricket, all the way back to the 1950s. The incongruity of the whole scene is such that what Gullit is actually saying seems to just float by, unheard. It is how he copes with the new situation that is more fascinating than any predictable pre-season platitudes.

There is an old football tale of one new manager, used to life as a player, who walked into his first press conference and proclaimed: 'I've been crapping myself more about this than I have about the match'. Football, after all, is what footballers do and understand. It is the rest of the panoply of modern professional sport to which they are unused, and usually untrained for.

But Gullit plays the press just as he plays the game, coolly, always in control. Like the children outside on the practice pitch, if the press stray into an area of questioning he dislikes, he quietly, politely, moves them back to where he is more comfortable. If someone steps over the line again, repeating the same question perhaps, Gullit smiles, shaking his head just enough to make his dreads bounce. Like the children outside, the questioner eventually complies. Watching from the side of the room, leaning against the tea bar, assistant manager Gwyn Williams, the former school teacher, observes quietly, ready to organise any special requests for player interviews, but, one suspects, equally prepared to step in and change the direction of the press conference should the situation require. Even so early in Gullit's honeymoon period as Chelsea boss, such precautions are unnecessary.

Already, Gullit's training methods had gained the acceptance of at least one senior member of his squad. Unlike Gullit, Mark Hughes's first season at Chelsea had not been an overwhelming success. As well as being unsettled by having to move south from his Cheshire family home, Hughes had been unhappy with the playing style of the team, the performances of some of his team mates, and the training regime. Gullit's ascension had seen most of his footballing concerns dealt with. 'As you get older and more experienced,' Mark Hughes said, 'you know what training you need. Because of the shape I am – heavy in the leg – I need a lot of speed work to keep me sharp, and the training this season has been geared to that much more, which has helped me. Under Glenn Hoddle, we concentrated on matchplay situations, playing 11-a-side games, which I didn't enjoy. Ruudi goes in for small-sided games and one-on-ones – a lot more of the quick, explosive stuff, which I need.'

Part of the reason Gullit was able to make such changes was his insistence on twice-a-day training, built around lunch, eaten by the players in the communal dining hall at Harlington. In one stroke, Gullit had contrived to bring the players closer together as a unit. Now, instead of the old routine of training, shower and drive home, the players would spend more time together, talking, eating and drinking football.

'Last year, I told the players what I was used to, and they know I won all these things,' Gullit said. 'I am not demanding things of them, like changing their eating and drinking habits, but some players are doing it by themselves.'

His chairman, Ken Bates, confirmed that Gullit's changes were fundamental, his influence profound even before he took the manager's job. 'He was an influence behind the scenes, even under Hoddle,' Bates said. 'Glenn was into reflexology, alternative medicine, a dietician. Gullit is into fitness. He brought in Ade Mafe and a different style of coaching. He bombed out the reflexologist, the dietician and the masseur.'

Gullit explained to Bates that he got rid of the dietician because the players rebelled against it. Gullit rejected the paternalistic approach to players, preferring to adopt an attitude based on trust and example, and, above all, self-discipline. 'If I say, "You must eat this," they won't eat at the training ground, they will go elsewhere and get it. You have to get them to realise the only person who can look after themselves is themself. If they don't realise that, they won't be in the team.

'These are not continental ideas, they are my own ideas. I have my experience, and I have played under many good managers, and I want to use that on the team. I want the players to think first of what they can do for the team. Everybody has an assignment. They have one for when we don't have the ball and one for when we do. It is like the pieces in a clock. If one piece is wrong, the clock does not work.

'It was the same with Milan. Every day the same thing, every day your assignment. The team move like that, the team move like that, the team move like that,' he emphasises the repetition, and his hair bobs again. 'All of a sudden, you could dream it. Without thinking, you did it. Then, when you had the ball, you could explore yourself because you were not thinking about it. Then you make a dummy, you score a goal, everybody is happy. Simple really, but only after the hard work has been put in.

'If I see on the faces of the players that they are enjoying what they do, then I have achieved what I want.'

Bates, though, was most concerned about how well Gullit might make the transition from player to manager. 'Some make the transition from player to manager easily, others find it a problem,' Bates said. 'John Hollins found it hard. As a player, he was one of the ones that took the mick out of the manager behind his back. Now his team mates were doing it to him.

'Most player-manager fail because, suddenly, instead of having to work for maybe ten hours each week, suddenly they find themselves having to put in 60 hours every week, and they can't cope. A football club today is not like it was 20 years ago – it's a big business. So we at Chelsea decided to let Ruud concentrate on his playing and coaching, and that's why we organised others to look after the administration and deal with the press and players' contracts.'

So soon into his managership, not all of Gullit's playing plans had been definitively formulated. Under Glenn Hoddle, Chelsea had experimented with the 3-5-2 system. Gullit was known to prefer such a continental approach, but nonetheless was not hidebound to keep to it. 'I have to see which formation they play the best. It was the same with Milan, we started with 4-3-3, then Marco van Basten was injured and we had to change something. It was against Verona, we played 4-4-2 and we played so good it was "Ah, we've found it". The same with Chelsea. I want to see what they do the best.

'This season is starting a new adventure. Every season excites me, but this one is different, there is more to do, more everything. You must always look for challenges in life, otherwise you will get bored.'

Yet one of the most obvious factors of Gullit's management at Chelsea passed completely unremarked by the press conference. For not only had the club appointed a foreigner to coach the team, Chelsea had also appointed the first black manager in the Premiership. Perhaps it is a sign of these relatively enlightened times that the colour of a man's skin can pass unremarked, an irrelevance when the man is properly judged for what he is. But in the case of Chelsea, that such an appointment can be made – indeed, was demanded by the vast majority of the Chelsea faithful – is indication either of the great esteem in which Gullit is held personally, or of incredible progress that race relations have made in Britain.

Chelsea, after all, is the same club where just ten years before, one gifted black player was hounded out of the club by the racist chants and abuse he received from his *own* fans, who would pelt him with bananas if he got too close to The Shed. The terraces at Chelsea were for a long time a productive recruiting ground for extreme right-wing racists groups, such as the National Front and British National Party. And if anyone suggests that racism in football is a thing of the past, they would be wrong. While anti-black sentiments may be rarely heard at Stamford Bridge these days, 'anti-yid' songs, even chants about the holocaust, taunting Tottenham Hotspur fans and offending many more, can still be heard, lustily sung by many in the 28,000 crowds. Yet it was here, at Chelsea, that Ruud Gullit was embarking on his managerial career.

Gullit rationalises. 'It's a game of emotions,' Gullit said, 'and if people call me names, call me a black bastard, it gives me a feeling of superiority. You hear things said from the crowd sometimes, but they are just working off their frustrations and I don't mind that because they will always applaud you at the end. Sometimes when I was at Milan they whistled at me when I was on the ball, but I took it as a compliment. I said: "You are afraid of me". It made me feel good. You have to be positive, because no one is going to resolve it for you.

'What I do object to is the kind of thing that happened when Ajax played in Hungary last season when people started making rude jungle sounds. That's abusive. When Ajax complained, UEFA imposed a fine, and that was right.'

Gullit's positive, self-reliant attitude probably comes from his father, who emigrated to the Netherlands from Surinam. 'He worked during the day and went to night school for eight years. It was not easy. He told me that to achieve things I would also have to work hard.

'The most important thing is talent, whether you are black or white. I was aware I was black but for me it was a stimulation. If I played with ten white guys and I was the only black guy, everybody would look at me, and for me that was an advantage. If you feel attacked by the way you are different, you have a problem.'

Thus, before he even started, Gullit stood out as a Premiership manager. He would soon discover whether he was outstanding as a manager in the Premiership.

Chapter 6

There had been so many new arrivals at Stamford Bridge during the summer of 1996 that the management might have had to give serious consideration to having a revolving door on the changing rooms. But a look around the dressing rooms soon made it clear that the appearance of Vialli, Leboeuf and di Matteo also meant that for others, opportunities in the first team would be limited, and there were not enough coat hooks to accommodate the kit of every member of the squad.

David Rocastle had won 14 England caps during his time as one of Arsenal's more creative midfielders. They rated him so highly at Highbury that vice-chairman David Dein had had a coffee table made for their boardroom with its legs shaped just like the player's. But after a disastrous move to Leeds United, where he hardly ever got a game, playing just 25 games in two seasons, and then a brief stay at Manchester City, Glenn Hoddle had signed him for Chelsea in the belief that here was just the sort of skilful player the side needed. It was not a unique perspective – after all, Hoddle with three other Premiership managers had spent a total of £6 million on Rocastle's three transfer moves – but the trouble was, it was not one shared by Ruud Gullit.

Rocastle's last game for Chelsea had been at Blackburn the previous November. A broken toe in a reserve game soon after had hardly helped him to force his way out of 'the stiffs', but he must have hoped that, in the pre-season under Gullit, he would at least get a chance to show his worth.

Then came the summons to Gullit's office. There used to be an old, black and white Western series on television in the '60s, called *Branded*, where a US cavalry officer was wrongly court martialled for cowardice and each episode saw him trying to regain his good name. The opening credits, though, were the most striking thing about the entire programme. Against a dramatic drum roll, the programme's hero was summoned forward and cermonially stripped of his badges of rank, with the final indignity, the big symbolic gesture, being his officer's sword

being broken in two. Rocastle was to suffer an equivalent fate at Chelsea
– instead of having his sword broken, he would not be allocated a squad
number for the forthcoming season. 'I was wheeled into Ruudi's office
and told there was only room for a squad of 22 and that I wasn't going
to be one of them,' Rocastle said. 'This was before a ball had been
kicked. I was so shocked, I couldn't speak.'

Such treatment can affect people in at least two ways. Some might
become so angry at their fate that they seize any available opportunity to
impress the powers-that-be. Others might be so upset by their treatment
that they recoil into themselves, the shock too much to overcome. After
his two previous nightmare stays at Leeds and Manchester City,
Rocastle would now fall into this latter category at Chelsea.

It was not that he did not get any playing opportunities in the pre-
season games. As Chelsea set off for a brief summer tour of the West
Country, Rocastle would get to play some football. But not so that
anyone would notice him. A week after the Kingstonian game, the
phoney war of pre-season matches saw Chelsea at Exeter. Even this
game was typical of Chelsea in many ways, disappointing from
beginning to end. Despite the assurances of Graham Rix in both the
national and local press that this would be the game in which both di
Matteo and Vialli would make their debuts, neither appeared. Vialli was
on the bench sure enough, as was Gullit, but neither was exactly dressed
to play football. Two games into pre-season, and already the whispers
and rumours about injuries were beginning to grow louder. Doubt, the
perennial partner of the Chelsea fan, was by his side once more.

Gullit, it seemed, would require some minor knee surgery before the
season proper got underway. This was hardly the sort of news to scotch
the scoffing of the Italian experts who had warned when Chelsea signed
him that 'Glass Knees', with his advancing years, might turn out for us
increasingly rarely.

At low-key games such as this, the atmosphere is sufficiently relaxed,
the game so totally unimportant, that there is a greater opportunity for
interplay between players and supporters. So it was that, when some of
the fans behind the Chelsea goal called out to Kevin Hitchcock to ask
where Vialli was, the goalkeeper gestured towards the stand and mimed
bowel movements, perhaps suggesting that his new colleague did not
have the stomach for this game.

At least the match provided an opportunity for Gullit to see how some
of his younger, less well-known squad members might perform.
Teenager Jody Morris, once a student of the FA's School of Excellence
at Lilleshall and already an England under-21 international, but still
looking to force his way into Chelsea's first team as a regular, carried the

responsibility of trying to control midfield. Quick, with good ball control, the Exeter players took delight in closing him down quickly and bustling his slight frame off the ball at every opportunity.

Behind Morris, the Chelsea defence was experimenting with David Lee as a sweeper. Basically, he would operate as a defender, but have the freedom to roam forward, making passes to set off Chelsea attacks. Lee's passing was a joy to watch at times, although he tended to favour the ball out to the right to Frank Sinclair, often neglecting the other wing-back, Andy Myers.

Sinclair is deserving of a special mention. He has been with Chelsea since the age of 11, joining the staff as a trainee at 18, and over the following seven seasons had convinced supporters that he would give his heart and soul for the club. 'He'd run through a door for Chelsea, rather than open it,' his club captain, Dennis Wise says. The club's Player of the Year in 1993, Sinclair is renowned for his great speed and as a phenomenal leaper at crosses. Yet, Sinclair's ability to make simple errors when on the ball had led some fans to cringe whenever the defender was presented with a pass and time in which to dwell.

Sinclair's speed had, in the 1994 FA Cup final, seen him assigned to cover the attacks down the wing from Manchester United's Andrei Kanchelskis. After holding United to 0–0 for an hour, Eddie Newton conceded a penalty that put Chelsea behind, to be followed only a few minutes later by Sinclair having a penalty awarded against him (even though replays would show that the tackle was neither unfair, nor committed inside the penalty area). The resulting goal came as a hammer blow to Chelsea's hopes that day. For Sinclair, after having had such an outstanding game up to then, it was a crushing blow.

'I still don't think it was a penalty,' he says. 'At the time, people said that just because you do everything together, you didn't have to copy Eddie at that as well. Eddie and I have spent almost every day together at Chelsea since we were 11, when we first met. I've spent more time with him than with members of my family. We're very close, we've both had ups and downs in recent years and we've helped one another through the bad times. 'Being defeated at Wembley just made all of us who played that day all the more hungry to get back there.'

Wembley was a world away from the picturesque St James' Park in Devon. Against Exeter, it seemed, Frankie was his usual self. Lee would drive the ball over to him, right to his feet, and Sinclair would somehow contrive to make the pass seem to be a bad one by failing to control it first time. 'You couldn't trap a bag of cement,' someone shouted from the crowd. The next time he got the ball, Sinclair would silence the heckler and make the rest of the crowd gasp in admiration, as he would trap a difficult pass stone dead, step inside two defenders, step over the ball, drag it back and then cross an inch-perfect ball on to the head of the old codger in row F behind the goal.

This was obviously a game which Chelsea believed (wrongly) they could win just by turning up. This suspicion was confirmed by the ease with which Chelsea managed to score after about 20 minutes. Lee sent another ball out towards Sinclair making another run down the right. Sinclair killed the ball dead, stepped outside one defender, and then as another approached curled a driven ball to the far post, swinging away from the keeper. Mark Hughes rose at the far post and knocked the ball back, across the keeper and into the goal.

What pattern there was to the game then set in. Chelsea knocked the ball around, making a number of long passing movements, working the ball from one side of the pitch to the other, all looking quite handsome, but also being quite ineffectual, lacking any direct approach towards the opposition goal. This was, after all, the team which had finished 71 places below Chelsea in the league system the previous season.

Exeter's eager Third Division players broke quickly, more directly. Most of the threat appeared to come down the Chelsea left-hand side, where on a number of occasions, the home side's speedy young winger got between Myers (never known for his tackling ability) and Steve Clarke and whipped balls into the near post where Erland Johnsen would head away for a corner.

It was at half-time, though, that matters became a little weird. The famous spoon-bender Uri Geller was introduced to the crowd, along with his son, apparently an Exeter City supporter. Geller's greatest celebrity had been some 15 to 20 years earlier, when he would get millions of television viewers across the country to concentrate on old, broken watches, which were supposed to come to life again through the power of positive thought. More recently, Geller had been applying these same techniques to the football team he supports, Reading, with suitable effect – Reading remain firmly stuck in the First Division. Now, at Exeter, when asked by the club's MC for a score prediction, Geller used his powers of positive thought to predict that the home side would equalise and, yes, then go on to win 2–1. The Chelsea fans in the ground, once they had finished laughing, sat back and waited for this Geller fellow to be exposed for the outrageous fraud that he obviously is.

In the second half, Exeter were attacking the end where their home support was based – The Big Bank (which, in fact, is not that big), where the supporters tend to huddle under The Cow Shed (which probably is a cow shed). This stirred the Devonians into great voice. The other changes were wrought on the Chelsea team, Morris and Gavin Peacock coming off to be replaced by Rocastle and Scott Minto. Peacock had looked fit and in form, eager to make a good impression on the new boss, and force his way into the reckoning. Which is more than can be said for at least eight of his colleagues, Rocastle in particular. Given an opportunity to prove his worth against opponents much inferior to his standard of play, the former England player just seemed to drift about the pitch as if in some sort of trance. Rendered speechless by Gullit's declaration that he would not figure in Chelsea's plans for the season, now Rocastle seemed completely unable to let his feet speak for him.

With Peacock gone, it was left to Dennis Wise to run the game for Chelsea. Wise was one of the few who seemed to want to actually play the game at more than a Sunday-afternoon-had-a-few-beers-let's-kick-a-ball-around pace. But it takes contributions from more than one player to govern a game, even against lower league opposition.

Exeter pushed forward, winning a penalty when Hitchcock brought down one player in the penalty area. Hitchcock saved the kick, but it was enough of a breakthrough to inspire the home team. The Exeter players seemed to stand taller, move quicker, pass better: they now believed they could beat this Chelsea side.

And so they did, just as Uri Geller had predicted with the sort of uncanny accuracy which many Malaysian businessmen might pay very handsomely for. The winning goal came in the final moments of the game, a shot across the face of the Chelsea goal – where Nick Colgan was now stationed, in place of Hitchcock – hitting the far post and rolling back across the line. Not that it seemed to matter to anyone, supporters or players. As they shuffled out, people moaned to those alongside and behind them, and one wag shouted, 'Ruudi, Ruudi, Ruudi: Out! Out! Out!'

Within 48 hours, Chelsea were playing again, this time against Plymouth, again without using their more expensive recent signings. But wheras against Exeter there had been a lack of urgency, this time the runs being made by Mark Hughes and Mark Stein were being picked out.

Peacock's goal had put Chelsea ahead at half-time, when Mark Nicholls – like Morris, a promising youth team player hoping for his big break – came on to replace Stein. Against a Plymouth back four that had performed well in the previous season's bottom division, making the play-offs and winning promotion at Wembley, Nicholls looked accomplished and skilful. He also showed an ability to take scoring chances, getting to the far post to connect with a hard, driven cross from Myers. Peacock, with an excellent solo effort, scored Chelsea's third to wrap up the game.

The next weekend, though, would prove to be a truer test of the new Chelsea. Umbro, the kit suppliers to the club, had begun organising a pre-season tournament to help show off the latest strips as worn by teams they supply – in 1996, they had gathered together Chelsea, Manchester United and Ajax at Nottingham Forest. Two games – semi-finals – on the Saturday would be followed by two games – final and third-place play-off – on the Sunday, with four groups of supporters enjoying a fun summer weekend of classy, enjoyable football, while giving the teams useful pre-season practice. That was the theory, anyway.

The sale of replica football shirts had become a vital, and large, cog in the workings of football clubs' economics. At £40 per shirt, these were no longer simply items of sportswear for kids – now they were part of the 'leisurewear' market, fashionable as never before after the success of Euro '96, and the supporter's imperative was to have the most up-to-date team shirt, home and away versions.

Overall, it has been estimated that sports retailing in Britain is worth some £500 million per year. This huge sector was at first driven by the boom in training shoe sales, but football shirts in the 1990s had helped to maintain growth of between 25 and 30 per cent every year. The marketing men had contrived to 'design' new kits once every year – one year would produce a new home kit, the next a new away strip. Any change of shirt sponsor would necessitate another change in kit. For the likes of Manchester United, even a *third* kit was also produced, so insatiable was the fans' appetite for the shirts. In total, merchandising and marketing brings in £18 million per year to Old Trafford, a big chunk of it – estimated at £3 million – provided by shirt sales. The rights to have such business cost Umbro something like £40 million.

Other manufacturers, too, would pay handsomely for the rights to provide other teams with kit. Nike, the American sportswear firm that already has basketball's Michael Jordan, track's Michael Johnson and golf's Tiger Woods on its books, was so eager to break into world soccer that it broke all records with its $200 million, ten-year deal with Brazil that works out as worth about £12 million each year.

In English club football, Reebok had just signed a £15 million deal to supply Liverpool until the millennium, with the club (in common with most such deals) set to receive a royalty for every shirt sold. Royalty figures vary from deal to deal, most being pitched at £3 to the club for every shirt; the Liverpool royalty was reported to be £10 per shirt. In the first nine months of the deal, Reebok sold £25 million worth of Liverpool replica shirts. In 1995, Newcastle managed to sell 500,000 replicas – enough to pay at least one-tenth of Alan Shearer's transfer fee.

Of course, the arrival of a player such as Shearer – or Vialli at Chelsea – would further boost shirt sales in the club shop even more, as football's fashion victims would buy new kit with their favourite player's name emblazoned across their shoulders.

Chelsea fans ought to have been grateful for a change of away kit in 1996, because it meant the demise of a hideous grey and orange away combo (seemingly selected simply because these happen to be the corporate colours of shirt sponsors, Coors). Yet matters of taste count for little to football fans – even Chelsea's grey-orange kit became a good seller. As John Williams, who has made an academic study of football at the University of Leicester, says, the shirts are being offered to a captive market. 'The supporters could refuse to buy the shirts, but they are trapped by their own allegiance and emotional links to the club,' Dr Williams said. 'The heart is ruling the head.'

But more important than any shirt was the quality of the man inside it, and at Nottingham's City Ground that sultry weekend, Chelsea fans would at last get to see the three new signings wearing their team's kit for the first time.

In Chelsea's first game, against Forest, Gullit opted for the three-man defensive unit, marshalled by Leboeuf, with wing-backs supplementing the three-man midfield, with John Spencer alongside Hughes. It was a case of perspiration over inspiration, though, as Forest's apparent reluctance to send players forward – apart from Dean Saunders, who was relentlessly booed by the Chelsea fans, who refuse to forgive or forget his career-ending tackle on Paul Elliott – saw the game drift towards a penalty shoot-out. Chelsea won that, just, and would face the winners of the next game, between Manchester United and Ajax, who were well supported by every neutral in the ground – about 6,000 of them. The support must have helped – Ruud Gullit had just managed to get Chelsea to their first final, suitably against Dutch opponents.

To deal with the hot conditions, and give a game to as many players in his squad as possible, Gullit made some changes for the match on Sunday, Hughes playing alone up front, with Vialli on the bench for the first-half. It was the other member of the Chelsea Azzurri, Roberto di Matteo, who lit up the match, his midfield play and superb passing including two telling through balls that produced goals. The first came after just six minutes, releasing Wise; the second, 11 minutes later, seeing Petrescu score. Chelsea 2, Ajax 0 after less than 20 minutes. A disbelieving Manchester United youngster, one of few who remained for the 'final', turned to his father to ask, 'Chelsea can't be better than Ajax, can they, dad?' a question which even Chelsea fans must have been asking themselves.

Things looked better still in the second half. Vialli appeared, his partnership with Hughes looking promising, exciting: the Italian, all flicks, power and subtle asides; the Welshman, undiluted aggression and a ceaseless eye for the opening. By the end of the game, even the Dutch drum and trumpeters were playing *Blue is the Colour*. Who, a year before, would have thought that the team squad would include two former World Players of the Year, and be managed by Ruud Gullit? Two weeks before the Premiership season was to begin, then, and Gullit had managed to win his first trophy with Chelsea. It may have been only the Umbro Cup, but it was achieved with more than a touch of style and élan.

Chapter 7

Beating Ajax in a pre-season kick-about is one thing, but challenging at the top of the table in after more than a month of the league season? Chelsea? Surely some mistake . . .

One of the great myths of football – possibly sport as a whole – is that certain clubs have 'reputations'. These myths take the form of assertions, repeated so often that they become accepted as fact. One demands that teams each have a distinctive style, a personality, if you like. This team's style, the reputation myth insists, passes down from generation to generation, from era to era at the club, as if there was some unseen, unacknowledged style-transfer genetic process going on between players. For instance, the reputation myth dictates that all Leeds teams are deemed to be dour, dirty and defensive, in the mould set by Don Revie in the 1960s. Or that Arsenal sides are always lucky, or boring (or both when George Graham was manager). In Chelsea's case, they had the reputation as flashy Cockney wide-boys, as flamboyant under-achievers.

It is, of course, all stuff and nonsense (apart from the bit about Leeds being dour). There is no reason why any one selection of 11 players wearing a particular team's shirts should perform in any way similarly to the same club's side of ten or 20 years before. If this were the case then according to this great football myth, somehow Mickey Droy must have 'inherited' certain playing characteristics from Jimmy Greaves. Or Clive Walker must have passed on his winger's genes to Frank Sinclair. Obviously, rationally, logically, this is complete bunkum. Except that, season after season, Chelsea sides – completely unrelated, except for the Wilkins brothers – somehow flattered to deceive, always living down to their reputation as the team with the all the solidity of a house of cards. For more than a quarter of a century, Chelsea teams fulfilled their reputation to the full by winning precisely nothing.

There was, however, no reason why Luca Vialli, Bobby di Matteo or The Beef would be aware of any of this – they had arrived as innocents in English football, ignorant of any prejudices or preconceptions about Chelsea. To them, Chelsea meant only a club based in west London, managed by Ruud Gullit, which paid good wages. They had probably never heard of Peter Osgood, never mind Ron Harris. Reputations meant nothing.

So, Ajax today, tomorrow the Premiership? Certainly, Steve Clarke thought better times were ahead. Chelsea operates a slightly odd system of having a team captain (Dennis Wise) and a club captain in Clarke, the club's longest serving player. Room mates when away with the club, the pair get on together very well, complementing one another, Clarke the mature ballast to the effervescent Wise's constant Cockney cracks. Clarke also has the responsibilities as the club's Professional Footballers' Association representative, the local union official (not that players on something like £15,000 per week-plus have ever been known for their militant tendencies).

Back in 1986, John Hollins paid £400,000 to St Mirren for Clarke, then a tyro left-back who had gained international recognition at under-21 level with Scotland. In and out of the Chelsea team under the succession of managers, Clarke developed in the later part of his career successfully into an all-round defender, first under Hoddle, playing at centre-back in Chelsea's new-style three-man defence, at one point even winning back a place in Scotland's senior squad.

The word 'stalwart' might have been invented to describe Clarke. 'Steve is as important to my team as a Vialli or Leboeuf,' Gullit said, but in such a way that you were certain he was not indulging in the usual managerial polite public platitudes. Gullit really meant it.

Clarke, who went the wrong side of 33 in the first week of the new season, is a family man who is never afraid to voice an opinion when required. More than most, after playing under five different managers at Stamford Bridge, Clarke was well placed to judge the changes at Chelsea. 'I'm in my 11th season here now, and it's like being at a completely different club. Everything about it has changed so much. In my first full season here, when I first came down from Scotland, Chelsea were relegated. We didn't play to sell-out crowds very often then. Now, you can't get a ticket at Stamford Bridge for love or money.

'In the old days, I used to worry about the games ahead. Now I look forward to every one. When I drive to the training ground now, I feel like a kid looking forward to Christmas. It's the best feeling in the world to pull on a Chelsea shirt, look around the dressing room and see yourself surrounded by class . . . *real* class. Ruud says we have to be more consistent. I thought we were beginning to find a bit of consistency under Glenn Hoddle, but Ruud wants more.'

What Ruud wants, often he gets – Clarke's performances, even in the earliest league games of the season, were those of a man more confident in his own ability than ever before, comfortable with his lot. Clarke, or any of the other senior pros in the squad, would confirm that much of this assured state of mind was due to confidence in their team mates – 'look around the dressing room and see yourself surrounded by class'. More than any time in his entire Chelsea career, Clarke could rely completely on the players to his left and right, both to do their jobs properly and, most importantly of all, to cover for him if anything went awry. This assurance and reliance within the squad was helping to build a strong team spirit and sense of identity. It was forging a belief in Chelsea.

On the field, Clarke's tackles were being timed to perfection, any attacking passes played into his zone of responsibility were intercepted with aplomb. At times against Southampton and Middlesbrough, Clarke made it look as if Gullit had two Leboeufs playing defence.

Had Vialli had a little more luck at The Dell, he might have scored two or three, but Dave Beasant was always there in the Southampton goal to stop anything. To think that when he was at Chelsea, Beasant missed the first few months of one season because he could not even hold on to a jar of salad cream, dropping it on his foot and breaking a bone. Now, all unlucky Luca could do was smack his bare forehead with his open hand out of sheer frustration.

Chelsea had to wait 174 minutes before their first league goal of the 1996–97 season. When it came, it was like a bolt from the blue.

It was a sultry summer evening at the Bridge. Somehow, midweek games at Chelsea always have that bit of magic about them – thousands hurrying through the capital rush hour to get to the ground which, with the floodlights on, stands out like a beacon in west London. Under the intense white light, everything seems somehow brighter, the players closer, the crowd bigger, the sound of their cheers louder. The effect of the concentrated brightness against the dark night skies helps somehow to raise the level of awareness.

So, after 85 minutes of Chelsea's first home game of the season, against Middlesbrough, with the sides stalemated at 0–0, when Roberto di Matteo picked up the ball near the halfway line before hitting it from at least 25 yards, all 28,000 people in the stadium must have heard the 'thwack' when his boot made its final, powerful connection with the leather of the ball, followed by a wooshing sound as it flew past the 'Boro keeper and settled into the back of the net.

The goal gave a handful of players the opportunity to show that they had been practising more than free-kicks down at Harlington – an elaborate, living frieze was created by di Matteo, Wise and Co., as they lay on the Stamford Bridge turf in repose, like latterday Roman emperors. 'Not at all,' di Matteo said. 'It was an instinctive thing, it just happened.' Whatever, they still looked like they enjoyed lording it over the opposition. This game, after all, had been seen as an important test for Chelsea, pitted against another side noted for its all-star line-up of foreign imports. The match was fairly even, Nick Barmby, Emerson, Ravanelli and Juninho failing to get past Leboeuf and Clarke, and on the rare occasions that they did, Dmitri Kharine, Chelsea's Russian international keeper, saved the only shot on target. Thus, three points earned with a late winning goal, something so unlike Chelsea, but it meant four points earned out of the first six of the season.

Since di Matteo's arrival at Chelsea as the club's record signing, he had enjoyed as high a profile as a member of Brentford reserves, most attention having been attracted by Vialli. But di Matteo's transfer was as important to Gullit's plans for success. Here was the first current Italian international to sign for an English club, a signal that all footballing roads now no longer led to Rome, but headed instead for London.

Dapper and handsome in typically Italian style, di Matteo's only previous contact with English football had been playing alongside Paul Gascoigne in Lazio's midfield. 'The only English Paul Gascoigne taught me was: "You reet ugly bastard",' he said on his arrival shortly after his £4.9 million transfer had been agreed.

Di Matteo had been part of the underachieving Italian side at Euro '96. He was one of the five players, the core of the side, who were rested against the Czech Republic when coach Arrigo Sacchi underestimated the opposition so badly that it cost Italy their place in the next round of the tournament. So, perhaps coming to arch under-achievers Chelsea was not such a wrench for di Matteo. Swiss-born, the young di Matteo never played in Italy until after he had won Swiss league title with Aarau and took the Swiss Player of the Year award as a sweeper, but it was his ball-winning tackles in midfield and a peripheral vision as wide as Cinemascope when it came to defence-splitting passes which were influential in helping Lazio to their third-place finish in Serie A in 1995–96.

It was this influence that Gullit was hoping di Matteo would exert at Chelsea, though in these first games for his new club, the Italian looked short of fitness. As a Euro '96 player, he had been spared some of the pre-season ritual, and in the latter stages of the games against Southampton and Middlesbrough, it showed. Gullit knew that there was scope for improvement. With Leboeuf running the defence and sending off pinhead-precise passes and di Matteo at the centre of things in

71

midfield, the Chelsea coach had obviously begun considering semi-retirement from playing. 'With a team this good,' Gullit, still working back to fitness after his knee operation, 'I won't have to bother playing again. I can sit on the bench and enjoy a cigar.'

Di Matteo had worked as a baker, a butcher and a mechanic before he signed for Schaffhausen in the Swiss second division at the age of 17. He was signed from Aarau by Lazio in 1993, but disputes with the coach there meant that by the summer of 1996, he was keen to leave. When he arrived at Chelsea, he asked for the Number 16 shirt – 'I used to wear it in Switzerland. It brought me luck.'

It did not take long for di Matteo to fall foul of the English press when he scrawled 'Fuck off' on an autograph-hunter's kiss-me-quick-style plastic bowler hat before the game at Southampton, hardly the act of someone trying to endear himself with a new audience. To make matters worse, the hat was a freebie distributed to fans by *The Sun*. Inevitably, the newspaper got to hear about the incident, and while di Matteo said that it was all just an ill-conceived joke, the next day's paper described it as 'a mindless act which showed he has the IQ of pond life'. Still, *The Sun* has got things wrong before . . .

Given that brush with the tabloids so early in his Chelsea career, it is perhaps odd that di Matteo said he had opted to play in England because he likes the anonymity and privacy the country offers, despite its notoriously intrusive popular press. 'On the pitch, there is little difference between here and Italy, but that changes off the pitch. There, there is a huge amount of pressure to speak to the media – they are always looking for a new story, but I like my privacy. London is a big city, but here you can walk around and have space to live. When I'm out, I like to be left undisturbed. So money certainly wasn't the only reason I chose to come to England.' Still, £800,000 per year in salary must have helped.

'I knew what I was letting myself in for. I had heard of Hoddle, Wise and Gullit. Then there was Vialli's move as well. It was very important to me that Gullit wanted me and the club did everything they could to buy me. I wanted to learn something new, from both a professional and a personal point of view. I am 27, I felt the need to go it alone. Here in England, I have more responsibility, you become more autonomous, more mature. More of a man.

'I can only speak highly of English football, of England and London. Football in Italy is changing. Older players say it has got worse. There, if you lose a game, it is like the end of the world. In England, pure sport still exists. It is not a cultural thing, it's the mentality that's different.'

Di Matteo found that he soon adapted to the English way of life.

When he moved into his luxury flat overlooking Hyde Park, the homecooking may have been Italian, but the ingredients were bought at Sainsbury's. As someone who already spoke German as well as Italian, from his time growing up in Switzerland, he soon found he was picking up idiomatic English. 'I wanted to go to school to study, but I never had the time,' he said. 'So I bought a book of grammar,' not a regular requirement of most players in the Premiership, 'and I studied a bit that way. The rest, I picked up at the training ground. The first English words you learn are for your job on the field: man on, time, turn, switch, squeeze. I've learned some Cockney, too. The black players speak the language slightly differently, they speak their own slang.' For a belting shot such as di Matteo hit that night against Middlesbrough, the language was universal.

After di Matteo got on the scoresheet against Middlesbrough, Vialli and Leboeuf did the same in a comfortable 2–0 home win over Coventry. The visitors made things slightly easier for Chelsea, when they contrived to have two players booked and another, Liam Daish, their big, lumbering centre-back, sent off for arguing with the referee, Paul Danson, a man notorious for flashing his cards. The gist of the argument was that, in the build-up to the goal, Dan Petrescu had handled the ball. Obviously, neither referee nor his assistant saw the offence, and the goal stood, and Mr Danson needed a police escort to get off the pitch at half-time.

The sole concern for Chelsea after this match was that more of the chances should have been taken, and the main culprit of wastefulness was Mark Hughes. The previous season, his first at Chelsea, had hardly seen him cover himself in goal-scoring glory, and already some observers were beginning to ask whether the new partnership with Vialli would really work. There was one moment in the second half when Hughes and Vialli both spun off their markers together, and both ran diagonally behind the defence together, as if they had been practising a football version of synchronised swimming or formation dancing, the only problem being that in football, there are no marks for artistic interpretation.

Perhaps Hughes and Vialli were too similar in their styles of play, too much like predators, trying to survive off the same scraps, when what might have been needed was a more complementary style of footballer, one who could create as well as score. With John Spencer, the Scotland international, straining at the leash on the subs' bench, it could surely only be a matter of time before one of Gullit's thirtysomething strikers would have to stand aside. It seemed highly improbable that it would be Vialli who would be giving way.

Three games, three big signings score, three cleansheets. Very un-

Chelsea-like, but going into September, the New Azzurri found themselves in second place in the Premiership with a trip across London to Highbury awaiting.

It would be fair to say that Chelsea do not have too high a regard for any other London side. None are disliked any more than the others – all are considered with the utmost contempt. While the north London derby, between Arsenal and Spurs, is possibly the nearest equivalent in the capital to Liverpool *v* Everton, United *v* City in Manchester, or Newcastle *v* Sunderland, for Chelsea it is their game against Tottenham which oft-times means the most to Chelsea supporters. Some have suggested that, down the years, because of the sheer number of London clubs in the top division – five in 1996–97 – and the resulting high number of derby games, the intensity and ferociousness of these games detract from any London side's chances of winning the championship. Liverpool, for instance, only have two bruising encounters with Everton to worry about. During the league season, Chelsea will have to overcome similarly tough matches with West Ham, Spurs, Arsenal and Wimbledon, home and away. It takes its toll, not just in terms of injuries or suspensions (bookings always seem more common in derby matches), but also in sheer tension and adrenalin.

So it is that, because of Arsenal's recent successes in the league, the annoying antics of their striker Ian Wright, their parsimonious defence and the Gooners' supporters endlessly repetitive mocking choruses of 'No silverware' (to the tune of Chelsea's 'Blue flag' song), getting one over on the Gunners had taken on added edge. Thus, 2–0 up, at Highbury before half-time with an exhibition of total football, things were really coming just right.

It was during this game that Gullit's manager's bench manner became most apparent. Legs stretched out, apparently relaxed, the giveaway at the churning going on inside the man was the way he chewed on the small, golden crucifix that hangs around his neck. Still, he is hardly the sheepskinned managerial archetype – that role at Chelsea must fall to Graham Rix.

Puffing intently on a Café Crème cigar, Rix's memories of that dug-out at Highbury are brim-full of successes, as he, as part of a 1980s team with Liam Brady and David O'Leary, brought back trophy after trophy to north London, much of it under the coaching supervision of Don Howe, surely one of the most successful English coaches of the 1970s and '80s. Perhaps Rix's role at Chelsea would be to bring some of Howe's grit to the oyster of Gullit's influence, with the end product being a cherished pearl.

Still fit enough to turn out for the stiffs if required, Rix could almost pass for one of the lads, though it is not all part of a 'good cop, bad cop' psychological management scheme he has hatched with Gullit. He prefers to refer to himself as 'a little buffer between the players and the manager – though I've been called other things, too. But we need someone like that. After all, Ruudi was a player only last year, one of the team, and now suddenly he's the gaffer who's got to pull somebody in and tell them their not playing. Some of the fellas get rather angry.

'So they come along to me, and say "Rico, what the hell's happening?" and I try to calm them down, get them to understand the reasons. Sure, there have been things he's done that I haven't necessarily agreed with, but we chat about it, he tells me why he's doing it, and I back him up 100 per cent. We've both been players, we know what it's like, if you're not seen to be strong as a management team, the boys will play on it. They can be rascals.'

Rix had always wanted to move into coaching when his playing career came to a close, but his reputation as something of a jack the lad may have made some believe he could not be serious enough. Even Rix's closest friends warned him when Hoddle, a friend from their days in the midfield of England Youth teams, invited him to take on the youth squad at Chelsea. 'Liam Brady, my mate, said, "Rico, whatever you do, take it serious." And I have.' But even Rix himself could not explain his sudden promotion to become Gullit's right-hand man when the Dutchman took over from Hoddle. 'Surprised is not the word. I'd never spoken to him about the job, never had chats about football. He was a first-team player, I was youth team coach. I don't know why he picked me. I've never asked. But once I knew we were going to be playing the same way as under Glenn, then I realised that being with the first team, working with someone like Ruud Gullit at a club like Chelsea would be a great experience. Being an ambitious sort of lad, it was a step I had to take.'

So it was that Rix found himself in the away team dug-out that night at Highbury, watching his new team, Chelsea, dominate his old team, Arsenal. Then old-style, throw-it-all-away Chelsea returned. Rix's new team had gone from being 2–0 up to being 3–2 down with just minutes of the match left. Wright, on as a sub, had got Arsenal's third at the end of some formidable pressure play from the home side. A potentially great away victory looked to be thrown away. Then Chelsea did something they had never been known for – they stole it at the end.

Deep into injury time, John Spencer – surely the player with the shortest legs in professional football since Billy the Fish – had come on as sub for the injured Leboeuf. The Scottish international chipped into the Arsenal penalty box and Wise skimmed on to it and lashed the ball into the top corner of the goal.

A point saved, or two thrown away? It is a debate as endless as the bar room discussions about pint glasses that are either half-empty or half-full, but the performance had been enough to confirm that not only was this Chelsea team capable of mixing it with the best in the division, they were also able to play some great football. Three days later, and it was a journey to Sheffield for a match against early Premiership leaders Wednesday. This time, Craig Burley and Andy Myers added their names to the lengthening list of Chelsea's scorers. Three points won away from home maintained the side's championship challenge and earned from Wednesday manager David Pleat the remark that Chelsea were 'possibly the best side we have faced', when his team had already played against Aston Villa and Newcastle.

But the game at Hillsborough was as significant for what went on in the Chelsea goalmouth as for the goals scored. Dmitri Kharine, the only Olympic gold medallist playing in the Premier League, had kept three cleansheets in the first four league games of the season, showing form that was worthy of Russia's international keeper. Not since Peter Bonetti in the early 1970s had Chelsea managed to find a consistently great goalkeeper, such a vital element in any successful side. At £400,000 from the old Moscow army team, CSKA, at the end of 1992, Kharine had seemed a bargain buy, but his early performances at Stamford Bridge had seen some dub him 'The Cat'. It was ironic humour from care-worn Chelsea fans, and nothing to do with Bonetti, who had been given the original feline nickname because of his agility. In Kharine's case, they called him The Cat because he kept getting in a flap.

Making the transition from playing football in one country to another is difficult enough for most western Europeans. But Dmitri Kharine suffered the epitome of culture shock, arriving at Chelsea from Moscow speaking not a word of English, used to a completely different alphabet, a different calendar and a different format for the football season. As if that were not enough, within an hour of moving into a new home, he found himself burgled. Gwyn Williams, now Gullit's assistant manager, had been the man deputed at the time to deal with the crisis. 'Dmitri had been in England six weeks, living in a hotel while he waited for his work permit to come through,' Williams said. 'Finally, it did, and on Christmas eve, my wife and I took his wife to their new house. They immediately went out shopping while I went back to the training ground to pick up Dmitri. When we got back, the police were there – he had had all his money and personal belongings stolen.

'It's Christmas, he's 3,000 miles from home, doesn't know anyone, can't speak a word of English and suddenly he needs a new front door . . . You can imagine the shock.' Armed only with a pocket

Russian–English dictionary, Williams then attempted to sort out the mess in Kharine's life. But nothing the goalkeeper had stolen that day was as valuable as what he was about to lose playing at Hillsborough.

Kharine's season was effectively ended just 15 minutes into his fifth game, after barely a month of the Premiership. Kharine had always, since arriving in England, worn a pair of tracksuit bottoms when playing. Some had mistakenly believed that this was somehow symptomatic of a soft foreign keeper who did not want to get his knees dirty. In fact, it was because a knee injury early in his career had forced Kharine to wear special supports to try to prevent a repetition.

But an awkward landing, a twist of the leg, and ligaments in the Russian's knee were damaged so badly that they would require three operations in the next six months. For the player, it was a blow which would take months of hard training for him to have even a hope of salvaging his career. For Chelsea, it was to be just the first of a series of injuries which were to hinder their progress.

Not that the Premier League makes any concessions for such setbacks. The following week, and Chelsea were at home to another club in the top echelon, Aston Villa, the game switched to the Sunday to accommodate Sky TV – Chelsea's second televised game of the season, showing already that they were being seen as a team to watch. Even with live television coverage, Stamford Bridge was only just short of capacity, for what might be euphemistically called a typical British, full-blooded encounter, illustrated by Villa's five bookings.

The match might have been closer to capacity had Chelsea given access to the ground to everyone who arrived that day with a ticket. Unfortunately for Diego Maradona, while he had a £250 ticket, he did not have a tie.

Maradona was in London for a promotion of street soccer sponsored by Puma, who bought the World Cup-winner and three of his friends £1,000-worth of tickets for the directors' box at Chelsea. As Chelsea operate a strict dress code, Puma also gave the four guests a Chelsea tie each when they were on the way to the match. Even this was not enough for Maradona, though, since he was wearing jeans and a T-shirt and refused to stop off in order to buy a collared shirt. In any case, what sort of football club would it be that would refuse him, Diego Maradona, entrance to the ground simply because he was not wearing a silly tie? Maradona was about to find out.

At the main entrance at Stamford Bridge, Maradona was asked by a young stewardess to wait while she checked out the situation. While he waited, the tubby Argentinian found himself mobbed by autograph hunters. Perfectly normal, you would think, for the one-time world's greatest player, but exactly not the thing craved by Maradona – undergoing psychotherapy for his drug dependency, the Argentinian's state of mind was so unbalanced at around this time that, when stuck in a hotel lift while in Alicante, he wrecked his suite out of fury and frustration.

Chelsea, meanwhile, kept him waiting. So Maradona took matters in to his own hand (of God), marched into the ground, entered the first room he came across, and immediately found himself besieged again. He fled the crush, pleading with his friends, 'Get me out of here.'

So by the time Chelsea officials had found him to show him to his seat – without a tie – it was too late, and so it was that one of a handful of footballers in history who had managed to raise aloft the World Cup was last seen at Stamford Bridge boarding a cab and heard to say, 'If I can't get into a football stadium, something must be wrong.'

The game itself was to set a pattern for many of the games against top opposition at Stamford Bridge during the coming season, the opposition prepared to get plenty of players between the ball and their goal in an attempt to frustrate Vialli and Hughes, in the hope of nicking something on the break. In this case, it was a free-kick just outside the Chelsea area which Andy Townsend, the former Chelsea skipper, hit hard over the wall for a goal.

It was a new Chelsea hero, Leboeuf, who got the equaliser, just before the interval, as he timed a run from deep to perfection to meet Petrescu's cross. With every game, the Frenchman's poise in defence, his passing and his ability to join in attack reinforced what Colin Hutchinson had said when his signing was announced: persuading Strasbourg to part with Beefy was like getting Southampton to sell Matthew Le Tissier.

A goal apiece, a point apiece, leaving Chelsea in third place in the Premier table, six games unbeaten, the best start to a season since 1986. Unbridled optimism was, for most hardened Chelsea fans, tempered with a dash of realism and a hefty dollop of experience. *Something* had to go wrong soon: next week, it was Anfield.

Chapter 8

The fizzy pop cup has never fired the imagination of players or punters, except, perhaps, when they have reached the outskirts of Wembley on the day of the final to discover that, stapled together with their match ticket, is a passport to Europe for the following season, conditional only on winning that day's fixture.

Not least among the credibility problems of the League Cup has been its many sponsored guises – from Littlewoods to Coca-Cola and, most ridiculously, the Milk Cup. As a midweek, two-legged affair, beginning for teams in the top division in mid-September, the League Cup in recent times has usually earnt nothing but the scorn of the leading clubs, particularly from sides with commitments in Europe. For them, the League Cup is now an unwanted obligation, nothing more than a chore that has to be done, endured, suffered. While it may be a useful fund-raiser for clubs in the lower divisions, the Coca-Cola Cup is a needless distraction for the top clubs. Unwanted extra games in an already over-loaded season. Such has been Manchester United's recent contempt for the competition, that even after an official reprimand for fielding a below-par team in one League Cup tie, they have continued to take the fixtures as an opportunity to rest senior players and blood youngsters. For them, bigger prizes await in Europe or after Easter. What happens at a pokey second division ground in mid-October has become the epitome of irrelevance.

For Chelsea supporters, one thing which the 1996–97 League Cup offered was a chance to go to Blackpool. Of course, for the team, it was still a two-leg chore that had to be endured, but for the fans it was the chance of a late summer trip to the seaside, a look at the illuminations, and a bit of a knees-up and a piss-up. So, with the Irish Sea breeze whipping up the empty chip papers outside Blackpool North station after the train had pulled in that Wednesday afternoon, it was an ill-wind for anyone who had not expected to be braced by the coastal air. Along the Golden Mile, things warmed up a little, mainly because of the thousands of fat friers busy at work along the sea-front, serving up fish and chips and greaseburgers to the thousands of late-season holiday-makers who were sampling the myriad delights of bingo huts, amusement arcades, 30-foot tall giant parrots and plastic dinosaurs. Had Steven Spielberg ever seen the prehistoric monster that is Blackpool, the capital of tat, he might never have bothered with *Jurassic Park*.

For a journey of such length, and with Blackpool hardly being on the Inter-City mainline, this cup trip demanded an overnight stop-over for travelling Londoners. Considering that Blackpool is the centre of the universe as far as B&B is concerned, and considering that demand for such facilities must have been on the wane because of the time of year, the number of 'No Vacancies' signs that had been put up when the first of the Chelsea fans arrived in town was uncanny. But if the rail fares and bed and breakfast charges were just extra expenses for the visiting supporters, at least they had the chance of cheap beer and food. Cod, chips, peas (mushy, natch), bread, butter and a steaming mug of stewed tea for less than £4 was an unlooked for bargain, as was beer at £1 a pint in a pub across the road from the homely (i.e. small) Bloomfield Road ground. And to think this was where Stanley Matthews, Stan Mortensen and Jimmy Armfield used to ply their trade in the First Division.

The beer and the fish had barely been digested before the Chelsea faithful were made to feel quite queasy: Blackpool went ahead in the first minute. No cause for concern, though (unless you really had deposited your dinner over some unsuspecting Lancastrian in front of you), as Chelsea then proceeded to find their feet and the Blackpool goal. What had begun as some sort of ordeal by cup-craft, with Chelsea seemingly set for an early exit at the hands of some lower league wannabes, ended in a 4–1 victory, including some good play, and providing an excellent excuse for the small band of travelling fans to go out into the night and enjoy the late licensing arrangements of one of the premier resorts in Europe (at least, that's how Blackpool is described in one of the local tourist brochures. Who are we to argue?).

It had not gone unnoticed, however, that the Blackpool goal had been conceded by a defence that, for the first time this season, had lined up without Frank Leboeuf. The Frenchman's influence on his new side had already become profound, and in his absence due to a hip injury and the assumption that Chelsea would overcome Blackpool with ease, he was missed as sorely as his aching side.

'He's the best piece of business this season,' Chairman Bates called Leboeuf. 'Frank can be one of the best sweepers this decade,' said his manager, who gave Leboeuf as the reason he need not rush his own return to the side. As a semi-pro playing in the south of France, Leboeuf had kept one David Ginola out of the SC Toulon team. But in eight years as a professional footballer, Leboeuf had never won a major trophy with Strasbourg, coming closest in the 1995 French cup final when his side was demolished by a Paris St Germain side which included Ginola.

Only injury and Laurent Leblanc prevented Leboeuf from playing at the heart of France's defence in Euro '96 – his ten caps had coincided with an unbeaten streak for his national side – something which Gullit considered to be to his, and Chelsea's, advantage. 'If Leboeuf had played for France in Euro '96, he would have been chased by a whole number of clubs and then his value would have rocketed,' Gullit said. All that was left for Gullit and Colin Hutchinson was to offer a better deal than Leboeuf's hometown team, Marseille, and they won their man. The player was already disillusioned with French football.

'The only thing that kept me going that last season was playing for France. Otherwise, I was just going through the motions,' Leboeuf said. 'In some league games I was bored and felt I was playing in the third division in small empty stadiums without any atmosphere. Once I came to Chelsea, things were so different.

'Playing in France makes it impossible for reputations to grow, such is the mentality there. You are either good, or bad, and that is how you stay.' Chelsea offered Leboeuf an escape, and a chance to play alongside his idol. 'I started as a pro in 1988, the same season that Ruud went on to win the European Cup with Milan. He had also been voted European Footballer of the Year. Back then, I could admire his talents when I saw him on television. But I thought that was as near as I'd ever get.

'The fact that I'm with Gullit at Chelsea means I have succeeded in something.' Not least was the way that Leboeuf immediately won over the Chelsea fans, with his crisply timed tackles, bravery in last-ditch situations, and sublimely accurate passing.

The Strasbourg fans protested long and hard when their skipper left, but Leboeuf needed a new challenge, to try a new role. 'When I was at Strasbourg, I was captain and I was a little bit like Dennis Wise, joking all the time. Now,' he adds, speaking in perfect, if accented, English, 'I must be quiet because I don't understand everything. I'm not the best joker in the dressing room, so I joke with Luca because we have the same bad English.'

The self-deprecation extends from his linguistic skills to his footballing ability. 'It is not a question of good technique,' Leboeuf says, 'because there are a lot of good players in England. Maybe the difference is about tactics. I think if you play against an Italian side it is very difficult for the English to win because the Italians have such a different tactical culture. It is a chess game for them, though it may be boring for the supporter. That is why the English game is so exciting, but you lose in the tactical sense.' And he reckons he was a bit like Dennis Wise?

Leboeuf says that the trick to his ability as a *libero* or sweeper, the defender who calls the shots, was taught to him by France's greatest footballer of the modern era, Michel Platini. 'Platini has said you don't need a big technique, but what you need is great vision. If you look around you before you receive the ball you have the time to do what you want. I have a very good understanding with the other Chelsea defenders, like Dan Petrescu, and I know when I am in trouble.

'I see myself a bit like the quarter back in American football because I receive so much of the ball. It's difficult and tiring, because I need to distribute the ball and also defend, but it is also very interesting.'

Graham Rix, the Chelsea assistant manager, put the Frenchman's rapid settling in down to his preparation. 'The advantage Frank had over the other two summer signings is that he put in a full pre-season. Roberto di Matteo had not trained for 10 days before the first game because of a back problem and Vialli missed much of the pre-season because he was carrying niggling injuries. Frank may not have been given the same sort of publicity as Vialli, but that doesn't stop him being a terrific player. He's a former captain of Strasbourg, so he's used to leading, to being dominant. He's strong, competitive, what I would call an intelligent defender.'

Evidently, momentarily against Blackpool, Chelsea missed that intelligence. But it was just the sort of shock to the collective system that was required, and the Londoners proceeded to end the seasiders' cup dream. After a result like that, there was no chance of Chelsea going out of the League Cup on the away goal rule this season, was there?

Like many fans who made a week of it, the Chelsea squad stayed in the north-west, prior to facing Liverpool at Anfield in the league on the Saturday. But just as the early goal at Blackpool had punctured Chelsea's Premier League superiority, so the game at Liverpool was to leave Chelsea's Premiership pretensions completely deflated.

From third place in the table to seventh, a 5–1 drubbing placing Chelsea's season in stark perspective, the limitations of the side best illustrated by the sheer, staggering gormlessness of the cushion header with which Andy Myers knocked the ball past his own keeper and into the goal on the stroke of half-time, to send the visitors to the dressing room 3–0 down. Myers was not the only one in the ground to hold his head in his hands after that incident. The cause lay in something which had happened half-an-hour earlier, when Myers had been comprehensively undone by Robbie Fowler, who had got on the far side of the defender to score the first goal. The doubts had been planted so deeply in Myers's mind that anyone could sense the uncertainty, perhaps even fear, going through his thoughts later in the match as the ball flew towards him at the far post. Myers was playing the game after having had pain-killing injections for some badly bruised ribs he had suffered in a training ground collision with Kevin Hitchcock earlier in the week; the pain of scoring that own goal was far worse than any physical suffering, though.

Myers, like the rest of the Chelsea team, was shattered and then swept away by a Liverpool team that looked as if it could go on to challenge Manchester United for the Premier League title. A fusillade of three goals in seven minutes either side of half-time broke any vestige of resistance from Chelsea. It was clear from this that any Premiership prospects Chelsea may have had were simply pipe dreams.

'No one likes to lose,' Ruud Gullit confided after the game, 'but for us maybe the timing was right.' The burgeoning optimism surrounding Chelsea's performances in the first six weeks of the season had obviously begun to spread among the players. They would not be over-confident henceforward. 'Maybe we were in danger of believing things that were not true. We couldn't think of titles before this game, and we certainly can't now.'

Gullit, too, may have learned a lot about himself that day. It was the first time his side had lined up with a back four, rather than the three centre-backs and two-wing backs. Liverpool showed comprehensively that it did not work, as the midfield was over-run and Leboeuf, of all people, appearing least comfortable with the new formation.

He was even more uncomfortable the following Wednesday night, when Blackpool arrived at the Bridge for the second leg of the League Cup fixture. An apparent formality, played out in front of the smallest home crowd of the season (11,732), saw Blackpool score three times from four efforts, hardly a reassuring start for Frode Grodas, the Norwegian international keeper who Gullit had signed on loan from Lillestrom as cover while Kharine was injured. A single goal by John Spencer was enough, but only just, to see Chelsea through. Suddenly, though, Chelsea's sublime form had deserted them.

Dominating a 1–1 home draw with Forest – a side without a win since the first day of the season – hardly helped to allay the suggestion that Chelsea had been a five-minute wonder. Slack marking and loss of concentration in the final moments of the game allowed Jason Lee to equalise Luca Vialli's third goal of the season. The Italian had twice hit the woodwork, as well, but in the end it amounted to two points thrown away. 'In the last two matches,' Vialli said, 'I have ten chances and miss nine. That is not enough for Chelsea. I have to score more.'

It was a view apparently shared by his manager, who dropped Vialli to the bench for the next game, away at Leicester. A win there hardly restored Chelsea confidence, as the young tyro forward, Emile Heskey, nicknamed 'Bruno' because of his heavyweight build, used all his physicality to intimidate Leboeuf, and managed to get the Frenchman and Clarke booked in their efforts to contain his strong challenges. Mark Nicholls got his first start of the season, but made way for Vialli at half-time. The substitution transformed Chelsea's performance in the second half, as they came back from being a goal down to score three goals, Vialli getting his within a minute of coming on. 'Before the game, I was a little bit angry,' said the Italian, 'because every player wants to play. Then I scored . . .' Vialli smiled at the thought of the goal. But the mere prospect of his not being in the starting line-up a year before when at Juventus was undreamt of – what was going on?

Leboeuf and Clarke's yellow cards were half Chelsea's allocation that day, bringing to 28 the total number of cautions thus far in the season, more than any other Premiership side, which in Chelsea's case was an indication of carelessness and sloppiness rather than them being a dirty side. Whatever the reasons for the cautions, they were sufficient to see Wise, Mark Hughes and Leboeuf facing suspensions, a loss of key players which could prove to be costly.

Already, though, there were rumblings of discontent among players, other than Vialli, and while the club was at pains to discount reports in the tabloids, it was not enough to dispel suspicions that things were somewhat short of complete peace and harmony at the Bridge. John Spencer, the Scotland international, had voiced his frustrations at being just part of the squad, 'I'm desperate to get in the first team,' he said. 'I really need first team football.' Others on the fringes were also restless: David Lee had a meeting with Gullit to discuss his situation, Scott Minto expressed his concerns for regular games, but it was Gavin Peacock, one of Hoddle's prized signings when he was at the club, who was the first to put in a transfer request. 'I'm not surprised if they moan,' Gullit said. 'If those people out of the team are not unhappy, then I would be worried.'

Gullit had already begun to add to the over-congestion in the Chelsea dressing room by occupying a peg there himself for a friendly match against Forest at the Bridge a couple of days before the Leicester match. Gullit wanted to use the match to see how fit Terry Phelan, Paul Hughes, Eddie Newton and Mark Stein were after various injuries. Peacock, who was playing his first game since suffering a deep wound under his knee, twisted his ankle and had to go off at half-time. Also substituted after 45 minutes were Gullit, Phelan and Stein. It was all part of a process of gradually building up match fitness, something no amount of training runs or practice games can recreate. It was still an odd scenario, with the vast ground empty except for some litter blowing through the East Stand, with a gaggle of journalists crammed into the limited seating in the press box. Such was the interest in the Chelsea player-manager's health and well-being. There were enough savvy journalists present there also to recognise Stewart Houston, the newly appointed manager of west London neighbours Queens Park Rangers. Just who did he have his eyes on?

Gullit managed to fit in another reserve game soon after, lasting 70 minutes the following week at Harlington against Fulham, where Phelan played for a full 90 minutes for the first time in months.

Then came Wimbledon.

Phelan, the flying Irish international wing-back, obviously felt that, having proved himself in the reserves, he was ready to return to the first team. The hamstring injury which Phelan had suffered in the FA Cup semi-final the previous season had taken a long time to heal. It had been an injury which had been crucial to that game, a turning point which saw Manchester United come back from being a goal down to win the match 2–1. Now, it seemed to Phelan, the injury was crucial to his career.

When, in the hour before kick-off against Wimbledon, the Irishman discovered that he had not even been named among the five substitutes to face his former club, the resulting row was fierce indeed, as voices were raised and doors slammed, the noise reverberating down the players' tunnel. Not being picked was all too much for Phelan, who had never managed to reconcile his life as a professional footballer with the demands of his private life. His injury was not his only worry: he had been attacked while in a night club by someone wielding a champagne bottle against him; and his marriage was in trouble. What Phelan did not need at this point was effectively to be told he was not good enough to play for Chelsea.

It was his troubled marriage which affected Phelan most deeply. 'People think footballers have a great life. But they don't appreciate the strain all the moving round puts on your family. Jo and I had been together since I was 18 and she was 16. She followed me from Leeds to Swansea, then on to London when I played for Wimbledon for five years. But I always wanted to return to Manchester, and we were delighted when I moved to Maine Road. We had a lovely house in Bolton, and the children were happy. When I left Manchester City to join Chelsea, Jo decided there had been enough disruption to the family. That move to Chelsea was to cost me my marriage.

'I was living in a flat in London while the family were in the north. Our marriage suffered. I used to travel home to see the kids whenever I could, but I was getting up at 4 or 5 a.m. to travel back to London for training. It all took a toll.

'When I started to have injury problems at Chelsea, there were times when I seriously thought about packing it all in, going back up north and just getting a job in a factory. The thing is, I want to do the best for my kids, and the way for me to do that is to stay in football.'

Phelan had talked about his problems with Gullit. 'His door was always open. When I told Ruudi, he was understanding and told me he'd had similar problems in the past. He told me that if ever I needed a couple of days off to see the children, there was no problem.' But the argument before the Wimbledon game marked the beginning of the end of Phelan's time at Chelsea. Gullit would brook no arguments over team selection, and Phelan was to start just one more game for the club before being sold for a knock-down £850,000 to Everton at the end of the year.

On the field, as well as off it, the Wimbledon game was to be one of flashpoints of the season. Gullit included himself among the substitutes, but dropped skipper Dennis Wise to the bench for the derby against his former club. 'My job is to win games for Chelsea, so I have to make decisions that are right for the club, not to make me popular,' Gullit said. He had certainly managed to do that.

'We never have reserves at Chelsea, just squad players. You've got to have at least 20 to choose from,' Gullit said, though some among his squad remained unconvinced. Within a month, Spencer and Peacock, two of the linchpins of Hoddle's 1994 FA Cup final team, had quit Stamford Bridge to join QPR. Spencer, Chelsea's top scorer the previous season, complained of being left in limbo under Gullit, forgotten and unspoken to, as the new manager brought in expensive foreign signings. 'No one at the club actually told me that I wasn't wanted. My whole career has been a fight for a place in the side. But you have to be given a chance. It's no good playing a game here and a game there. You need a run in the side, and that hasn't happened.

'Every club is bringing in foreign players now, so you have to accept it is going to happen. The foreigners Ruud has brought are all great players. I admire these guys. It's great to watch them work. They are players you can learn off. But it's no good me being on the bench learning off them.

'I'm 26 and I've not started a Premiership game this season. There's a World Cup coming up. I was involved in Euro '96 with Scotland and I want to be involved in the World Cup – so I need to be in the first team.'

Spencer had at least got on to the pitch against Wimbledon, though only when Chelsea were having to chase the game as the south Londoners' robust approach left the home side reeling, literally. The game was won within four minutes, when, after a Vinny Jones long throw, an apparent foul on Hitchcock in the Chelsea goal was allowed to pass by the referee (David Elleray, the Harrow schoolmaster so despised by Chelsea ever since he awarded two penalties to Manchester United in the 1994 Cup final), resulting in a goal by Robbie Earle. The die was cast.

You might have thought that the Chelsea coaching staff would have been sophisticated enough to anticipate the opposition's tactics: high balls, long throws, intimidation and muscle. High balls were duly bombed into the Chelsea area at every opportunity, and the defence began to resemble the Keystone Cops, as they chased about haplessly, falling over themselves in their disarray. Leboeuf suffered *lebump*, and played most of the game with a bandaged head, dazed and confused, one clumsy error gifting Wimbledon another goal. Uncertainty and lack of organisation contributed to Wimbledon's seventh successive league victory in an impressive run of results, as they out-fought and out-thought Chelsea to win decisively 4–2.

It was the fourth home sell-out of the season, with the gates closed at 1 p.m., two hours before kick-off. Chelsea were now being considered sufficiently big a draw that even this game against Wimbledon, notorious for having little support (average home attendance: 14,000, a figure artificially boosted by the 25,000 London-based Manchester United fans who had taken out Crazy Gang memberships in order to watch their first league match of the season) could be a sell out.

In fact, the demand for tickets for probably Chelsea's most attractive league game of the season, against Manchester United, had all been sold in October – four months before the game. Tickets for other key matches were also now only being sold if bought together with tickets for less obviously attractive games. Good gates, of course, meant good revenue, essential to provide the funding for the top players' wages. But what would happen if, as against Liverpool and Wimbledon, the results started to go against Chelsea? And what would happen if internal strife among players unhappy at being left out of the side were to affect the side's performances detrimentally? Such questions were already being asked, and a long trip up to Bolton for the next round of the League Cup would be crucial in providing some answers. No one, though, could have surmised the deeply profound and tragic changes that would be wrought at Chelsea over the next week.

Chapter 9

'We'll just have to win the FA Cup now.' Those were his last words as he left the directors' box at Burnden Park, after witnessing another premature cup exit by his beloved Chelsea. Then Matthew Harding scurried off into the night. He had a helicopter flight to catch, so that he might be back in London for the start of business on Wednesday.

Just a few hours later, being blown around a Cheshire field amid pieces of scattered, twisted wreckage, was a copy of that night's Bolton match programme, the *Trotters Review*, charred black around the edges and torn. One of the firefighters at the scene in the grey pre-dawn autumn mists bent down and picked it up, the first clue that the victims of the helicopter crash might have been football fans.

It is unlikely that the cause of the crash will ever be known with any great certainty. Small aircraft such as the twin-engined Eurocopter Squirrel, call sign G-CFLT, which crashed that night are not required to have the sort of black box flight recorders which are carried on larger, commercial aircraft, to tape the pilot's radio messages and so help to determine the cause of such accidents. So the final moments in the life of the pilot and four passengers on that helicopter that night will probably remain a mystery. All that is known for sure is that Matthew Harding's sudden death, on the night of 22 October 1996, brought about an outpouring of public grief and respect from the football community which is normally reserved for national heroes.

A manager of another club, in another time, once said that football wasn't a matter of life and death: it was more important than that. Perhaps, for a rare moment, Chelsea fans, together with a broad cross-section of football supporters across the country, realised that such epigrams were really little more than that, and that football is, after all, just a game, and that the lives of the people in and around that game can be far more precious than a simple scoreline.

Death and sport are not easy companions. Too often, sport delves into the vocabulary of real tragedy to describe moments in what ought to be, after all, just a game. Yet sport demands danger, of the spectator as well as the participant. For if you commit yourself to supporting a team, you dabble with the danger of disappointment. But the death of Matthew Harding came as a surprise and a shock to English football because it was so out of place, with the vivacity of the man himself, and the vivaciousness of sport. Sport is not supposed to be about death. It is meant to be about life, affirming the glories and joys of living, celebrating the very act of drawing breath, of making effort, of striving again to succeed, sport is supposed to be about excitement, risk and confrontation. Sport is about the stuff of life itself. And football was the stuff of Matthew Harding's life.

Yet in the midst of his successful business, the joys of his children, and his pleasure at seeing a rejuvenated Chelsea, at the age of 42, Matthew Harding was killed.

Mick Goss, the pilot, had returned to the helicopter before the Bolton match was finished to make some routine safety checks in advance of what was expected to be a straightforward, 90-minute flight back to Heathrow. Earlier in the afternoon, en route to Bolton, they had stopped off at Oswestry, Shropshire, to visit Per Lindstrand, the hot air balloonist who was planning a daring round-the-world flight attempt with another high-profile millionaire businessman, Richard Branson. Harding was providing some financial backing for the project, and was keen to see how things were getting along with Lindstrand's new balloon. This was all provided, of course, the visit did not stop him watching Chelsea play that night.

Lindstrand had taken a liking to Harding, and warmed to his encouragement and enthusiasm for his project: 'The word *can't* was not in his vocabulary,' Lindstrand said. But the word can't was in Lindstrand's, and he thought that the thick fog that had enveloped his balloon factory in the Welsh Marches that afternoon ought to have stopped Harding's helicopter from flying on. 'It was zero visibility,' Lindstrand, an experienced pilot of more than just hot air balloons, said. 'There was a lot of fog. It was not a night to be flying a helicopter.'

But fly Harding and his party did, and half an hour after leaving Lindstrand they landed safely at a makeshift helipad in the car park of a Bolton bakery, where they were met by local businessman Jonathan Warburton. On that helicopter with Harding was Ray Deane, another fanatical Chelsea fan and a friend since their schooldays at Abingdon; John Bauldie, a journalist from *Q* magazine who shared Harding's enthusiasm for Bob Dylan, having written several books about the musician, and who had been invited to travel north with Harding because of his support for Bolton Wanderers; and Tony Burridge, another insurance executive whose ability in the markets had so impressed Harding that he had recruited him to run one of his subsidiary companies. Burridge was also a friend of Warburton's since they had been at Millfield School together.

The party went off to have a few drinks and a meal before the match, though Harding turned down the offer to visit a local pizzeria, saying he was too nervous before games to be able to eat. 'I'll pick up something at the ground,' Harding said. He was in great spirits just minutes into the game, too, when Scott Minto went on a solo run down the left-hand side of the pitch, cut inside two Bolton players and launched a swirling shot from more than 20 yards to give Chelsea an early lead. 'When Chelsea scored, Matthew was jumping up and down,' Warburton remembers. True to form, being in the directors' box did not diminish Harding's facility for showing his joy at Chelsea success. 'Being a Bolton fan, I told him to sit down,' Warburton says.

Warburton would soon have plenty to cheer about himself, as Chelsea's vulnerability at corners, so evident on the Saturday against Wimbledon, was now exploited by Bolton. Gullit had included himself in the starting XI for the first time this season, but even his brand of footballing magic, including a cross-cum-shot which glanced off the bar, could not stop Chelsea going out of the League Cup.

Despite seeing another Chelsea defeat, as he left Burnden Park, Harding was still in a convivial mood. According to Ken Bates, as they parted, Harding wished him a safe journey home. Back at the helipad, Goss had completed his checks and had got a favourable weather report from the Met Office. At about 10.40 p.m., the helicopter took off for the southward journey, the route largely following the M6 motorway. Then, little more than 10 minutes into the 90-minute flight, there was an explosion and a crash.

Witnesses in in the small farming town of Middlewich – and more than a dozen telephoned the Cheshire fire brigade to report the explosion – spoke of hearing a low flying helicopter, perhaps circling, possibly in some difficulty, before the sound of the explosion. In a nearby old people's home, Leslie Anderson was on night duty as an auxiliary nurse. All was quiet in her ward when she heard the helicopter, 'I thought it was the police chopper, and I wondered what they were doing,' she said. Then, 'All of a sudden, there was this huge bang and a screaming sound. It sounded like World War Three. I phoned the police to report the noise, but didn't think any more of it until I heard police sirens and saw flashing blue lights coming from across the fields.'

Tom Broad, a retired farmer, was in the living room of his house, watching television with his wife Marion, when they heard the helicopter struggling to remain airborne. 'The engine seemed to be coughing and spluttering. We heard the aircraft above, and we still heard the engine jumping as we ran outside to see what was going on. We saw the trees on the top of the ridge overlooking the house burst into flames.'

'We heard what sounded like a loud explosion,' another witness, Amanda Boyse, said, 'and then there was a bright light in the sky across the fields.'

To search for the crash site, the police themselves used two helicopters, one scrambled from Manchester and another from a nearby RAF base. They flew over the countryside near Middlewich, between the A530 and A54, using thermal imaging equipment to identify where the helicopter may have come down. Within 30 minutes of the first call to the emergency services, the wreckage had been spotted. There was a couple of small fires in the undergrowth of a wooded area between Norcroft Farm and Sutton Hall Farm. The search party soon discovered five bodies among the wreckage. They knew there was no chance of any survivors.

Before the explosion, there had been no mayday message, no hint that the helicopter was in any difficulty. Even the expert aircraft crash investigators at the scene the following morning could only speculate at what might have caused the accident. Nearly 40 of the French-made Squirrel helicopters have been in service in Britain since 1980, many of them operated by the police and military, and they had an exemplary safety record. The actual aircraft involved in the accident had been used safely enough just three weeks before by Tony Blair, the leader of the Labour party. The two-engined version of the Squirrel, which this helicopter was, is supposed to be especially safe, since in the event of one engine failing, the other is capable of keeping the helicopter airborne until a landing site is located.

Thus, at least one possible cause seemed to be ruled out immediately. From the deep gouge marks running nearly 100 yards across the field, with four cuts in the turf where the main rotor blade had hit the ground, leading to the burned-out wreck at the edge of the woods, it was clear that the machine had not just dropped from the sky – some suggested that tail rotor failure might have caused Mike Goss to lose control of the aircraft, lose altitude, and perhaps hit an electricity power cable, bringing the aircraft down. Although the helicopter's route had been south-bound, the aircraft had crashed when travelling in a north-easterly direction, suggesting that Goss had been circling, perhaps looking for a safe place to make an emergency landing.

The largest piece of debris found at the crash scene the following morning was one of the helicopter doors. This had come to rest more than 80 yards from the rest of the fuselage. The passengers, too, had been scattered about the field, all killed on impact by multiple injuries.

It was not until later the following morning that the bodies were identified – indeed, early reports had suggested that there might have been a woman on board the ill-fated flight. But news of the crash and its location meant that those at Chelsea and at his Benfield's insurance firm who knew of Harding's travel plans for the Bolton game were quick to draw their own sad, sorry conclusions about the possible victims. The first reaction, invariably, was less of sorrow, more of disbelief.

It was the early hours of the morning when Graham Rix got home. It had been a long, sorry journey south, typical of those subdued drives after a disappointing defeat away from home. Rix was tired, perhaps half-asleep, when the phone rang. 'I got a call from a journalist, not confirming anything but asking me to confirm what happened. I'd had no idea. I think it was about half past three that morning. I spoke to Gwyn Williams, then he spoke to Colin Hutchinson,' Rix said.

'I didn't know Matthew really well, but what you see is what you get. He was a great Chelsea fan. I knew he was a great friend of Graham Bell.' Bell, like Harding, is a City businessman who had become a benefactor of Chelsea. Bell had helped to finance the Chelsea youth team which Rix had been coaching until his recent promotion alongside Gullit. On hearing the news, Rix took it upon himself to call Bell.

Few of the players wanted to talk, or could talk, of the tragedy the following day. As they arrived at the Harlington training ground, the gates were shut behind them to exclude the curious and the press. Most of the players had known Matthew as an effervescent character who might show his head in the dressing room before the game, but more often than not would choose not to intrude, and only approach the players after games in the club bar. 'He always had something nice to say, it didn't matter if you'd had a bad game,' Steve Clarke remembered of Harding. 'He was always positive, even if we'd had a bad loss, he was a positive influence for Chelsea. Every time I spoke to the man, I came away feeling better.'

Although the players reported for training on the Thursday morning, it was almost impossible for them to get back to work, to behave as if it is was business as usual. 'You can't, can you?' said Rix, 'a tragedy like that, it affects everybody. We've got a game on Saturday against Spurs, and we've got to approach the game as Matthew would have wanted us to. Especially against Spurs. That is the one game he'd have wanted us to win.'

For Clarke, the routine aspects of the footballer's life, the warm-up, stretching, the training session, was a welcome diversion from the shattering sorrow. 'It was good to get back to training. It was probably the first time since yesterday morning that I hadn't thought about what happened. It is a good release to get back on the training pitch, try to get back to normality.'

Harding's last interview had been on Michael Parkinson's BBC Radio 5 Live programme the previous Friday. The other guests on the programme were television commentator Brian Moore and former Liverpool, Spurs and England goalkeeper Ray Clemence. The topics of the hour-long programme ranged far and wide in the footballing world, from Paul Gascoigne (who was in the news because he had been sent off earlier in the week and, it had been alleged in tabloid revelations, had been beating his wife) to agents to the standard of play in England.

Harding's comments on Paul Gascoigne's publicly aired problems were perhaps personally revealing. 'I have a certain sympathy for anybody who finds themself in the goldfish bowl that he's found himself in. If only he could surround himself with people that really care about him and want to harness that talent to its best effect, rather than so much of what seems to happen in the world of football . . . I find that a pity. Of course, we can all sit here in judgment, and of course the newspapers are going to love every minute of it. But I feel sorry for him above all else,' Harding said of the frustrating, frustrated talent that is Gazza.

Harding, of course, had his own public image to contend with. Because, beyond his involvement with Chelsea and his acrimonious business spat with Ken Bates, Harding found himself a subject for news reports because of his immense wealth, his sometimes maverick approach to the usually staid London insurance markets, his role as a benefactor to the NSPCC, for his £1 million donation to the Labour party and, above all for the prying tabloids, the complicated conduct of his personal life.

He had established a lifestyle which saw him visit the family home in Ditchling, Sussex, at weekends, spending time with Ruth, his wife of 20 years, and their four children – Hannah, 18, Luke, 14, and 12-year-old twins Patrick and Joel – while he set up home in Wimbledon with Vicky Jaramillo, 17 years his junior, the Ecuador-born mother of their two-year-old daughter, Ella.

Harding had managed to keep the affair out of the *papparazzos'* lenses, often compromising some of his closest friends by letting them in on the secret and expecting them to remain silent about it to Ruth. But once he and Jaramillo had been seen in public together, going to Chelsea matches where once he had been accompanied by his wife, and attending premières and parties where they were photographed by the press, Harding had been forced to 'try to sort something out' with Ruth.

Possibly because he was being mindful of his own personal situation, in the Parkinson radio programme Harding refused to make a moral stand over Paul Gascoigne. Parkinson, in his best, provocative, Yorkshireman-over-a-pint-glass mode, pressed the Chelsea vice-chairman. Would Harding be prepared to take on a player, such as Gascoigne, who had admitted to being a wife beater? 'I just can't begin to answer that question,' Harding said. 'I just think it ill-behoves a lot of us to sit in judgment on what goes on behind closed doors. In his case, his doors are open, not closed . . .'

The discussion then broadened out, moving along to a more general debate about the sort of circumstances which can 'create' a Gazza. They spoke of the pressures of the modern game, the immense rewards often available to young players, and those same young players' ill-preparedness to cope with the demands of the modern, media-driven football industry. Harding pointed out that, were it not for changes forced on English football by the disasters at Heysel, Bradford and Hillsborough, and the resulting Taylor Report, the infrastructure at the grounds would have remained largely unaltered.

What followed from Harding seemed to be a most pointed condemnation of old-style football directors. 'Those that have been responsibile for owning and running football clubs over the last 25, 35 years, have done absolutely *nothing* to put any money back into the particular clubs over which they've exercised their fiefdoms. And all of a sudden, what we have found, in the space of a short time – what amounts to two or three, maybe four seasons – clubs have had to jump two or three business generations. From the most squalid conditions which I grew up on – worse than Victorian conditions, the urinals, the standing, the lack of cover for weather and the catering facilities – it was disgraceful. OK, we all loved it, probably because it was half of the fun and we didn't know any better.

'Then we had to move three business generations in about three seasons to build all-seater stadia, and it was too much for people. So we've seen this rush at it, which has seen a lot of people hanging on to the clubs they run, or hanging on to the positions that they've got, hoping that the Football Trust will provide all the finance. Now of course, Sky's come along and done so much for football. I remember when I joined three years ago, people thought I was a bit crazy – they probably still think I am – to get involved as I did, but now, three years on, and getting involved in a serious football club is seen to be, for reasonably financially astute businessmen, it seems to be quite a sensible thing to do. Whereas three years ago, I would have needed to have my head examined.

'Now, football is getting itself ready to be part of the serious sporting leisure world of the 21st century, and to that extent, the more exposure it gets on television, the more it captures people's imaginations. I think the state of English football, with what the Premiership has become, has put football in a healthier state and a more positive state than it has been for a long, long time. The continentals now recognise that the English Premier League is now the most exciting and dynamic football league in Europe, and to that extent, that's where they want to be.

'Go back before the Taylor Report, go back say seven, eight years. Can you honestly say that in the world of English football, with 92 clubs, that there was a body politic, a financial structure that made sense?'

But what, Parkinson asked, about those clubs in the Premiership who are over-spending? 'You've got to ask yourself whether there are any clubs in the Premiership that *aren't* over-spending,' Harding answered. 'I don't think it makes much sense, but every game in the Premiership now is a six-pointer. It is worrying, but the fear of failure is high, the stakes are high. Whether football is ready to get into the cut and thrust of the business leisure world is something I'm not sure about, but sure as apples is apples, that's where it's going.

'The amount of money Sky are making available from the start of next season is an enormous inducement for clubs to think on a broader horizon, to consider becoming publicly quoted. Of course, the arrival of pay-per-view television could make the Sky money look like pocket money.

'I am a little bit concerned about the plc route for football clubs because I happen to believe that there's going to be the thick end of 20 clubs who'll be publicly quoted within 18 months to two years, probably most of them in the Premiership, I think it's inevitable. And I just watch with interest the people who find themselves with the controlling shares of those clubs because in the main what I think you're going to find is that the shareholders are not necessarily dyed-in-the-wool fans of the particular club in question. To what extent then do clubs get traded a bit like footballers?

'As a Chelsea fan for the past 34 years, I've got used to players coming and going, and you love 'em the day they join and cry the day they leave, but you soon forget them. But clubs must remain and retain their own integrity and I'm interested to the extent which we could find that media interests and business interests will come in and buy up a club, and possibly trade a club to buy up another, bigger club. I think that's worrying for football.'

Harding would die with the concern for football, and for Chelsea, ultimately unresolved. Perhaps, had he lived, Harding might have found a solution to the dilemma. Certainly, Glenn Hoddle, the Chelsea player-manager with whom Harding had become so close during his time at the club, was of the opinion that, more than merely money, Harding could contribute to the sport. 'It is just unbelievable that the game should lose somebody who had so much to offer,' said the England coach on the day after the helicopter crash.

Disbelief as much as sadness, shock before grief – it was the reaction of many of the people who visited Stamford Bridge over the next four days, placing flowers, scarfs, shirts or simple letters of condolence on hastily erected steel fencing that soon extended for more than 100 yards from the main gates of the ground, up towards the East Stand. 'We have lost a hero, but football has lost a champion,' read one message stuck between the wire mesh. 'We used to chant "loyal supporter" in The Shed. Well, Matty was the loyalest of loyal supporters. We must not let his dream die with him,' read another. There was even a message from a Millwall fan: 'We all want a Walker or a Hall, but most of all, we'd want to have a Harding, someone who puts his money in for no other reason than a love of the club.'

The club received messages from abroad – America, Norway, Canada, Japan, Australia and Hong Kong, among others. The owner of Wimbledon, Sam Hammam, brought a small wreath of blue carnations to Stamford Bridge personally, and supporters from even Chelsea's fiercest rivals – West Ham, Arsenal, Liverpool and Manchester United – were among the many who visited Stamford Bridge that week to contribute their own small token in a temporary shrine to Matthew Harding.

Harding's death drew the sort of impromptu reaction normally associated with the death of a great manager, like Liverpool's Bill Shankly, or a great player, like Bobby Moore. Like Shankly at Anfield and Moore at West Ham, Harding would also have a more permanent memorial to his contribution to Chelsea Football Club, with the decision announced by Ken Bates to re-name the North Stand as the Matthew Harding Stand. At a hurriedly organised press conference at Stamford Bridge the day after the crash, Bates said, 'This is one press conference I never wanted to chair. We are still stunned, trying to come to terms with Matthew's death. At times like this, words don't mean much.

'It's a sign of the mark Matthew made in football that we have been inundated with messages of sympathy and condolence. We are all rather helpless, as our sympathy goes out to Matthew's family and the other four families caught up in this tragedy.

'Matthew was the catalyst of the rebuilding of Stamford Bridge. It was his enthusiasm and loan that allowed us to build the North Stand.

'Ere, boss, what's the Italian for "Clean them boots"?' Chelsea's new managerial partnership, Ruud Gullit with assistant Graham Rix. Gullit would prove the master of delegation as well as inspiration at Chelsea. (Stu Forster/Allsport)

'Luca, is it true that you want to be known as the most expensive substitute in world football?' Vialli meets the British press during pre-season, 1996. Ironically, considering the saturation coverage given to the £20,000-per-week-plus striker's travails, Vialli stated that it was the more relaxed nature of the British media, compared to Italy's, that he liked about being in London. (Clive Mason/Allsport)

Painful lessons. When Chelsea's outstanding young defender, Michael Duberry, ruptured his Achilles tendon, ending his season, he turned to former England midfielder, John Barnes, for advice on how to battle back. (Michael Cooper/Allsport)

Bridge of Tears. A young fan hangs his contribution to the temporary memorial to Matthew Harding, Chelsea's vice-chairman, who was killed in a helicopter crash in October 1996. (Gary M Prior/Allsport)

Can't keep a good man down. Mark Hughes enjoyed an Indian summer to his career, his strength and skills providing the perfect foil in the second-half of the season for Gianfranco Zola. (Ben Radford/Allsport)

From Hammersmith to Wemberlee. Dennis Wise and Franco Zola congratulate local lad Eddie Newton on his Wembley goal, which sealed the game and helped to erase Newton's not-so-fond memories of his previous Wembley final three years earlier. (Shaun Botterill/Allsport)

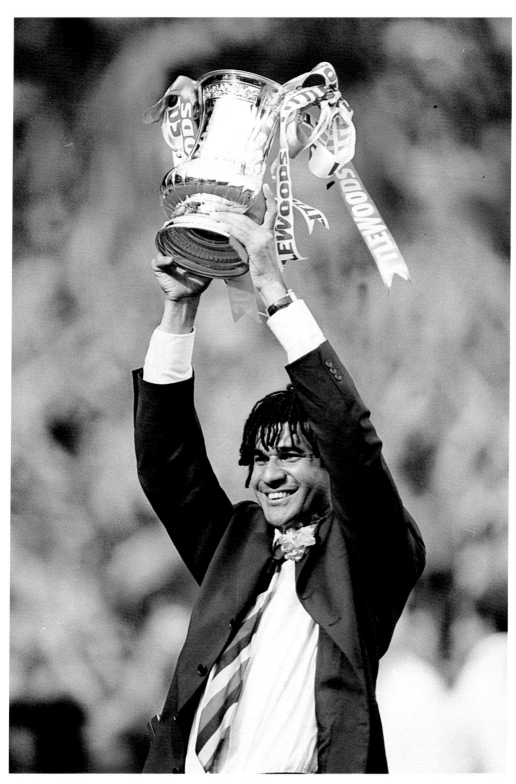

Back in the big time. After 26 years, Chelsea had again won a major trophy. According to Ruud Gullit, he always wins things when the side he plays for wears white socks.
(Shaun Botterill/Allsport)

We'll keep the Blue Flag flying high. Massive crowds blocked the Fulham Road on the morning after the FA Cup final to give Chelsea a heroes' welcome. (Ross Kinnaird/Allsport)

Without that it wouldn't have been possible. Re-naming the stand is the least we can do when you think of all he has done for the club.

'Matthew's death will not affect our future plans. Such was his dedication to the club that his promised financial commitment to the club was totally in place in the shape of the southern complex, which you can see rising. It was the next stage of achieving his and all Chelsea fans' dream of having a world-class team in a world-class stadium.'

Seated alongside Bates at the press conference was Ruud Gullit. Gullit has long been regarded by football folk as one of the more sensitive, cerebral of their kind, even something of an enigma. On this day, the normally elegant Dutchman looked slightly crumpled, a little careworn. Unshaven, wearing a black suit and a light blue, check shirt, unbuttoned at the neck, no one could catch his eye – his gaze was cast a thousand miles away, anywhere else other than Stamford Bridge, here and now. It was clear that he had been very deeply affected by the events of the previous few hours.

Eventually, Gullit's attention turned to the meeting at hand, and he addressed himself to a question. He seemed near to tears as he answered. 'It has been a strange week. I have felt strange myself. I have felt depressed and have not slept for two nights. I could not work out why I had not slept the first night. Perhaps I know now. All this is so hard to take in.'

It was decided, despite an offer by Tottenham to postpone the match, to go ahead with the league fixture on the Saturday. 'It will be a very emotional occasion – and I honestly have no idea how it will turn out for everybody,' Gullit said. 'I will be asking my team to do their best but I also know people have to be given the opportunity to express their grief. There are no special demands I can make on people in an environment like this.

'I have been to church and prayed to God in the last couple of days because I felt I needed to. I am not a Catholic, a Christian, a Buddhist or whatever, but I believe in God and I am comfortable with that. It is good to have something to give you relief in circumstances like this. I wanted solitude and I wanted the time to ask questions about life. This is my way of coping but I don't know how others will cope. It is an individual thing.

'I remember when I was with Sampdoria in Italy and the club's president died. It was very emotional and although I did not know the man very well I felt the effect because I could see the grief of those who did. This is a similar set of circumstances but I can only cope in my own way and let people cope in theirs. What we all must do is pray for the soul of the poor guy and his family.'

Steve Clarke, too, was worried about the sense of unreality of the approaching game. Football had been put firmly into context this week. 'It's been a strange build-up during the last couple of days. I must admit the feeling is missing for the game but we have a match to play and we've got to prepare for it the best way we can. I think it's better to have a collective show of grief straight away, get this game over and allow people to pay their tributes.' The catharsis of grief would affect not only Chelsea's next game, but the rest of Chelsea's season.

Chapter 10

There is something uncannily eery about the sound of 28,000 people being silent. It was verging on the surreal. It was unnatural: there was not a cough, nor a rogue shout, not even a passing train or a car driving along the Fulham Road just before three o'clock that afternoon to be heard inside Stamford Bridge. The opposing fans from Tottenham had been exemplary in their behaviour, though by now it was clear that respect for Matthew Harding was widespread and absolute among ordinary football fans, regardless of what colours their team happened to wear on a Saturday afternoon.

The names of the accident victims had been read across the public address system just before the unforgetting minute began: Harding, Deane, Burridge, Bauldie and Goss. The minute seemed to last an age. A crow somewhere over in the bare trees of the Brompton Cemetery, the other side of the railway tracks from Stamford Bridge, cawed coarsely. Then, as if anyone in the ground needed reminding of the reason for this tribute, somewhere in the distance could be heard a rhythmical whirl, the steady beat of a helicopter, perhaps taking off from the nearby Battersea heliport. It could not break the solemnity of the moment, and as Roger Dilkes blew his referee's whistle to mark the end of the minute's silence, the first sound heard was a collective sigh of regret before the fiercely loud chant went up, one sensed led from those on their feet at the northern end of ground under a freshly painted sign which read, 'Matthew Harding Stand': *Matthew Harding's Blue and White Army* . . . It was a chant that would become familiar in football grounds throughout the land over the next seven months of the season.

That match day in and around Stamford Bridge had already been remarkable. Instead of turning up barely an hour before kick-off, supporters had been arriving in small, subdued groups from mid-morning. Some had tickets, some were prepared to pay well above face value to get a ticket, and others just came along to view the ersatz memorial and pay their respects. A short guy, with a red beard and red

Arsenal shirt, scurried along among the blues and whites carrying a small bunch of flowers, which he placed carefully by the fence, waited for a moment, turned on his heels and set off back to Fulham Broadway, presumably to catch the Tube to get him to Highbury for his team's match that afternoon.

Pinned to the wire fencing nearby was a tribute from someone signing themselves 'Russ, a Brighton Blue', one of many which tried to express what Harding had meant to them.

> You'll remember Tottenham and Palace in the FA Cup,
> You'll remember going away to win to keep us up,
> You'll remember the journeys to the Twin Towers,
> You'll remember football in the sun and winter showers.
> Now we will remember you, the great man who shared the dream,
> You gave us more than any other and that we will never forget,
> Every time we are in the ground you will be there to keep an eye,
> Every time we sing a song, you will lift the blue flag high.

Across the King's Road, in the Imperial Arms, a perfectly pulled pint of Guinness stood on the bar, untouched, as if waiting for Matthew to walk in at any moment. Cornelius, the landlord, had pulled the pint, which was bought by Peter Osgood. Harding, whenever he met with Osgood in later years, would greet him as 'The King' – as a boyhood hero of Harding's and so many others who had watched Chelsea in the late 1960s and early 1970s, Osgood had truly earned the title. Osgood's relative lack of international recognition remains one of the great unsolved mysteries of the footballing world, but equally extant is Osgood's goal-scoring record for Chelsea and his feat of scoring in every round of the FA Cup in 1970, something no one has matched since.

'Matt was just a true blue and the people loved him for that,' Osgood said. 'They also knew that this man could, just might, give them what they so desperately wanted: a winning team. Now this. There is a bloody curse on this club. We have never been closer to the good old days when I was playing. I just hope it is not all lost again.'

By one o'clock, about the time Harding would normally leave for the directors' box, Osgood's pint of Guinness had been joined on the bar by another dozen.

For Osgood was not alone in visiting the Imperial that lunchtime, Harding's favourite pre-match haunt for a cheese and pickle sandwich or oysters to go with his Guinness. Before midday, the bar was packed. Harding's sister, Grace, was at the centre of a small huddle of friends and business acquaintances, but the bar-room babble was quietened once

Football Focus came on the television screen in the corner. Harding had always managed to get the pub to be quiet whenever he wanted to watch this section of the *Grandstand* programme. There was no question that he had achieved that again on this day, as Gary Lineker introduced a sombre item. Not for the first, or the last time that day, the images of Matthew Harding as his ebullient self, inter-cut with clips from the crash scene three days before, and footage taken at Stamford Bridge in the aftermath, prompted tears. There were tears from grown men who probably had not wept in years – one pair of brothers, both big men, in their 40s, hair shorn tight to their heads, wearing Chelsea's bright yellow away shirt and clutching a wreath of blue flowers, were reduced to red-faced, sobbing boys by the thought that they would never see Matthew alive again

'The only difference between him and us,' said one, 'is that he had a few million quid, and we don't. If it was his round, he'd buy. But if it was your round, he'd make sure you got one in, too.'

Beside him, another Imperial regular, his own pint barely touched – it's difficult to drink with a lump in your throat – said, 'He would ask your opinion about the team and tactics, and you knew he'd go back upstairs to the boardroom and put your point across. He listened to what the fans said.' When Len Shackleton wrote his book on football, he famously included a blank page under the heading: 'What the average club director knows about football'. Shackleton had obviously never met Harding.

'I had to come here,' Matthew's sister, Grace, said, after standing by the bar for a while, listening to the compliments and condolences. 'I wanted to be here with them all. I had heard so much about this place and how they loved him. I am not a football person, but I feel like one now.'

The people Grace Harding met for the first time that day were a mix of people who had met Matthew Harding, who knew him well, and people who had only ever heard about him or read about him in the newspapers. The grief had spread far wider than just friends and family. David Lacey, writing in that morning's *Guardian*, said: 'Something precious died with Harding. His appeal among Chelsea fans lay primarily in his visibility. Not for him the executive box behind darkened glass. His pre-match visits to a local pub, moreover, recalled an earlier, gentler age when dusty, musty old Stamford Bridge attracted football's promenaders.

'Whatever happens to the Harding fortune, the passion which persuaded him to plough £26.5 million into Chelsea died on Tuesday night and cannot be replaced. He was the 89th richest man in the kingdom. Stamford Bridge would be fortunate indeed if the erstwhile 90th was to be found in the King's Road this afternoon humming *Blue is the Colour*. Somehow, one gets the feeling that Chelsea are not that lucky.'

Lacey is probably the finest football writer in Britain today, yet on this occasion he got it wrong. The loss of Matthew Harding somehow managed to galvanise the club – players, backroom staff and fans – with a passion which would be carried forward for the rest of the season, starting that afternoon against Tottenham. As Ruud Gullit put in his programme notes that day, 'A very nice person has passed away, but his spirit will always be a part of Chelsea'.

Ten minutes before kick-off, Gullit had gathered his players together in their dressing room, just as he would before any game to give them the pre-match team talk. This time, he said nothing, the footballers just being encouraged to stand, hand-in-hand for a moment's reflection. Nothing needed saying.

The atmosphere in the ground had been strained and sullen before the minute's silence, when Dennis Wise, Kevin Hitchcock and Steve Clarke carried out a wreath with 'Matthew RIP' in white carnations, which was placed on the pitch in the penalty area in the shadow of the Harding stand. The Chelsea players gathered around the D for the minute's silence, holding hands again and holding back their tears.

The match got underway with only two seats in the place not taken – those which would have been used by Harding and his guest at that game. The club had had to draw the line, though, before the ground had become so overwhelmed with memorials that it would be turned into a mausoleum. 'We had to say no when someone rang wanting to sponsor a military band to play *Abide With Me*,' said chief executive Colin Hutchinson. 'It was reaching the stage where it would have become difficult for the players.'

It was difficult enough as it was. The uneasy atmosphere clearly affected the first few minutes of the game, the Chelsea players uncertain, the Tottenham team looking as if they had long before decided not to compete with the occasion. A cross from Gullit and a dynamic leap and downward header by Michael Duberry which brought about a finger-tip save from Ian Walker in the Spurs goal after 11 minutes seemed to crack the reverie. Perhaps it was the subdued nature of the Tottenham midfield, but Gullit seemed to have more time than usual to send his precision passes all around the park.

It was Gullit who helped to instigate the first goal, after 27 minutes, releasing di Matteo down the right, from where he crossed and Mark Hughes's header seemed goal-bound, until it found the foot of the far post. Gullit's passion play had seen him race the length of the field, though, and he was there, in a spin of dreadlocks to hit home the rebound.

Tottenham equalised five minutes before half-time, though, as Hitchcock flapped at a long throw and Armstrong turned the ball into the undefended goal. Gullit was immediately on hand to pick the ball out of the back of the net, to get the game underway once again. The angered look of contempt he gave to his goalkeeper as he made his way back to the centre circle would have withered weaker men. The second half, though, was all Chelsea, one move, in particular, encapsulating the brilliant football that the New Azzurri seemed capable of: Gullit, down by the right touchline near the halfway line, shimmied and feinted to pass by his man, before passes between Vialli and Hughes released Scott Minto storming in on the Tottenham area on the left-hand side, his volley from 20 yards making the crossbar vibrate.

It was left to David Lee to restore the lead from the penalty spot, and di Matteo slid home the clinching third goal into a narrow gap between Walker and his post, after Vialli had hit a perfect cross. Still unbeaten by rivals Spurs since 1990, this 3–1 win would have delighted Matthew Harding. 'I suppose it was scripted for us to lose,' Gerry Francis, the Spurs manager, said.

Not that the game was completely divorced from painful reminders of reality. David Lee, a centre-back with a licence and ability to roam, broke his leg in a tackle as he galloped upfield. It was the end of his season. And in the matchday programme, chairman Ken Bates had attempted to leaven the lofty tributes when he wrote of the two men's first meeting, 'I think we were fascinated with each other, so alike and yet so different, with one thing in common – Chelsea.

'He wanted to be loved by everyone, had many acquaintances but had few close friends . . . Matthew died still a mystery, an enigma, because behind the veneer of *bonhomie* he was a loner, a deep thinker. Very good company, a star in the cut-and-thrust of friendly repartee but given to monosyllabic replies if you probed deeper.' Some letters to the national papers had also questioned the devotional nature of some of the press coverage – 'He had a public school education, and his well-connected father found him a position in that most socially useful of industries, the re-insurance market,' one correspondent wrote to *The Guardian*. 'He amasses a small fortune by the time he is 40. A modest proportion of that is then spent on indulging a childhood fantasy of immersing himself in Chelsea Football Club. Sadly, Matthew Harding meets an early death travelling by helicopter.

'We are then met with a barrage of media coverage that would have us believe one of the nation's truly great citizens has been prematurely ripped from us. Sorry, but have I missed something?' Someone else pointed out that press coverage that week had made Harding seem like some sort of Father Teresa, but that his financial input to Chelsea had all been in the form of loans, and that he was now receiving £1.5 million per year in rent from the club.

Yet, while Harding was a businessman, what set him apart was that he had a heart. There is the story of how, when John Dempsey – a member of Chelsea's 1970 FA Cup-winning side who now works with disabled children – approached Harding for a contribution towards a new minibus for the kids, Harding's reply was, 'Buy the bus and send me the bill.' No hesitation, and no great fanfare to herald the contribution (although Harding was not always a shrinking violet when it came to his expenditure: he had a habit of having his tax bill framed and then hung on his office wall, for all to see).

There was also the time that a sitting tenant in a property owned by a Chelsea subsidiary had been ordered to leave, even though she needed just another few weeks in order to find alternative accommodation. A written appeal left at Harding's City offices brought a response within 24 hours, Harding having brought up the matter at a board meeting that same day – the tenant was given the extra time needed to find a new home.

Even Ken Bates's own account of his dealings with Harding confirmed that, within a week of being asked for money for ground development, Harding had stumped up £5 million, and within a month of that, work had begun on the building of the new North Stand. It had been Harding's money which had made so much of the re-building, of the ground and of the team, possible.

Of course, just like the ground, the re-building work of the team was still in progress, and at times, Gullit's side closely resembled the Stamford Bridge arena: open at one end. But apart from Hitchcock's one aberration in the Tottenham game, Gullit had just been part of possibly his side's best performance of the season so far. Fittingly.

'I never dreamed of a tribute like this,' said the Dutchman, physically and emotionally drained by the day's events. 'The vibes were really, really strong and the team responded to give something back. You'll never forget a day like this.

'I was more happy about winning for him than winning for Chelsea. Today wasn't about playing a football match for three points. In a game like that, you don't talk about tactics – you just hope that everyone gives more than they've got, and they did that.'

Harding's funeral was the following week, and just like the Tottenham game, was attended by both his wife, Ruth, and his girlfriend, Vicky, and all his children. This time though, they were unable to be nearly lost among thousands of football fans – Ditchling's picturesque 13th century St Margaret's church was packed with barely 100 mourners there. Thus, the funeral of Matthew Harding brought the two grieving women together for the first time. They did not sit together, not a word was exchanged, and minutes before the service ended, Vicky slipped away from the church in tears.

The storm-grey clouds above the Sussex village where Harding had had his home reflected the mood of the mourners as they arrived, people drawn from the worlds of sport, politics and business. Harding had said that his dream for the millennium was for Chelsea to win the championship and Labour to be in government, so it was fitting that among those there that day was John Prescott, deputy leader of the Labour party, and Tony Banks MP, one of Chelsea's more colourful celebrity fans, while representing the football club were Ken Bates, Ruud Gullit and Glenn Hoddle, the manager Harding had fought so hard to keep at Stamford Bridge.

Francis Maude, the Tory shadow minister, and a member of the board at Benfield, had first met Matthew 30 years before when they had started together at Abingdon School. Maude remembered his friend in one of the addresses given in the small, ancient Sussex church that day:

A good friend of mine prints on all his letters the legend, 'One life to live – no time to waste'. No one lived that maxim so thoroughly as Matthew. It turned out that he was granted only half a lifetime. But he did more in that time than most can hope for in the full span . . .

What was he? Complicated, driven, clever, funny, generous, impetuous. He wanted to make a difference, and what a difference he made.

You all know the story. Benfield. Chelsea. His work for charities. His family, whom he loved, and who for so long gave him the strength to build his life. It sounds conventional enough. But Matthew did it all differently. He didn't want to do things the way others did. He was a true contrarian.

As a schoolboy, not an academic failure as some have said. Fearsomely bright, intensely hard-working when the subject engaged him, he left most of his A-level papers unfinished. Those he did complete were so good, he was offered the chance to resit the same papers again. But by then, mentally, he had moved on. He passed by the academic prizes for which the rest of us strove. In some odd way that I think even he never understood, all that was too easy for him.

A contrarian in business. He succeeded by doing business differently. By innovation. The status quo was an affront to him. He loathed complacency, the assumption that things should carry on just because that's how they'd always been. For Matthew, the only success that was worthwhile was what he earned by doing things better. Benfield's business success came about in the old metaphor, because they built a better mousetrap. They gave their customers a better product with better service. They made their market work better. In an age that carps at rich rewards for high success, Matthew was unashamed in rewarding himself and his colleagues handsomely. He answered to the market every day of his business life, and the market, a demanding judge, gave him and his partners consistently high marks. They may feel bereft, but it never was a one-man band, and I know that his surviving partners will build successfully on the powerful franchise that they have built together.

Contrarian in politics, too. For many the epitome of the successful Thatcherite entrepreneur, even what the vulgar might call a fat cat, he did what people who didn't know him least expected. And extravagantly, too. I told him that if it was publicity he was after, my party could have got him just as much for a lot less than a million.

Again, his approach to Chelsea was different. For Matthew, Chelsea was no rich man's plaything. He was a childhood supporter who one day found how he could *really* support his club – and he did it abundantly. The extraordinary and moving scenes at football grounds around the kingdom last Saturday, unique in my memory, were a tribute to his magic.

And his work for charities was different. He wasn't interested in just writing a cheque and walking away, although he did write cheques, and big ones, too. He wanted to be involved – to make more of a difference than just financially. Not just on the national scale – but helping local enterprises, and even our old school. There, as well as his generous financial help, he went every term to talk to senior boys about life after school, an undertaking that, in the light of Matthew's approach to his own final exams, the school treated with some trepidation.

What are my own memories? Being taken by him and his father to a match at Stamford Bridge 30 years ago, cheering at the wrong moment, and never being invited back.

The school cricket team we played in for five years, together with Ray Deane who too was stolen in the same disaster.

Doing Greek O level together – which I failed and he passed.

More recently, our regular two-bottle lunches, the last two long weeks ago, when we talked of everything and nothing. How after divulging his latest plans and schemes, wiping away the tears of laughter, he'd say, 'Isn't it fun being me?' – and who was I to argue with what was so obviously true?

I recall his delight at being godfather to our baby daughter. His fierce belief in his friends, that would shore you up when you doubted yourself. Himself a stranger to pomposity, how he relished puncturing it in others, so you learned not to give him the chance. How he never wasted time, but always had time for his friends.

Matthew was driven, competitive, creative, touched with a bit of genius. And like many people who are born with the capacity to do great good, he could also cause hurt. But there was some magic in Matthew, and it touched all who loved him.

Although he seemed indestructible, he lived his life as if each day might be his last. So when that shocking, wrenching day came that *was* his last, he had already built more, done more, made more difference, touched more lives, than falls to most people in a whole lifetime. That accident, that stole five men before their time, put out a bright light in our lives.

His voice breaking with emotion, Maude was close to the end of the valedictory for his friend:

'Never look back,' he used to say. But we *will* look back, with love and thanks for an extraordinary man. And when we grieve for his going, as we mourn his loss, let's remember him as he was – and smile through the tears.

Chapter 11

In the week that followed the Harding traumas, things were only a little calmer at the Bridge. Even before the vice-chairman's ashes had been allowed to settle over the pitch at his beloved Stamford Bridge, it was the state of the club's finances, the identity of possible replacement directors, and the state of Harding's will and life insurance policies which generated greatest attention at Chelsea.

Sitting at the breakfast table of his home counties farmhouse, Ken Bates must have nearly choked on his Sunday morning cornflakes the day after the Tottenham match. After turning from the sports pages, full of glowing tributes to his former rival, Bates then read in the business section of *The Sunday Times* that his own time as chairman of Chelsea FC and Chelsea Village was nearing an end. Harding's death had, the paper claimed, robbed Bates's redevelopment scheme 'of credibility in financial circles', and Chelsea Village investors were keen to see 'an independent chairman with a financial background' installed in place of Bates. It seemed more than just mere coincidence that, elsewhere in the same paper, was a sympathetic profile of Peter Middleton, the former head of Lloyd's of London, who told how he had cheated death by refusing a ride in Harding's helicopter due to another engagement on the night of the Bolton match. Middleton was a relatively new board member of both the football club and Chelsea Village.

Middleton had been brought in to the Chelsea conundrum earlier that year when Bates and Harding were attempting to patch up their public dispute. In his youth, Middleton had at one time trained to become a monk, and also trained to become a member of Britain's Olympic athletics team – neither endeavour was seen through to fruition. In City circles, Middleton became known for riding a big-engined motorbike into the normally discreet Square Mile. Here was a man who liked to be noticed in a world where anonymity was often a prized asset.

Middleton had been introduced to Harding by Paul Miller, the former Spurs player-turned-City executive with Kleinwort Benson. He and

Harding were never close friends, but after Harding's resignation from the Chelsea Village board, Middleton was seen as being able to provide the sort of worthy, City ballast that multi-million pound schemes – such as the £22 million rebuilding of the West Stand, the final phase of the Stamford Bridge redevelopment – are often seen to need.

Middleton, as the head of European operations for the Wall Street merchant bank, Salomon Brothers (on a reputed salary of £1 million per annum), was thought to be just the sort of figure who would inspire confidence in potential investors, and when Bates and Harding hammered out their peace deal at a private meeting in Drake's Bar at Stamford Bridge the previous summer, it was Middleton who was present. Some time after that meeting, Bates wrote to the new non-executive director, suggesting that when the time was right, he would stand down as chairman of Chelsea Village and hand over to Middleton.

But at the end of October 1996, Bates certainly did not believe that time was now, and as he saw the value of his Chelsea Village shares dip in the aftermath of Harding's death, the accompanying newspaper speculation about his own future spurred him to take direct action. Bates effectively controls Chelsea Village through his own 25 per cent shareholding and also because he speaks for the mysterious Rysaffe trust, based in Hong Kong, which holds 36 per cent of Chelsea Village, the largest single holding. Within 24 hours of the press reports appearing at the weekend, Bates had called an emergency board meeting, where, in his own, robust style, he demanded the other directors to put up or shut up.

None was prepared to challenge him, and Bates emerged from the meeting to say, 'I have just received the total support of the directors of Chelsea Village. They are 100 per cent behind me, and that includes everyone. I repeat, *everyone.*' Middleton seemed to endorse that statement when he said, 'Nothing will happen at Chelsea unless Ken Bates agrees with it . . . there is no way Ken Bates will cease to be chairman of Chelsea Village plc unless he chooses to do so.'

As he battled to steady the Chelsea ship which had been rocked by this sudden loss of confidence, Bates went on to the London local television news that night to make a bold statement about his company's financial standing. 'The club is well financed, the development is continuing and we have no financial problems,' Bates said, decrying what he described as 'ill-informed, somewhat ghoulish, press speculation'.

Bates said: 'I am aware of the contents of Matthew's will. It is totally supportive of Chelsea and it asks his executors to do all that they may need to do to help us. But, without diminishing Matthew's contribution in any way, I should point out that we are already ahead of schedule in our rebuilding at Chelsea. We have spent over £66 million in completed works and contracts since 1992 and Matthew's valuable contribution is £15 million. That means we have raised over £50 million from other sources, including our own cash generation. That puts it in perspective. We do have other loans, we do have other shareholders and we are continuing to talk to other people who want to be part of the Chelsea story.

'I'm very sorry that Matthew will not be here to see it, but if he is looking down from above he will have the satisfaction of seeing it completed.

'There has been speculation over the last few days over the chairmanship of Chelsea Village plc, but under the articles of association of the company, it is for the directors to elect the chairman. I have the unanimous support of the rest of the board to complete what I want to do.'

Early the following morning, Bates moved again, issuing a stock market announcement asking for traders to ignore the comments of financier Paul Miller (a business acquaintance of Harding's) – whom Bates suspected of being the source of rumours that City confidence had been undermined by the death of Chelsea's vice-chairman. 'Miller has nothing to do with Chelsea whatsoever,' Bates said. 'He's just an insurance salesman.'

At least a degree of uncertainty was resolved at Harding's funeral the following day, when Bates's claims about his vice-chairman's will were confirmed. In an announcement by an official from the Benfield insurance company, it was revealed that Harding had left a fortune of £202 million – over £30 million more than had been estimated – in trust for 'numerous beneficiaries'. These included his wife and children and his girlfriend and her children, as well as the business which Harding had strived so hard to develop, and, of course, Chelsea. 'Matthew requested that his wife and her children and girlfriend and her children are properly provided for and will continue to live at their respective homes,' the spokesman told reporters waiting in the rain outside the church where the funeral service was held. 'Matthew Harding has expressed his clear wishes to the trustees that they support, for as long as it is deemed appropriate, both The Benfield Group and Chelsea.'

Amid all this, the players at Chelsea Football Club had to somehow try to get themselves back to some form of normality. The weekend ahead presented them with possibly the most severe challenge in the Premiership: a contest against the defending champions, Manchester United, the outstanding English team of the 1990s, in front of 55,000 fans at their Old Trafford ground. Somehow, the inspiration of the previous week had been retained, perhaps even extended, because Chelsea that day produced an even better battling display, and what their coach himself described as 'the best game we've played this year'.

What was so satisfying for Gullit was that, as Chelsea won 2–1 at Old Trafford (the United goal being nothing more than a late consolation effort, achieved with a flukey deflection), the goals were provided not only by one of his big-name signings, but also by one of Chelsea's own, outstanding home-grown players. As Michael Duberry himself said after the game in which he had risen above the United defence at a corner and sent Wise's deeply crossed ball into the net with a piledriver of a header, 'Doing something that silences 55,000 people can't be bad.'

Some of them needed silencing, too, as elements among the Old Trafford crowd at one point resorted to some sick taunting of the few thousand Chelsea supporters among the crowd by chanting the *Dambusters* theme and making helicopter gestures. United fans have had to endure similar taunts for 40 years, ever since the Munich air disaster, so they, more than most, ought to know better. But the atmosphere at Old Trafford is, in any case, somewhat strained and strange these days. At one point during the season, United's manager had had to put an appeal in one of their home programmes for the fans to make some noise and create some atmosphere to lift their team, an extraordinary and unprecedented step. Meanwhile, official appeals for supporters to remain in their seats had somehow dampened down the usual fervour encountered at Old Trafford, and throughout the Chelsea game, the visiting fans – probably less than one-tenth of the overall crowd – were heard singing *Carefree* and *There's only one Matthew Harding*, above any feeble chanting of the home supporters. The last half-hour even gave rise to a new song – to the tune of *That's Amore*: 'When the ball/hits the back/of the Old Trafford net/That's Vialli!'

The silence of the home support at the stadium of dreams was blamed by one stalwart on the creeping gentrification of the United faithful, and the manner in which newcomers, attracted to the club by the successes of recent times, were less passionate in their support. In an angry open letter published in one local Manchester paper after the Chelsea game, someone calling herself 'Red Lady' wrote to United's fairweather fans: 'Go away. We don't want you. You are killing off what was once a fantastic atmosphere at Old Trafford. Going to a football match is not like the theatre you know, you have to *give* as well as receive. Giving is singing and shouting your heart out for the team . . . I was at Man U for the Chelsea game on Saturday. No one was really getting behind the team. The Stretford End was like a grave. Years ago the roar was deafening whether we were winning or losing.

'If you are not a person who is prepared to go to a ground and live and breathe every kick of the ball and shout on your team, then stay away and your tickets can be used for a true fan who is not a glory hunter and who gets behind the team to help lift them out of this bad time. Stay at home and watch it on your Sky TV with your posh friends instead.

'A conversation I overheard on Saturday, a London woman on her mobile after the game: "I don't come up here to see them lose you know. It's disgusting!" Well sorry . . . Please, unless you are truly a football fan, stay away from Old Trafford. And all you true Man United fans: please, sing your hearts out at Old Trafford in future. Fifty thousand Man U fans and a few thousand Chelsea fans and all you could hear was the Chelsea chant all the way through. Where were the Stretford Enders on Saturday? Don't let the theatre of dreams die on its feet.'

In fairness to the Stretford Enders, they were silenced by an outstanding display from Chelsea, though that was hardly any consolation to the glum Alex Ferguson, on a weekend which was supposed to be the start of celebrations marking his tenth anniversary in charge at United. His team's fans were a similarly hang-dog lot, milling around outside the megastore after the game, wondering if anything would ever see their side regain the dominance that had so fleetingly been theirs so completely. Defeat earlier in the week in the Champions' League – ending a 40-year unbeaten record in European competition at Old Trafford – had merely compounded some dreadful league form, in which the champions had conceded 11 goals in their previous two games, defeats at Southampton and Newcastle.

Only a lack of quality crosses prevented greater domination of this game by Chelsea, as the midfield of Wise, Di Matteo and Burley was creating space for themselves, slowing the pace of the game and then accelerating almost at will. Gullit, still nursing a knee injury, had brought the young Scot into the side in place of himself. Although on the bench, the player-coach clearly regarded himself only as emergency cover, because never once did he engage in the squad's communal stretching. But then, the way his midfield trio dominated, Gullit must have felt he could provide nothing more. 'I'm happy to be on the bench,' Gullit said, relishing the vicarious pleasures of management, 'because that shows the side is playing well. I'm enjoying management much more than I thought. Life is an adventure, and you have to see what brings you joy. This job does. I have surprised myself. To see my players' faces after they score a goal is fantastic.'

Gullit's counterpart at United, Ferguson, was much gloomier. Missing Giggs, United were unable to play the sort of counter-attacking game, at pace, which has been so successful for them. Even at this relatively early stage of the season, it had become clear that United's two much-heralded foreign signings, Poborsky and Cryuff , were nowhere near as successful acquisitions as Chelsea's veterans of Euro '96. This saw them all the more reliant on established players such as Giggs and Cantona, but with one injured and the other in woeful form, the Big Red Machine could not get out of first gear.

After Duberry's goal, Chelsea really did dominate the game. On several occasions, when coming forward, there was a straight line of five Chelsea players across the width of the pitch, overwhelming the outnumbered United midfield. Burley had a magnificent game, energetic, forever making well-timed runs which kept catching out the United defenders. Try as he might, Keane was over-run and could not galvanise his side, and Cantona was no help: one air shot when unmarked in the Chelsea penalty area provided a particularly embarrassing moment in an otherwise unremarkable performance for the Frenchman.

Long balls and crosses from deep by United failed to unlock the Chelsea defence, as the back three either set off the offside trap, or Duberry rose above everyone else to head the ball away from danger. It was from out of defence that the second, decisive goal was produced, Leboeuf intercepting a United pass and, almost in one movement, sending the ball 50 yards upfield into the path of the accelerating Vialli. In the clear, one-on-one with Schmeichel, the best keeper playing in the Premiership, the Italian shimmied one way, then the other, and hit the ball through the stranded goalkeeper's legs. His fifth goal of the season, one sensed it was the one Vialli enjoyed scoring the most.

David May's header, deflecting a long shot past Kevin Hitchcock, made the final ten minutes anxious ones for Chelsea, but they survived for a famous win. Three years before, when they had last won a league game at Old Trafford, it might have been fair to say that Chelsea rode their luck. Not this time: if anything, United were flattered by the final scoreline, as they went down to their first home league defeat in nearly two years. Chelsea's was a performance of organised class, determination and flair. As John Motson said in the BBC television commentary, 'Playing like this, you can't rule Chelsea out as title contenders'.

Dennis Wise explained that Chelsea's game plan had been to deny Cantona any chance to shine. 'People know the way to stop United is to stop Eric,' Wise said. 'He goes through stages in a game when he can be unbelievable, but we didn't allow him time on the ball and pushed him deeper.'

Ferguson could not quite bring himself to praise Chelsea's tactics, but he did give a grudging acknowledgement that his side had been undone. 'There are a lot of teams changing things now,' Ferguson said. 'It's not your 4-4-2, status quo, humdrum football. You're getting a lot of imagination at the moment.

'Their two front players coming short was a major problem for us. It meant their midfield could run in hope in the acres of space behind us. I thought that was the deciding factor in the game.'

Of course, one of those front two Chelsea players was a player whom Ferguson himself had sold, thinking his best days were behind him; Mark Hughes. But back on his old stomping ground, Hughes was in rampant form, using his strength and power to make him like a rock when in possession – completely immovable. Only a tendency, shared with Vialli, to over-elaborate outside the United area possibly denied his new side more goals.

The United match marked the return to top form of Michael Duberry, effectively cementing his place in the new defensive formation alongside Leboeuf and Clarke. A youth team product, Duberry had made his senior debut for Chelsea 18 months earlier, and had soon become a regular in the first team – just after his 20th birthday – when a string of injuries had forced Glenn Hoddle to throw him in at the deep end along with David Lee and Andy Myers. Extraordinarily, the combination worked, and worked well, and only the acquisition of Leboeuf, an injury to Duberry during the summer, and Lee's broken leg, had ended that trio's partnership.

Duberry has all the natural attributes to be a great footballer. He is tall, strong and very quick, so quick, in fact, that on the training pitch he has been known to outsprint fitness trainer Ade Mafe over 50 or 60 yards. While Mafe may have retired from competitive athletics, you do not make the final at the Olympic Games if you are a slouch. Added to Duberry's natural attributes, though, was an ever-growing confidence, an ability to control the ball, pass it and direct it where he wills, all the product of intensive tuition and encouragement first from Hoddle and then from Gullit. Duberry also has intelligence, wit and imagination. Ask him what the difference is between Hoddle and Gullit, and he smiles that beamer of a smile again, contains a laugh, and lifts an eyebrow as he asks, 'You mean you don't know?' Then, with the timing of a Ronnie Barker or John Cleese, he delivers the knock-out blow: 'Ruud's the one with dreads.'

It had taken Duberry a while after the close season to get himself back to full fitness, but once that was achieved, he became an automatic choice for the England under-21 squad that was assembled for a game in Georgia. After seeing his mature performance against the champions, some pundits even called for the youngster to be instantly promoted to the full England side for their World Cup qualifying match. 'As far as I'm concerned, I'm still some way off the full squad,' Doobs said, dismissing such suggestions with a broad smile that recognised that, surely some time soon, his time would come. For a lad who just a year before was on loan at lowly Bournemouth, he was prepared not to rush his progression, and to make a suitable impression on the England under-21 coach, Peter Taylor. 'At the moment all I'm thinking about is trying to impress Peter, because I know that if I do well, then the reports will get back to the gaffer. If it happens in a couple of years, then great, but I'm just pleased to be here.'

Playing alongside Duberry in the *espoirs* defence was Phil Neville, at 19 already with one full cap to his name and the experience of having been in England's Euro '96 squad. 'When you see what he's done,' Duberry said, 'it makes you tell yourself, "I can do that". But we've got to do it at this level first. Of course, whenever you represent your country you want to do well, but we don't get too nervous, don't put too much pressure on ourselves. After all, when you're in the squad you know that you're one of the best young players in the country, and that you've got to do yourself justice.'

With the man in charge of the full England squad being the same person who gave him his first chance at Chelsea, Duberry also seemed to be blessed with the sort of serendipity that sees him in the right place at the right time in his career as well as on the pitch. He also claims to have been lucky that the changeover in club coaches had worked out so well. 'It must have been one of the smoothest handovers ever. Almost nothing changed. I was a bit worried about a new manager, but all that has altered really are a few small things that outsiders probably wouldn't notice anyway.

'It's part of a manager's job to bring in new players. I would say that the new arrivals have had a positive effect already because, apart from being good players themselves, they have made everyone else step up their standards. The attitude of domestic players to foreign signings has to be: "Fair enough, you might be Italian and you might be good, but you aren't going to walk into the side here".

'In terms of technique, I think the continental players probably are superior to us. They spend longer working on it, and it's worthwhile because in Europe you are allowed that bit more time on the ball. Here, you aren't, and foreign players need a little time to adapt to the sheer pace of our game. I like our style of football, because I'm big and it suits me. But I think I can learn, too.'

When Gullit is conducting the masterclass, the opportunities to learn are legion, and Duberry was already enjoying being a pupil. 'Ruud wants us to behave responsibly, represent Chelsea professionally and to enjoy playing our football. I particularly like the last bit: ever since I did my loan spell at Bournemouth under Mel Machin I have been impressed by anyone who tells his players to go out and enjoy themselves. It might sound an easy thing to say, but it's more difficult for a manager to really mean it when he has results and all the rest to worry about. If you can transmit that sort of enthusiasm to your players, though, they will respond.'

Not, however, that Gullit is all sweetness and light, the joking TV pundit who impressed the blokes with his football analysis and wowed the women with his charm during Euro '96. 'When he needs to get his point across, Ruud changes,' notes Duberry. 'He has a different manner and a different tone of voice. He's the boss, you don't question his authority. That is the real him you see on television, and we see a lot of that guy, too. But when he needs to, Ruud changes.

'What Glenn and Ruud have made us do is think like footballers, even when we're away from the ground. It all boils down to remembering you are representing the club and looking after yourself. We do go out and let our hair down, but we don't get drunk, don't get silly. Now we hardly know any other way to behave.

'It's like the diet. I have a weakness for doner kebabs, and I have one from time to time. There's nothing wrong with that, or the occasional burger. But pre-match, I eat chicken, rice, pasta. I've been doing it for so long now, I probably would choose it anyway. Knowing what's good for me influences my choice. I'm a footballer, I can't eat like a slob every day.'

The new professionalism has its rewards, such as a four-year extension to his contract for Duberry, aimed at keeping him as a Chelsea player at least into the next century, or to attract the sort of transfer offer which could make the young man possibly the most expensive defender in English football. The new contract for Duberry was negotiated and signed a year before his existing deal expired – a sure sign that Duberry is viewed as a very valuable commodity at the Bridge. The value to Duberry of the deal – a total of more than £1.5 million, or £6,000 a week wages – also showed the player's perceived worth to the club, and was enough to put Duberry out of reach to predatory managers from other clubs, including Manchester United's Ferguson, whose admiration for the youngster pre-dated his latest Old Trafford performance.

Duberry was more than happy with his lot at Chelsea. 'This is going to be one of the top clubs in the country and when you are offered the chance to stay here, you're going to want to sign it,' Duberry said. It was a view which Duberry was about to discover was shared by another player, already established as one of the world's great internationals.

But first, there was to be another, final twist in the tale over the backroom struggle for control of the parent company that runs the football club. As Duberry and the others in Chelsea's squad were scattered around Europe for their midweek international duties, Stamford Bridge was the scene of another boardroom battle, resulting in Peter Middleton walking out of Stamford Bridge after a meeting of directors which he had summoned.

In the two weeks since Matthew Harding's death, and despite Ken Bates's best efforts, the stockmarket had remained uneasy about Chelsea, uncertain whether Harding's trustees would try to sell off his 28 per cent stake. Various names had been bandied about as possible new, big-money investors – from George Soros to Mark McCormack to Mohammed Al Fayed – but nothing could allay the market's concerns. The share price continued to drift downwards, all the time eroding the value of people's holdings in the club, all the time diminishing Bates's ability to raise other capital to pay for his development plans. Middleton's resignation from the board would only make matters worse.

Middleton had called the meeting in order to present a memorandum which put the view that the only way Chelsea Village could continue to raise the funds for development was to have an influential executive figure on the board who was clearly seen as independent of the chairman, Ken Bates. Middleton told the meeting that he did not necessarily have to be that chief executive figure, but he threatened to resign if he was not considered to be the company's big hitter. Middleton then requested further information about the company, its accounts and its mystery shareholders, at which point Bates was said to have 'gone ballistic', accusing Middleton of waging a clandestine campaign over the two weeks since Harding's death in an attempt to usurp the chairmanship.

When Bates refused Middleton's demands, the City banker gathered up his paperwork from the table and left the offices, leaving Bates to make the formal announcement of the resignation the following morning. Middleton's board meeting had taken less than a quarter of an hour, but it was enough to wipe millions off the valuation of Chelsea, as shares in the trading company fell by another ten per cent, leaving them at 96p each. That was still nearly double the value of the shares when they were initially issued (at 55p each) that March, but once on the slide, could anything be done to shore up the valuation of the stock?

One thing was certain – Ken Bates would do what had to be done to make sure his own investment in Chelsea Village was safeguarded. The ageing bruiser who had already seen off the Mears family and Lord Chelsea, who had fought off the grasping clutches of property developer John Duggan, and who had managed to outlive Matthew Harding, had now seen off another challenger to his control of the Bridge. Nothing, it seemed, would shift him, and now Bates was about to find the £4.5 million finance for a player deal which would turn Chelsea into the side *everyone* wanted to watch and, into the bargain, make his own position even more secure.

Chapter 12

The match was in full flow, but out on the pitch, the player could not concentrate on the game. He could not get the image out of his mind. He had seen him, there, in the directors' box, well wrapped up in a warm winter coat, up there, watching. Watching *him*. There could be only one reason why Mario Stanic, the Croatian international, had been invited to watch Parma's game against Internazionale that day, Gianfranco Zola reasoned, and that was to see what it would be like when he took over his own place in the side. It was then that Zola determined that he needed to move on.

As an established, experienced Italian international with 26 caps, a winners' medal from the *Scudetto* with Napoli and a UEFA Cup-winners' medal with Parma, Zola might have expected better treatment from his club. But he and Carlo Ancelotti, Parma's new coach, obviously differed in their view of the role Zola could play for the side. 'The Parma team was not built to choose between three players for two places,' Zola reasoned when he found himself the odd-one-out. 'If, at the beginning of the season, they had told me that I would have to change roles, I would have discussed it and probably we would have found agreement.' That there was no agreement between the two men was clear when, after being substituted during one *Serie A* game, Zola stormed off the pitch, ripping off his shirt and throwing it at the coach in disgust.

Zola felt that his place in attack had been usurped by the close season signings of Enrico Chiesa and Hernan Crespo. The short Sardinian with a face which would not look out of place in a pre-Raphaelite painting felt that the insult to add to his personal injury was when Ancelotti got him to play deep on the right-hand side of midfield in the game against Inter, while having his replacement, Stanic, looking down from the stands.

With Parma out of the Italian Cup and already knocked out of Europe, and the Bosman Ruling making Zola's potential transfer value to his club depreciate by the day, a deal was hurriedly arranged. Chelsea, the club which had declined to pay £10 million for Zola barely 12 months earlier, now jumped at the chance to sign the player for £4.5 million.

The deal was announced on Italian television on the Friday afternoon, before the two clubs had formally agreed terms. It had not taken so long for Zola to decide to take the Chelsea offer. He was introduced to the British public the following Monday at an impressive press announcement held at Stamford Bridge.

There had been a time when new signings would be photographed by a snapper who was helping out the local rag ('I do a good line in wedding pictures, John. Good price. Bar mitzvahs, too.'), the shot usually showing the player with a pen in a hand that was being guided by his new manager, after which one or two reporters would go through the routine of hearing the player recite his way through a series of identi-kit platitudes of mind-numbing tedium – 'Yeah, I've always wanted to play in Colchester/Barnsley/Port Vale.' 'I wouldn't have joined if I didn't think we could win something this season.' 'I've been really impressed with what I've seen of the set-up at the club.' And so on, 100 times over. Only occasionally would something genuinely interesting be revealed, or would a brick be dropped. When Neil Shipperley, the former Chelsea striker, was signed from Southampton by Crystal Palace, he was undone when he remarked, 'I've always admired the Seagulls,' probably because, down on the pitch, the Palace fans' chants of 'Eagles' could easily be misheard. The remark did not make Shipperley's first few games for his new club any easier, though.

Zola's press conference, by contrast, was a carefully orchestrated media event, and showed just how far English football – specifically Premiership football – had moved on from the old days, as the player emerged in Drake's to be confronted by a posse of TV news crews, a table bristling with microphones, and a press contingent more cosmopolitan than the United Nations Security Council. When asked why he had chosen Chelsea, Zola, in understandable if slightly hesitant English, did not reply that it was because they had offered him wages of nearly £25,000 per week, or that the tax rules in Britain are more favourable than in Italy, or that he could stash his savings in a Channel Islands tax haven while playing at the Bridge. It was, he said, 'Because Chelsea believes in me.'

Zola's transfer illustrated exactly the sort of expensive international dealing that has become so commonplace in the English Premier League. To sign Zola, over a contractual period which runs to June 2000, was to cost Chelsea about the same again in wages as they had paid for him in transfer fees. At the end of the contract, the player would be a free agent, able to take up employment with any other club outside

England (and possibly, by then, any club in England, too), leaving Chelsea unable to recoup any of their initial £4.5 million purchase price. For Ruud Gullit, Zola's new coach, it was a price worth paying. 'Matthew Harding had a dream,' Gullit said, 'and Zola will help us achieve it.

'Zola has vision, technique and is a game-winner. When he has the ball he can create and will give us that little bit extra that we need. For us, this is a golden opportunity. At Parma this season he has been a victim of a change in the playing style. If Parma didn't want to use his quality, I knew I'd like to have it. You don't get an opportunity like this every day and when I heard he might be available I knew that I wanted him to come to Chelsea.'

Not everyone was so convinced of the merits of bringing in highly paid foreigners. Dave Webb, one of Gullit's predecessors as Chelsea manager, and a Stamford Bridge hero of the 1970s who had by now moved on to manage Brentford, felt that the whole strategy was too risk laden. 'You're telling me the development of the Chelsea team is better because they've gone and got this fella Zola? I can tell you,' Webb warned, 'that it will blow right up in their faces, because in a minute you'll have them foreign players sitting there getting their £20,000 or £30,000 a week, and a guy there getting £3,000 per week – which is still good money. It'll all go boss-eyed.'

Howard Wilkinson, the former Leeds boss who was soon to be appointed Technical Director of the FA, was also heard to comment that he would not want to be a youth trainee at Chelsea. Gullit just laughed at this. 'We had a foreign legion before I arrived,' he said, 'There were Scots, Welsh and Irish.'

Gullit, though, denied that he did not want to sign British players. 'Everything over here has gone out of proportion, and class foreign players cost less than class English ones. We would love to have some English players, but when you have to pay £15 million for players like Alan Shearer, that takes them out of the reach of even most of the top clubs. But it's not for me to say it's ridiculous.'

Gullit left that to Colin Hutchinson. Chelsea's managing director offered an explanation which suggested that there was a problem with domestic transfer deals worth barely one-hundredth of Shearer's fee. The vast sums of cash being paid by Sky TV to clubs in the Premier League had created a sellers' market for domestic transfers, as the small clubs endeavoured to maximise the income from the few assets that they had – principally young talent. Hutchinson explained how Chelsea had approached one lower league club, interested in signing one of their players, an untried, unproven youth who had only been a first-team professional for half a season. A flat fee of £500,000 was demanded. 'There's no £100,000 down and staggered payments according to progress these days,' said Hutchinson. Despite having just agreed a £4.5 million transfer for Zola, Hutchinson also felt able to describe some of the demands from English clubs for lesser players as 'crazy money'.

After all, Chelsea had learned an expensive lesson from their experience with Paul Furlong, a promising enough young striker in the first division with Watford, but of unproved ability at the very highest level. Only after Chelsea had signed him was it shown that the player was clearly not good enough when thrust into the Premiership. Yet to sign him, Chelsea had had to spend more than £2 million, what was then a club record. It was an expensive gamble. 'Until the Bosman ruling applies domestically, it is clear that the best bargains are to be found abroad,' Hutchinson said.

Later in the season, Graham Rix, Gullit's assistant coach, would be able to point to five youngsters to whom Chelsea had given their first-team debuts that year, despite the presence of Zola, Leboeuf, di Matteo and Vialli. Delving into an inside pocket, Rix produced a photograph of Paul Hughes and Michael Duberry with Zola. 'That is ideally the way you want things – Zola being the icing on the cake. We are investing a lot of time and money in our youth programme.

'Manchester United appear to have it right. They have their foreign players – Cantona, Schmeichel, and others – but look at the excellent English ones as well like the Neville brothers, Scholes, Beckham and Butt. Ryan Giggs is home-grown as well. It is the sort of situation we want here at Chelsea for the long-term future of the club.'

The concept of bringing in a highly paid foreign mercenary to pass on valuable lessons to emerging home-grown talent was also, after all, something that had helped Zola in his own career. For Zola had learned a great deal himself from working with Diego Maradona, the man from whom he inherited the Number 10 shirt at Napoli. Zola was an untried, unknown quantity when he arrived at Stadio San Paolo in Naples in 1989. Maradona was the most famous footballer in the world. 'But he was always fantastic to me. I will never forget the help he gave me,' Zola said. 'He was the best player in the world and I learned so much just from watching him and training with him.

'He would stay behind after training every day for 20 minutes, showing me how to curl the ball at free-kicks. The first time I replaced him in the team, we were playing Ascoli and I was having a nightmare. Everything was going wrong for me. I could hardly kick a ball straight. Then, right at the end of the match, we got a free-kick and I pleaded with my team-mates to let me take it.

'After I hit it, I thought it was going to hit the corner flag. Then, suddenly, the ball curled and went in. I just turned around and there were 60,000 people going mad.'

After he arrived at Chelsea, just as he had been taught by Maradona, Zola would stay behind after training at Harlington, practising his free-kicks. Three or four lifesized plastic cut-out figures would be placed ten yards in front of him, as he lined up the ball around 20 yards from goal, and the little man, swaddled in several tracksuit tops to keep out the bitter cold that was blowing across the open tract of land near the airport, would hit ball after ball, sometimes for as much as an hour, curling and swerving his shots around the artificial wall. Some missed, some hit the woodwork, but only after Zola had hit a satisfactory number into the back of the net would he pack up the balls into a mesh bag and trot off the muddy pitch to the changing rooms, where he could warm his frozen body in a hot shower.

The fruit of such practice took some time before it was witnessed in a match, but in his fourth game for Chelsea, Zola got his first goal. It came from a free-kick, taken 20 yards outside the Everton goal, the sort of outrageous skill which bamboozled Neville Southall and had another entire stadium on its feet, applauding, amazed at the apparent magic which the little Italian has managed to conjure up. It was the sort of natural skill that takes hours of practice to hone to perfection.

'He makes me look ordinary,' Luca Vialli said of his erstwhile Italian international team mate. 'Of all the Italian players to come here,' Vialli had predicted generously, 'I have the feeling he will be the best.'

For Vialli, Zola's arrival at Chelsea offered more than just another team-mate who spoke the same language. Vialli also relished the possibility of linking up with a player who could perhaps provide him with the sort of service that would help him improve his own strike-rate. Zola agreed: 'I think we can play well together and we won't have any problems. I believe I can help him to score goals and that with him I can help the team to reach our aims. If Chelsea want to win the league then I want to be part of that. I certainly think that this team will be in Europe next season and perhaps even better than that.'

Zola's arrival did prompt speculation, though, that other Chelsea players would have to make way for the new superstar signing. Mark Hughes was prominently linked with a move to Bolton, back to the north-west of England where his family was still living, while the futures of John Spencer, Gavin Peacock and Mark Stein were all thrown into doubt. After all, not all of them could play in the first team.

Publicly, Gullit played the peacemaker. 'Nobody has to go,' he said. 'If you look at our last few games, Mark Hughes has been outstanding, a great help to the team. What's been better for him is that he's been playing with better players and finding that fun and we've now got even more better players with Gianfranco here.'

The Everton game in which Zola and Vialli both scored was Chelsea's third draw in four games since Zola had joined them, the other result being a defeat against Leeds at Elland Road. This sequence of results – three points out of a possible 12 – had seen Chelsea drift from fifth place in the Premiership to seventh by the beginning of December, gradually losing contact with the league leaders and, possibly, losing out on any chance of European football the following season. With the worst of the English winter – and English football's winter pitches – still to come, and despite an excellent display of skill by the little Italian on his home debut against Newcastle, people were already beginning to ask questions about whether signing Zola might have been a mistake, whether the pace of the Premiership was too quick for him, and whether, at just five-feet five inches tall, he could cope with the English game's physically demanding nature. Being the best Number 25 that had ever played for Chelsea was one thing, but it was a long way short of where expectations had been raised to when Zola had arrived.

Gullit, though, was obliged to be patient with Zola, to give him time to get used to the set-up at his new club. Meanwhile, and despite his public statements to the contrary, Chelsea's player-coach was conducting something of a mini-clear-out among his fringe players to make way for his new Italian signing. Spencer, unsettled by his inability to get a regular first-team place, was sold for £2.5 million to west London neighbours QPR, and was joined there, initially on a month's loan, by Gavin Peacock. Mark Stein was also put out on loan, to Stoke City.

Spencer had been the club's top scorer the previous season and a member of Scotland's Euro '96 squad. A prolonged spell in Chelsea's reserves, the wee man had reasoned, would jeopardise any chance he might have of playing in the 1998 World Cup. His prospects had not improved with the arrival of Zola, and just ten days after the Italian deal had been announced, Spencer had become an ex-Chelsea player.

Spencer was highly respected by Chelsea fans, who had come to admire his wholehearted determination for their team since he joined from Rangers nearly five years before. His goal against Austria Vienna during Chelsea's European excursion in 1994–95 was a highlight for him and his fans. As the ball ricocheted out of the Chelsea area after an Austrian attack, Spencer was first to react, running 70 yards with the ball, chased by two defenders who had been upfield for the corner, before flicking the ball over the keeper. It earned Chelsea a 1–1 draw and passage into the next round courtesy of the away goals' rule.

In return for such goals, Spencer's career at Chelsea had rewarded him well, and with the proceeds he had bought a large, genuine reproduction mock-Tudor house at Gerrards Cross, a typical footballer's home, with its gym, wrought iron gates and two Rottweilers. Spencer, his wife and two children, were obviously more than comfortable. In any other walk of life, you might expect someone to recognise a good thing when they had it, and carry on with Chelsea, playing out their time in the reserves, cashing the generous pay cheques every month, and using their spare time to reduce their handicap at golf or to establish a business sideline of some sort. Not Spencer. He chose to move to a club at the wrong end of the first division. The comfortable living he had earned when at Chelsea meant that he could afford to pursue his ambitions.

'I was sad to go,' he said, 'but I had to for my career. I know people talk about squads, but when I didn't play I was so unhappy. Moving was nothing to do with the club. I loved it there. I've got lots of memories, I'm just sad I had to go in order to play.'

Spencer and Peacock had been such key figures in Glenn Hoddle's Chelsea side, it was perhaps strange that they should be discarded so speedily by the new player-coach. While there was no overt ill-will from the departing players, quotes from Spencer in one tabloid that Gullit had not spoken to him for eight weeks before he was transferred suggested that, perhaps, all was not total harmony in the Chelsea dressing rooms.

It was a view with which Craig Burley, another Scotland international unable to command a regular place in the Chelsea side under Gullit, apparently concurred. 'I played in the first 12 matches of the season and was told by the management that I was doing a good job,' Burley said in an interview with *The Sun*. 'Since then I have been out in the cold. It appears that home-grown players are having to make way for the foreigners who have come into the club.'

Dennis Wise, too, was apparently unhappy with Gullit's tactical approach to matches – both he and Burley were being given different tasks in different games, never being allowed to settle into one particular task from one match to the next, as the new player-coach experimented with the blending of his squad's talents. The murmurs of disquiet from Wise soon came to an end, though, when at the beginning of December the former England international, just about to celebrate his 30th birthday, signed a four-year contract.

It was not just morale that was being hurt among the Chelsea squad. Jody Morris, the teenaged midfield prodigy, had already lost his place in the side when a dust-up outside a London nightclub saw him admitted to hospital for a broken jaw. It would keep the 17-year-old sidelined for the next two months. Then there was Jakob Kjeldbjerg. The Danish international defender had been ruled out of playing for more than a year through a succession of injuries, a persistent knee problem finally forcing him to give up hopes of resurrecting his career. Kjeldbjerg was just 27, and even being presented with a Rolex, bought after a whip-round by his team-mates, could not make him feel anything but hard done by.

There was a moment in the game at Leeds when Mark Hughes, too, feared for his livelihood. Chelsea players have suffered probably more than their fair share of career-ending injuries, the one which curtailed Paul Elliott's days as a player being the most notorious, since it resulted in a legal case fought in London's High Court, in which the defender sued Dean Saunders for damages over the tackle which had broken his leg. Elliott's case failed.

Whether Mark Hughes would have been any more successful in a legal action against Brian Deane will forever remain a hypothetical question, although on the night after the match, the evidence against Deane was fairly compelling: six stitches detailing the four-inch gash in Hughes's shin, down which the Leeds forward had stamped his studs. Even if such a tackle is not deliberate, by one professional on a fellow professional it would surely qualify as negligent.

'I feared the worst when it happened,' Hughes said. 'He came in high and when that happens you can be in real trouble. I think I got away with it, because if the challenge comes in over the boot you really are risking serious injury. It could have broken my leg.' Hughes had to be carried from the Elland Road pitch on a stretcher, yet according to the referee, Deane's challenge had not even rated a booking. In a game where the referee brandished his yellow card seven times – including, in separate incidents earlier in the match, to both Deane and Hughes – the challenge on the Welshman was clearly the worst in an overtly physical game.

For some, the outcome of Chelsea's defeat at Leeds confirmed the view that the highly paid continental mercenaries could not handle the meat and heat of the English game. George Graham, the Leeds manager, certainly thought that way. Under Graham as manager, his Arsenal sides had developed a reputation for defensive parsimony to the point of miserliness, the price of which was a lack of flair or invention. Now 'oop north' with Leeds, it was as if Graham relished the chance to fulfil every sort of stereotype about him and his team. Against Chelsea, Graham adopted the role of a latterday Corporal Jones from *Dad's Army*, suggesting that, a bunch of southern softies such as Chelsea 'Don't like it up 'em'. 'It was our attitude to impose the pace of the game on Chelsea,' Graham said. 'I just wonder whether they wanted to come up here in all the wind and the rain.'

Part of Graham's tactics was to deny Chelsea time and space, and he assigned Lucas Radebe to a man-marking job on Zola which was effective in diminishing the Italian's effectiveness. In 1994, when Zola had played for Parma in the European Cup-winners' Cup final against Arsenal, Graham had used the same tactic, with Tony Adams marking Zola out of a game which the London side won.

Gullit, for once, expressed outrage and anger at the way in which his side, and Hughes in particular, had failed to be protected from the close attentions of Deane and his team-mates. Hughes, Gullit thought, suffered more than most simply because of his strength and balance kept him on his feet even after the direst of challenges. 'I'm fed up with it,' Gullit said, 'If they kick him, they always seem to get away with it. Sure, Mark is not the sweetest character on the field, but I think he pays a price for it.'

It was a game that had been won and lost in the first ten minutes, yet even Leeds's first goal was achieved only after Ian Rush made a late challenge on Dennis Wise which went unpunished by the referee. From that challenge, Rush passed to Deane, who went on to score, and Rush – who had not scored before for Leeds – added a second soon after. The Chelsea defence of Leboeuf, Duberry and Clarke was a mess, and every time the ball was played behind them, they were rattled. Yet to achieve such an aim, Leeds had resorted to an approach which had Rob Hughes, football correspondent, thundering in the next day's *Times* about the need for the players' union, the Professional Footballers' Association, to take action to prevent reckless and vicious tackling, which can jeopardise the careers of fellow professionals. 'The FA Carling Premiership is in danger of serious regression into malice if the match at Elland Road between Leeds United and Chelsea yesterday is allowed to become any kind of benchmark for appalling foul play and refereeing that is an abdication of the rule book,' wrote Hughes.

Despite Brian Deane's best efforts, Hughes would miss just one game for Chelsea, the home draw against Everton (where in his absence, Gullit played up-front alongside Vialli). Yet he managed to be 'fit' (that is, have the four-inch gash on his shin well padded to minimise the damage should he suffer any similar challenges) to allow him to play the last half-hour in the defeat at Sunderland. Hughes's robustness was already legendary, so perhaps it was not really necessary for him to prove it by turning out for Wales in a World Cup qualifier in Cardiff just 24 hours before the Roker Park game. But he did, injuries and all.

At Roker Park, the side depleted by international call-ups and the suspension of Leboeuf, was clobbered 3–0, dropping to eighth place in the table just before the critical period of Christmas games. Among the absentees that day was Luca Vialli, who had flown back to Italy earlier in the week to get treatment on his injured hamstring. Of course, there is no such thing as a good time to be out of a side, but it would soon become clear that the Italian striker had chosen the worst possible time to vacate his place in the Chelsea team.

Chapter 13

In the shallows of the English Premier League, there lurks a great white shark. Known for his fierce, biting tackles, when this man-eater scents blood in the water, he glides in for the kill, disposing of his prey with a ruthless efficiency. One snap, and they are gone. But when Gianfranco Zola went fishing in Premiership waters against West Ham four days before Christmas, he caught Julian Dicks hook, line and sinker . . .

When commentators complain about the lack of 'characters' in the game these days, often, as well as lamenting the loss of mavericks, they often mention of how the league no longer has the sort of hard men like the Bremners, Harrises or Storeys of the 1970s. In so doing, they conveniently overlook West Ham's Julian Dicks. While hard man icon Norman Hunter was known as 'Bite Yer Legs', Dicks is the sort of tackler who swallows opposing forwards whole. It was said that when he was transferred to Liverpool, Dicks had thought the Number 23 shirt in the dressing room was his because it had 'FOWLER' written across the back.

Dicks had done nothing to soften his image, either, when he had had his head shaved. As he emerged at Stamford Bridge on the Saturday before Christmas, in the gloaming that passes for daylight in the afternoons in late December, with the solid bulk of his body beneath his grey head with its dark, sunken eyes, he had the look of a Hammer movie monster let loose on a football pitch.

For all his fearsome reputation, Dicks is not just a clogger. He is an accomplished player, with an ability to pass the ball accurately and hit long-range free-kicks that fly like ballistic missiles, skills which are lacking in many left-sided defenders who have been preferred to him in the England team. 'I'm not the brainiest person,' Dicks had once said. 'I ain't got no O-levels, nothing. I didn't go back for my results because all I ever wanted to do was play football.' It was something at which he excelled. Defensively, Dicks is at his most impressive, which was why the contest this day between him and Zola would be so instructive. If the little Italian really did not 'fancy it' in English football, if he lacked the necessary 'bottle' to cope with our physical game, then Dicks would surely uncover it.

It was Dicks, after all, who had (literally) walked all over John Spencer's head in a previous encounter between the sides. This time, would he walk all over Zola? Perhaps even the Chelsea management was a little worried about the psychologically damaging effect Dicks might have on their new signing. Hopeful that Dicks's reputation had not travelled as far as Italy, before the game no one warned Zola about the West Ham defender. Perhaps someone should have warned Dicks about Zola.

For Zola chose this particular confrontation to produce an exhibition of his rapier-like skills which, as if he were a footballing Zorro, saw him carve a metaphorical 'Z' in the middle of Dicks's forehead.

The game was only ten minutes old, and Chelsea were already a goal ahead, when a pass out of defence from within his own side's half sent Zola racing into space on the right. Travelling at pace, Zola immediately took the ball under control. Meantime, Dicks loomed up on the Sardinian to challenge. As he closed in on Zola, you could almost imagine hearing the theme music from *Jaws*. But just as Dicks went to take his first bite, in one, unseen movement, Zola turned inside Dicks. As the West Ham player turned back, Zola jinked outside him, and gained two or three yards, and now he headed for goal.

Still Dicks was not completely beaten, and he scurried back to the edge of his area, where he caught up with Zola. Again, the Chelsea forward beat his man, this time putting the ball between the defender's legs – 'nutmegging' him. There was something symbolic about this. This was no ordinary defender upon whom Zola had chosen to conduct this almost ritualistic humiliation, to whip out the player's innards with all the unblinking, instinctive efficiency of a Billingsgate fish gutter. This was Julian Dicks – nutmegged in front of 28,000 people. It must have been the utmost gesture of contempt possible to conjure up. To top and tail it all, Zola then sent a shot into the left-hand corner of the West Ham goal, where Ludo Miklosko was apparently as dumb-struck by the display as the spectators in the stands.

This game against West Ham would prove to be a defining one in the shape and outcome of Chelsea's season, of Zola's season, and of Mark Hughes's season. Indeed, in this moment of confrontation against Dicks, barely ten seconds of an entire game, Gianfranco Zola turned around his Chelsea career, winning the adoration of the Stamford Bridge crowd and probably, in his own mind, dispelling any apprehensions about his future in England.

Fear is supposed to be all in the mind, an awareness of danger supposedly as dangerous as danger itself. Thus Zola really was blissfully ignorant of Dicks before their encounter. It was not until after the game that the Italian was appraised of his opponent's chew-'em-up-and-spit-'em-out reputation. 'I wished they'd told me that before,' he said, 'I would have played on the other side of the pitch.'

If he had had any residual doubts or fears about English football, then this match was when he conquered them. Not only had Zola scored a spectacular goal, he had also scored a psychological victory over the most feared defender in the Premiership.

'Today I played a good game,' Zola said. 'I think I could score more.' On at least a couple of other occasions he swept through West Ham United's incoherent defence and narrowly missed. In fact, Dicks otherwise played a good game, twice saving his team in extremis and once almost scoring with a header. But West Ham could never recover from being two goals down within ten minutes. Their team, too, was as cosmopolitan as Chelsea's, but they performed as if they had been introduced to one another in the airport arrivals lounge that morning, and they spent the last 80 minutes of the game strolling around the pitch as if shellshocked. Chelsea had bombarded them on two fronts, Zola's light cavalry charging in after Mark Hughes had fired the big guns.

With Vialli away in Italy getting treatment on the hamstring injury he suffered when playing against Everton, the Chelsea line-up against West Ham saw Zola paired with Hughes up front for the first time. Someone once suggested that the single most important thing to possess in order to be a successful football manager is luck, and when he brought together Hughes and Zola as a strike partnership, Gullit proved he had luck by the bucket-load.

There was something fateful about the whole thing: the immediate understanding between the two; the nature of their play, one providing for the other. The partnership was devastating. 'I think both strikers were world class today,' Gullit said. 'I think they made it very difficult for the opposition.' Hughes, holding the ball up to lay off for Zola or the on-charging Chelsea midfielders, seemed to known where his team-mate would be with such unerring accuracy that the possibility of ESP being at work could not be ruled out. Where Hughes and Vialli had at times seemed too similar in their style of play, sometimes duplicating their efforts, the combination of Hughes and Zola seemed to complement one another perfectly, like claret and stilton.

Hughes had his best game for ages. Until this game, he had not scored a goal at Stamford Bridge all season. Here, he scored twice, after six and 36 minutes, and could, like Zola, have had more. From Zola's subtle flick, Hughes pivoted and hit a low shot that crept in between Miklosko and the left-hand post. His second was headed in from a long cross from the right by Petrescu; but where was Rieper, where was Bilic? The tall centre-halves were surely obliged to head such balls away. Bilic, a widely respected and admired Croatian centre-half, showed he had learnt enough East End English when he summed up his side's game: 'I would say I was crap, the defence was crap and we played crap.'

In Hughes, Zola had discovered his foil, and his protector. 'If I am having a problem in a match, I say, "Hey, Marco, come here," and Marco looks after me.'

In many respects, Hughes had as much to prove at Chelsea as his most recent strike partner. Hughes arrived at Chelsea with a reputation which, in many respects, was as awe-inspiring as Gullit's, who had joined the club on the same day. Hughes has been described as 'the centre forward with the on-pitch disposition of something let loose on the streets of Pamplona'. Rugged, hard-working, impossible to shackle or stop, Hughes possessed all the skills of an old-fashioned-style British forward, but with an extra touch of flair and skill. In a 14-year professional career, he had enjoyed seasons with Manchester United when he had bagged two dozen goals, although later in his career he had fulfilled more of a role as a provider and creator than a simple goal-hanger.

Such attributes, though, had been virtually unseen at Stamford Bridge in the season and a half that Hughes had been a player there. Expectations had been high – Hughes, after all, was attributed with 'winning' the FA Cup from Chelsea in 1994, not so much because of his goal in the final, but more by virtue of his late strike against Oldham in the semi-final. Without that, it was reasoned, Chelsea would have beaten the Latics in the final.

Once at Chelsea, though, Hughes seemed to be missing something. Clearly, the Welshman did not enjoy playing alongside Paul Furlong; John Spencer's role playing 'in the hole' had too often seen Hughes left isolated, a lone striker; joined by Luca Vialli, the two men had found themselves too often racing for the same pass, occupying the same space, their striker's instincts too similar. Among the Chelsea faithful, Hughes became known by a bizarre acronym – HTBUW: Held The Ball Up Well. Too often at the end of games, that was all that could be said of Hughes – he had Held The Ball Up Well, but nothing else could be remembered. Not his fault, perhaps, he could not help it if the rest of the team failed to support him. Still, it was a long way short of what might have been hoped for . . .

At 33, with his wife, Jackie, and children living in a purpose-built house in Cheshire, it was not surprising that with the arrival of Vialli and then Zola, rumours began circulating that Hughes might be 'unsettled' at Chelsea, that he might be looking for a move. Certainly, Bolton's manager Colin Todd had made enquiries about Hughes's availability and there had also been a suggestion that Blackburn, sans Shearer, had looked to pay £2 million to Chelsea to get the player to fill the void. But the player himself would always maintain that he had never sought a transfer.

Hughes had been born in Ruabon, a small town in Denbighshire, north Wales. This is a football-playing part of Wales, where the landscape in the 1960s, when Hughes was growing up, was dominated by slagheaps, the man-made mounds of black ash and residue from the coal pits. Somehow, these pointed mini-mountains could be seen from every vantage point in the town, whether looking skywards or down at a reflection in a tar-black roadside puddle, serving as a constant reminder of the area's dependency on King Coal. By the time Hughes was into his teens, that reminder was all the sharper, since the demise of the coal industry had seen all but one of the pits close. Jobs here would be scarce from now on. So for a lad who could play a bit, there was no hesitation when, six months before his 15th birthday, he was offered schoolboy terms at Old Trafford.

His mother, Jenny, worried about young Mark when he moved to Manchester. 'He was always so quiet at home that I was worried about him going to live away when he joined Manchester United straight from school. I remember telling him that if he was to make it he had to impose his presence, not just hide away in a corner.' Young Hughes took heed of his mother's advice, at least on the pitch, and made a career of imposing himself. Off the pitch, he has remained quietly spoken, relaxed and friendly, not at all the forbidding, belligerent figure that appears on the pitch. He is a family man who enjoys a couple of pints with his mates or a round of golf. On football, he has developed a mature wisdom about the game with a sense of proportion about its importance in the overall scheme of things. His dedication to his profession, though, has seen him develop a muscular game which has been imposed on opposition defences with whatever team he is playing for – United, Barcelona, Bayern, Chelsea or Wales. Defenders around Europe have been kicked from penalty spot to far post by Hughes down the years, without ever realising it was his mam who taught him to play that way.

'I need to be physically involved in a tough match, otherwise I don't feel any sense of fulfilment,' Hughes says. 'But nobody ever gets seriously hurt against me – they know they are not going to get crippled high across the knees or have an elbow smashed into the face.'

His Welsh team-mate of ten years' standing, Ian Rush, calls him 'the enforcer'. 'If any other player was being given some rough treatment, Sparky would sidle over and sort out the offender. One bone-crunching tackle was nearly always enough. His power and strength made him the enforcer in the team.' At Chelsea, Hughes would become the perfect bodyguard for Zola.

Hughes had determined to leave United when it became clear that his future would see him wearing a benchcoat more often than a red shirt. 'It was a difficult decision, but once Eric Cantona decided to stay after his ban it was clear he would start up front with Andy Cole and I would have been on the outside of things.' Hughes's eyes twinkle when he thinks of what has developed at Old Trafford since his departure. 'Looking back, I would like to think I would have played more games than I imagined I was going to, though I've no regrets.'

At Chelsea, and under Gullit, Hughes had been relieved of some of the more utilitarian responsibilities which he had been expected to shoulder at United. 'I used to chase full-backs and tackle midfielders all game,' he said. 'It looked good, but it took something away from me as an attacking force. I'd be too tired to get into the box. I'd expended my energy in other areas where I wasn't hurting teams. It drained my energy.

'This season, Ruudi said early on he didn't want his strikers to tire themselves out in other areas. He wanted them to be fresh and sharp in the penalty area, and it's made a terrific difference to my game. It's taken me 15 years to realise I've been playing the game the wrong way.' At Chelsea, the Pamplona bull was unleashed to charge at goal.

Perhaps, above all else, what Chelsea had bought when they recruited Hughes was a winner, a player who knows little else besides. Could Hughes teach Chelsea's nearly men the winning habit? 'When a club hasn't won anything for a while it's always breaking the cycle that's the difficult part,' he said. 'At Manchester United there had been a dreadfully long wait to win the league but, once we did it, it made it easier for the teams that followed to be successful.

'Once we overcome that feeling of being there and not quite doing it, once we win that first trophy, I'm sure more will follow. There are similarities with United. When I rejoined them from abroad they were at a similar stage to Chelsea now. Then Mr Ferguson went out and bought some quality players, as we have done here, but it took two or three seasons before the team gelled. I'm very happy now, playing with Zola. If you can't play with a man of his ability and technique, there's something wrong with you.'

That Zola was becoming more at ease with his lot at Chelsea was clear. 'If a club buys Zola, Zola will play the way Zola knows how to play.

My football has certain properties, and I cannot change that.' Having Hughes alongside him allowed Zola to play his own game.

Christmas is a hard time for footballers in England, where there is no midwinter break as there is in other European leagues. While everyone else is sitting down to turkey and all the trimmings, British players find themselves just embarking on a frenzied period of back-to-back matches, providing holiday entertainment for the crowds and very often serious answers to the outcome of the league title for the pundits. So, no sooner had Dennis Wise unwrapped his musical slippers (which played *Que Sera Sera*, which Wise took as a clear indication that Chelsea would be playing at Wembley), than he also had to unpack his boots for a training session under lights on Stamford Bridge's pitch on Christmas evening, while virtually everyone else in the country was settling down to watch *Only Fools and Horses*.

The extra training worked, for in the Boxing Day game at Aston Villa, Chelsea came away with three points, two goals and one cleansheet. Villa Park is never an easy ground at which to get a favourable result, but with the home side in fifth place in the league table, having won their previous four games, including beating third-placed Wimbledon 5–0, this fixture had looked daunting indeed for Chelsea. Yet by the end of the match, it was the visitors who were playing keep-ball. 'The build-up play was magnificent,' babbled a thrilled Eddie Newton that night before setting off back down the motorway for home. 'It's starting to become vintage Chelsea football now, getting the ball, passing it, can't get in on one side, come out the other way, go out the other side, can't get in there, but keep the ball, keep the ball, if necessary we go back to the goalkeeper. Be patient.

'I think the crowd are beginning to appreciate it now because we've been playing it for three or four years. Certainly the players are appreciating it because they don't want to do anything else, just play football.'

It was Zola who got the two goals, in the space of four minutes just after an hour's play, but Gullit gave credit elsewhere. 'He supplied the bullets but the gun was really being fired by our midfield.' Gullit himself had acted as master of ceremonies, conducting events at a leisurely pace from the position of sweeper (Leboeuf was nursing a groin strain). If Gullit, Zola and di Matteo – who was outstanding in this game, having been dropped from the side earlier in the month – really do deplore the English habit of having their footballers play over the Christmas period, they had an odd way of showing their disaffection.

In truth, Villa's Australian goalkeeper, Mark Bosnich, thousands of miles from the warmth of Bondi Beach, had frozen. Two elementary handling errors gave the game to Chelsea, whose control emanated from defensive solidity. 'We have worked very hard over the last two weeks about our defensive job,' Gullit said. 'That doesn't mean we have to be defensive, but I am very happy with the competition for places, and I know Zola, now that he is settled with his own house and he feels appreciated, is very happy because, as a midfield player, it is a great feeling when the defence is solid behind you.'

Two days later, and the visit to London of Sheffield Wednesday surely offered Chelsea the opportunity of further progress in the Premiership. But despite leading from the eighth minute (Zola), extending the lead soon after (Hughes), hitting the woodwork once, having two goals disallowed for offside, and still being in the lead going into the 90th minute, somehow Wednesday contrived to get a late equaliser, just as Forest, Newcastle and Everton had done. The season before, under Hoddle, Chelsea had led in 19 games which they ultimately only drew or even lost. Now, under Gullit, that same bad habit seemed to remain as, even before the turn of the year, they had managed to squander what amounted to eight home points through conceding late equalising goals.

'The way we played, we deserved more,' said Gullit. 'David Pleat had to change things because we were all over them. After he changed, still there was no threat. They got two goals from 30 yards out of nothing.' Clearly, the manager was not happy at the eventual result. But he also felt progress was being made. 'You have to go step by step, and we are only on the second step. If I can make the third step to have more stability in the team, so we can do it week in, week out, then it will be different.

'But we are still building, still creating something. There are a lot of steps! You have to learn, always be better than the last game. It's something you have to do slowly, slowly. Everybody thinks, "Oh, you have all the good players, here you go," but it's not like that, you have to work every week very hard and make them aware that it's all about team spirit.

'I'm not stressed about it, I'm very happy about the job,' Gullit said. 'To people who don't understand why, I already have won everything, I have everything, I am a happy man. I was offered the job, I just took it and I will take it how it comes. I have no stress, no pressure. Ambitions? Yes! But what do I have to lose?'

As had happened at Elland Road (when Zola had been marked so closely by Lucas Radebe that the Leeds defender had had to be persuaded not to share the shower with the Italian after the game), the opposition changed their tactics in order to use tight man-marking as the answer to the threat from Zola. Atherton was assigned to the task for this game, prompting Zola to remark after the game: 'I prefer my wife.'

The Wednesday manager, David Pleat, who had already praised Chelsea's play once before this season, was impressed by his opposition again. 'I enjoy Liverpool because the way they play is patient, passing, working; chess-like, not too direct. Chelsea are becoming like them, a very good team too.'

Also watching the performances of Zola and Roberto di Matteo that day was Cesare Maldini, the new coach of the Italian national side, who, too, was impressed by what he saw. Afterwards, he discussed the form of the Italians with their club manager. 'He is very impressed about the way people here live the game in a different way,' Gullit said. 'He said it was very nice to see this game.'

So after three games over Christmas, seven points, a deal which, had it been offered before the Christmas lights had been turned on in Oxford Street, most people involved with Chelsea would have accepted. All that remained was to kick-off the New Year with a game against the Premiership leaders, Liverpool.

After a Christmas-less Christmas, how do footballers see in the New Year? Often, they will be ensconced together in a hotel, where they can be supervised by the coaching staff, so that they can ensure not too much is drunk, nor does anyone stay up too late on what is, after all, the evening before a big game. Ruud Gullit, though, saw things differently. 'There were people at the club who wanted me to take the players to a hotel on Tuesday night, but I wanted to give them the freedom to stay at home and enjoy New Year's eve. They wanted to have the festivities and I thought I could give them the responsibility of being with their families.' His players responded to his trust.

In certain respects, what the Chelsea team produced against Liverpool was final confirmation that Gullit's strategy, his blending of players, had worked. They had taken that extra step. For this performance was not the cavalier Chelsea of old, where they would throw players forward with abandon, ignoring defensive duties and walk away from the ground afterwards with a shrug that would say, 'We may have lost, but at least we entertained. There were seven goals . . .'

No, this was a completely professional, ruthless performance that was determined to give nothing away. Chelsea outdid Liverpool at what Liverpool had always been best at.

There is a theory among some observers of Premiership football that home advantage is no longer worth as much to teams as in the past. This is based on the premise that, increasingly, teams are being organised to specialise in counter-attacking: football's equivalent of the hit-and-run, a smash-and-grab where the team is able to absorb any amount of pressure, but once possession is won, it can break into attack, and break quickly. Compare, if you will, the relative successes of Manchester United – a side which thrives on the counter – and Newcastle under Keegan, a team built to attack, and attack gloriously, but which never seemed to have learned how to defend. Counter-attacking was a tactic which had well served the great Liverpool sides of the early 1980s, when they used it most effectively when playing in European tournaments, but it had been adapted effectively in domestic competitions by Arsenal under George Graham, and then United.

Such an approach depends on a rock solid defensive unit, on tireless midfielders and on forwards who can break at great pace. For 90 minutes at Stamford Bridge on the first day of 1997, while the temperature might have been below freezing, the watching Chelsea fans glowed warm with delight as their side showed that they, too, could control a game out of its defence.

It takes supreme confidence to concede possession to Liverpool, but this is what the Chelsea midfield was able to do, closing down the opposition players whenever they brought the ball into the Chelsea half, denying them the opportunity to fashion any useful move, and ready, at all times, to pounce on any errors. It was as if the Chelsea midfield cut off the oxygen supply to Liverpool's dangerous attackers, Fowler, Collymore and, later, Berger. Unable to breathe, goalscoring life was choked out of them.

Central to this ploy was Frank Leboeuf, returned to the side after suspension and injury, and back at his very best. His ability to transform defence into attack perhaps influenced Liverpool's approach: they showed restraint, caution, and did not commit wholeheartedly to attack as they might have done. It was as if they knew there was a trap waiting to be sprung, it was just that they were unsure when, or how.

In the 43rd minute, it happened. Mark Hughes harried the young substitute, Dominic Matteo, and he passed to Michael Thomas. Thomas found himself in possession just inside his own half, but with nowhere to go. So he played a pass square across the pitch towards Mark Wright. The only problem was that Thomas had not looked up, for if he had, he would have noticed Roberto di Matteo between him and his team-mate. The Italian midfielder successfully intercepted the ball, and with no covering defence between him and goal, was able to take the ball into close range and sidefoot past David James. The chance was taken with a coolness as icy as the day, and finally fulfilled Gullit's expectations of the player. 'I spoke to him a few weeks ago and told him that I hadn't seen what I'd expected from him in some games. Perhaps it was a reaction from Euro '96 – I'm aware of that sort of thing because I've been there myself – so I gave him a couple of weeks off and he's rewarded himself and me.'

Di Matteo admitted he had taken longer than he had expected to settle into the English game. 'It's not easy if you come from a different country, having to learn a new language, a new mentality,' he said. 'But now I've found some friends in London, who have helped me settle, and my team-mates have helped a lot as well.'

If anything, di Matteo's goal was exactly the sort of strike which Liverpool had exploited so well in their 5–1 drubbing of Chelsea at Anfield earlier in the season. Having taken the lead, Chelsea then played the second half as if they were almost daring Liverpool to take risks and come forward in an attempt to take the game. For a side that had failed to keep a cleansheet at home since August, it was a strategy as daring as all-out attack.

It was a challenge Liverpool evidently felt incapable of accepting – Fowler was carrying an ankle inury, Collymore was ineffectual, and in defence, Liverpool had already lost Ruddock to injury early in the game. Since then, Hughes had proceeded to take Matteo for a guided tour around Stamford Bridge. Hughes might have made it two goals for Chelsea, when Wise hit a 40-yard pass to the Welshman, who found himself without any support and so took the only option left to him, a crashing shot. Had James not got a finger-tip to the ball, sending it up on to the bar, the match would have been sealed there and then. As it was, the second half was 52 minutes (the referee somehow managed to add seven minutes of injury time) of anxious watching: could Chelsea do it? Could they defy Liverpool this way? The answer, eventually, was 'Yes'.

'We keep surprising ourselves with the way we perform,' Hughes said. According to Gullit, Hughes must have been surprising himself. 'I think Mark Hughes is playing one of his best seasons ever,' said Gullit. 'You can see it in his face: he is very happy. He's fit. He's one of the leaders.'

Not that Gullit was satisfied, yet. 'The team is like a rough diamond, we have to work on it.' It was an interesting analogy coming from someone born in Amsterdam, and one which raised a question: what new facets would he cut into the Chelsea team structure going into 1997?

Chapter 14

Stunning. Sensation. Resurrection. Breathless. Scintillating. Memorable. Tumultuous. *The Times* is not noted for sensationalising its coverage of sporting events. If anything, its editorial style strives for understatement. Needless adjectives are frowned upon, subbed out of copy with the computer-aged equivalent of a sharp blue pencil. Yet in its report of Chelsea's second encounter with Liverpool during January, in the fourth round of the FA Cup, even the old Thunderer found it nothing but completely appropriate to include the words 'stunning', 'sensation', 'resurrection', 'breathless', 'scintillating', 'memorable' and 'tumultuous' in its Monday morning match report. In this context, such words demanded to be included in the report if it was to come close to conveying the extraordinary nature of the match, what many considered to be the most remarkable turnaround in cup history.

By the end of the game, the Chelsea fans had put into song their own summary of events. 'Two-nil down/Four-two up/Knocked the Scousers/Out the Cup/La-la la-la, la-la-la, la-la!' they sang, as they danced and jigged and jumped around in the Matthew Harding Stand. For they had first endured, then enjoyed, the ultimate sporting experience. In less than two hours, they had seen their initial high hopes trampled, any flicker of life seemingly stamped on. But then they witnessed the embers of their ever-present hope being gently fanned, then fuelled, catching light and burning bright, the fans' despair and disbelief being transformed into delight and delirium

It had already been an outstanding weekend of cup football, marked out by a set of results which, if they did not all quite qualify as 'giant-killing', had certainly seen some of the bigger clubs left bruised and battered. Non-leaguers Hednesford had led at Middlesbrough before going out 3–2. Woking had managed to hold Coventry to a fourth-round draw and lowly league side Wrexham dumped West Ham out of the competition altogether in their third round replay. Then there were the goals, works of craft that are rarely seen in a lifetime, but which somehow this weekend seemed to fly in from all angles, from all ranges. Probably the two which will remain in people's memories longest were scored by skilful players at opposite ends of their careers: Chris Waddle hit a left-foot curler home from 30 yards for Bradford City as they dismissed Everton, and QPR's Trevor Sinclair scored with an extravagant bicycle kick from the edge of the penalty area.

With Nottingham Forest, despite struggling in the league, knocking Newcastle out of the Cup at St James' Park, the world's oldest cup competition had already begun to look wide open even before Chelsea and Liverpool took to the pitch at Stamford Bridge that Sunday afternoon for a match which the BBC had chosen to televise as the 'tie of the round'. Often, such selections of televised games are doomed to dullness. Rarely have the Beeb's sports executives been so richly rewarded for their choice.

Yet it could have all been so much of a foregone conclusion after barely 25 minutes, when Stan Collymore added a second Liverpool goal to the Fowler effort scored within the first ten minutes. Chelsea's defence had reverted to (disorganised) type, looking haplessly ill-equipped to cope with players of the class of Steve McManaman. And with ten minutes of the first-half left, McManaman had the opportunity to send them out of the Cup. He cut in from the left, hurdled a challenge from Leboeuf, made himself space and had only Kevin Hitchcock to beat.

Instead of crossing the ball to an unmarked team-mate, or hitting it with pace past the keeper, McManaman tamely side-footed it towards a relieved Hitchcock. Had it been 3–0 then, Chelsea would have been on their knees and surely with no way back. Anyway, McManaman must have reasoned as he jogged back with a shrug, at 2–0 up, Liverpool could not possibly lose this one. Nothing to lose sleep over. In the commentators' box, David Pleat, the Sheffield Wednesday manager, watching the slow-motion replay, must have placed a curse of insomnia on McManaman: 'There'll be a nightmare tonight, that Steve McManaman will have, if Chelsea wrest this game from Liverpool's grasp'.

Where John Barnes and McManaman had organised and controlled affairs in the first half, the second 45 minutes were under the direction of Gianfranco Zola and Mark Hughes. It was Hughes's introduction after half-time which was the signal change in Chelsea's approach.

Scott Minto was substituted by Hughes, as Ruud Gullit abandoned his 3-5-2 principles. This was cup football, after all, all or nothing, and two goals down with 45 minutes to play, Gullit gambled everything he had on turning the game around. Gullit's starting line-up, after all, had been surprise enough, as he had kept Hughes on the bench and opted

141

for the first time to play his two Italian international forwards together up-front from the start of the game.

But the Vialli–Zola combination, for whatever reason, was unable to affect the game in the first period. Vialli, who had not started a game for nearly six weeks, was starved of service, while Zola spent his time chasing the game, chasing the ball, unable to exercise the sort of commanding performance which people had come to expect of him. Dwarfed by the Liverpool defenders, Zola's path too often found a red-shirted dead-end.

Hughes came on and cleared all obstructions. Immediately, he provided the touch of aggression Chelsea so desperately needed in the final third of the field, scoring within five minutes of being on the pitch. It was an archetypal Hughes goal, the sort of goal he had scored dozens of times with Manchester United. He was in the Liverpool penalty area, back to goal, the ball was chipped in to him from the left, he took it down, controlled it, shrugged off the attentions of a defender, turned and shot. His attitude galvanised his team-mates – no fancydan celebrations now, but the clenched fist, the call to arms, the belief that an impossible position could be transformed into a winning one.

It was Hughes's feisty, distracting presence which helped to liberate Vialli and Zola, who were to score the other three goals. Where the Chelsea defence had seemed vulnerable in the first half, now it was Liverpool's turn to be made to appear clumsy, edgy, even anxious every time another wave of blue swept towards them.

Behind Hughes and Vialli, with Zola operating 'in the hole', another tactical tweak by Gullit had helped to stem Liverpool's supply of possession. John Barnes may not be as mobile as he once was, but his ability to pass a ball is undiminished, and it had been his distribution in the first half which had so often set in train attacks from McMamaman or Jason McAteer down either wing. Gullit has said in the past that he dislikes the idea of man-marking, of the essential negativity in the approach which demands that one of your own players is designated to specifically stop an opponent from playing his own game. But this is effectively what the Chelsea manager opted for in the second half, as Roberto di Matteo denied Barnes the time and space to orchestrate matters for Liverpool. 'This,' said Gullit, was the 'vital change.' According to Gullit, 'Barnes couldn't have the ball.' Effectively, Gullit made sure that Barnes was a conductor without a baton.

Chelsea started with a 12th man playing a role in the second half, as the home support tried to rally their team. The club had taken record receipts for a match of £585,000 for this sell-out, upping the price of its special 'bumper issue Matchday Magazine' ('programme' to most people) by 25 per cent to £2.50 and selling every available copy of that, too. It would have all been short-term profit, though, had the club been knocked out of the Cup now. The fans knew this, and wanted more, so for the entire second half, they gave more, too. It had been suggested, at parliamentary level, that in order to bring back some atmosphere at football grounds, there should be some reintroduction of terracing at grounds. The second half at Stamford Bridge that day showed that there is no need for such a retrograde step. The seats in the Matthew Harding Stand went unused for the full 45 minutes, as the Chelsea fans stood, jumped, bounced, slapped hands, hugged, shouted and cheered their side on.

After Hughes's goal, Chelsea's players and supporters could sense a fear running through the Liverpool team. Possession football, passing the ball down one flank, across the penalty area, down the other side, as red-shirted defenders lined up across the 18-yard area to halt Chelsea's progress, but not to deprive them of the ball. In one such move, Barnes had the ball just outside the Liverpool area when Hughes, with all his might, stuck out a boot to deflect the ball towards the on-charging Zola. The ball raged past James. Two-all.

Two minutes later it was 3–2, after Petrescu chipped perfectly into the path of Vialli, the sort of pass the Italian striker had been waiting for since August. Having shot over the bar from short range in the first half, this became a test of nerve for Vialli, as well as the crowd. What happened next was Arctic-cool: almost unseen, a flick from the outside of Vialli's boot, the least controllable of kicks, and the Italian, arms outstretched like wings, banked away in celebration. Three goals in 13 minutes. Chelsea were flying now.

Liverpool, meanwhile, were in freefall. Not since 1964 had a Liverpool team squandered a two-goal lead, but now they were in a state of collapse. From a free-kick out on the right, Zola floated the ball over and Vialli, charging in from the edge of the penalty area like an English centre forward, hammered home the header unmarked. James's first movement in the Liverpool goal was to collect the ball from the back of the net. Mark Wright, the former international centre-half, stood nearby, stock still, hands on his hips, his eyes glazed in disbelief. What had happened, he seemed to be asking, and how?

The epitome of a game of two halves. What had Gullit said over the half-time orange segments? Had he read the Agincourt speech from *Henry V*? 'I said to them, if you score in the first 15 minutes you will win this game,' Gullit revealed. 'But I never thought it would be like that.

'I had faith, and also the crowd participated a lot. I heard our players say that when we scored the first goal, the Liverpool players were really afraid of what was going to happen. If you feel that as a player then you can really take advantage.'

Roy Evans, Gullit's downcast counterpart from Liverpool, attributed a lot of the credit to the role Hughes had played. 'He changed the game,' Evans said. 'Instead of defending on the halfway line, second-half Hughesy kept forcing us, and we're defending on the edge of our own box against players of quality.' Accurate insight, though some were prompted to ask why he, as the team's coach, did nothing to reverse this approach. 'Our dressing room was not a pleasant place to be after the game,' McManaman said.

While the tea in the Liverpool dressing room was left to stew and cool, the players too choked to be able to swallow, Chelsea's players drank a deep draft of exuberance. 'I will remember that match for a long time,' Luca Vialli said. 'It was unbelievable. We put on to the pitch all our capacity, our quality, our art. We deserved to win because our second half was fucking unbelievable.' Though perhaps not as unbelievable for Vialli as what would happen to him the following week.

Since returning to England following treatment for a hamstring injury and then a Christmas-tide dose of flu, Vialli had been only substitute in the third-round FA Cup tie against West Bromwich Albion and for the league games at Forest and at home against Derby. Despondent at not being able to win back his place in the side, the Italian hero of the Cup victory over Liverpool must have thought that, after scoring twice in such a game, he would be in the starting line-up at White Hart Lane the following week. He could not have been more wrong.

Perhaps it had all started with the third-round tie, when First Division West Brom arrived with their record signing, £500,000 Shaun Murphy, in their team, while Chelsea's team sheet revealed that their millionaire rivals had two winners of the European Champions' Cup, in Gullit and Vialli, among the substitutes. 'We couldn't believe it when we saw Vialli was only on the bench,' said West Brom's Ian Hamilton.

The Italian came on for Mark Hughes towards the end of the match, and might have scored but for the woodwork. A week later, in the league game at Nottingham, and Vialli's introduction in place of Myers early in the second half signalled a revival in Chelsea's performance, but with Zola man-marked into oblivion once again, no goals meant no points. An emphatic win at home seven days later against Derby, and there was not even a cameo appearance for Vialli.

Not playing in the first team, for Vialli, meant no football at all. His omission from the starting line-ups was beginning to worry him, as his fitness would begin to spiral downwards if he failed to get to play regularly – no amount of training can compensate for 90 minutes' worth of adrenalin-pumped activity. Had he not shaved it off, he would have probably been tearing out his hair.

Vialli had himself espoused the concept of the squad system which was now keeping him sidelined. 'No longer is it a question of selecting 11 players from 15,' Vialli had told one interviewer before Christmas, when he was still assured of his own place in the first team. 'Now there are 20 good players at the manager's disposal. While this is good for Ruud Gullit, it is not so good for the players. Sure, they get angry when they are left out of the team, but that is a bad mentality. If you want to win something, you have to have more than 11 players.

'Milan is a great example. For the first time in Italy, they had something like 22 great players. From that moment, they won everything, and that is what Ruudi is trying to do at Chelsea. He wants the best – and he wants lots of them.'

Understanding a system when you are a working cog in the machinery is one thing, tolerating being a spare part is something else. One disgruntled interview too many drew a public reproach from Gullit. 'If someone can't cope with a new situation, there's only one solution,' Gullit said on the eve of the home league game against Derby. 'There is no star status here. Vialli is a friend but I can't let that interfere with the running of the team.' On the bench the following day, Vialli cut a lonely, depressed figure, until Dennis Wise, scorer of Chelsea's equaliser that set up the victory, rushed over to the dug-out and lifted his team shirt to reveal a vest with the legend: 'Cheer up Luca, we love you!' The gesture put a smile on everyone's face, including Gullit's. 'Wisey summed it up for all of us,' said the manager. 'We all want him to be happy here. Luca knows my plans and he has agreed to fit in with them.

'Look at Dennis Wise, the effort he put in today. He has been in the same situation as Vialli. Wise showed Vialli how he should cope with it. It was the best sign you could have.'

A week later, and an hour before the Liverpool Cup game, as the squad was gathered in the changing room at Stamford Bridge, tying up boot laces and putting on their gloves before going out for the warm-up, Gullit broke the news to Vialli that he would be playing from the referee's first whistle. He was delighted. He had a chance.

His first six months in England had not been easy. Niggling injuries had been a problem, and at one point Vialli had resorted to popping painkillers before games to deaden his aching hamstring in order to play. Finding somewhere to live had also taken longer than he would have liked. Above all, adapting to the robust style of play had had its tougher moments: 'The referees never seem to blow their whistles, so the tackles are harder,' he said. 'When we played at Leeds, it was like playing rugby.

'The difference between here and *Serie A* is that in Italy, you don't just play the other side. You play against yourself. You are always nervous, you are always under pressure. The mental side of it is much tougher.' As he lined up for the start of the match against Liverpool, then, Vialli's own mind game was just about to kick off.

Having conquered his own nerves and then helped to conquer Liverpool, Vialli was entitled to think he might have played the following week, perhaps as part of the three-man attack which had destroyed the league leaders.

But if a week is a long time in politics, then for Vialli, it must have seemed like a lifetime as during a series of training sessions at Harlington, a pattern emerged into which the Italian did not fit. Worse still, a straw poll of the squad confirmed the manager's tactical inclinations, and by the Thursday everyone, including Vialli, knew that Gullit would revert to the 3-5-2 pattern of play at Tottenham. Even after a couple of days to brood on the decision, it seemed all too much for Vialli. He could barely bring himself to sit on the bench with his manager, and for a time skulked in the tunnel, watching the match in isolation, taking the occasional nervy puff on a cigarette. The distance between player and manager was only a matter of yards. Symbolically, it was a gaping chasm.

A 2–1 away win, capped off by a rocket-fuelled long-shot from Roberto di Matteo, and Chelsea moved up to fifth in the Premier League table. It all served to confirm the manager's judgment. 'I think we showed today that we have to play like this,' he said. 'You can't all the time argue about whether he's playing or not playing . . . I have three strikers and I can only put two in there. The important thing is the tactic. You have to find a way that is comfortable with your players. So in training we tried three different ways. And it was obvious. I was not surprised. Everyone looked more comfortable in 3-5-2, and so that was how we started against Tottenham.'

After the game, as the various newspaper journalists, many of them from Italy, chased around for a story, Vialli diplomatically made himself scarce, slipping out of the ground as quickly as possible. He did not relish the attention he had attracted a couple of weeks earlier when, after he had given an interview for an Italian television station, it was transcribed, translated and republished throughout Europe. 'I'm not very happy on the bench,' Vialli had said on camera, 'I think Gullit should play me because I deserve to play.'

Later, though, he elaborated. 'I signed for three years, but I don't want to spend the next two years sitting on the bench. I'm happy here, but only 75 per cent happy. I don't want to move. It's not true that Gullit and

I have had a fight. It's not true that I refused to sit on the bench at Tottenham, it's just that there wasn't enough room on it for me. As soon as I said, "I'm not playing, so I'm not happy" on Italian television, all the newspapers really got on the case.

'After all, it's not as though money can buy you happiness. I'd play for nothing. Life is not only about football. There are many other things. I am really happy until about an hour before the games on Saturday, and then very happy an hour after the game. When I have to be on the bench, I feel a little low . . . But now I have a new house, and my girlfriend. I'd be stupid to be unhappy just because I'm not playing much. I know football, so I know that it goes up and down. So it's important to stay on a level, and I'm sure that, after a while, the good times will come again. 'It is only normal to feel fed up when you love to do something and you can't do it.'

Vialli, at least, might have played. Michael Duberry, however, would be entitled to feel completely fed up when his season was curtailed after an accident in training on the Thursday before the Derby match. The frost had bitten hard into the ground at Harlington, and there was no give in the turf. Duberry set off in a chase for a ball, slipped and fell. 'I'd chested the ball, went to pass it with my right foot, and it felt like someone had booted me in the Achilles. But there was no one around me . . .'

There would be plenty of people around him soon enough, as he had to be carried from the pitch on a stretcher, thence to an ambulance, and then to hospital, where the surgeons diagnosed a ruptured Achilles tendon, and operated the following day.

It is an injury which can terminate a sporting career, whether that of a footballer, a sprinter or a rugby winger. For a defender, such as Duberry, renowned for his pace, it could curtail his career markedly. After his operation, to aid the recovery, his leg was put in plaster over his knee, which meant that when he returned to Stamford Bridge ten days later, he had to hobble up to John Barnes on crutches, rather than put in a crunching tackle on the Liverpool captain. Duberry sought out Barnes because he, too, had suffered a similar injury, but had managed to get back to playing for his club and country. 'He told me what he did to recover from his injury. He showed me the scar, it's in the same place. He said he had to do some specific exercises, but that the tendon was thicker and stronger, and that it shouldn't rupture again.'

Duberry was obviously frustrated, having been enjoying a run of excellent form in a winning side, something which his former club manager, Glenn Hoddle, had been observing from afar as England coach. With the World Cup finals in France 18 months away, Duberry was entitled to think he might have worked his way into the full international squad from the under-21s. The injury obviously was an immense set-back. Instead of having the next four months mapped out for him as a combination of cup and league games interspersed with international duty, Duberry now had his daily schedule dictated for him by his doctors and physiotherapists. It would be nearly three months after the operation before he would be free of the plaster cast, and able at last to begin full rehabilitation exercises and some swimming to regain fitness. The best prognosis was that he might, just, be ready to start proper training again in the pre-season routine the following July.

For Chelsea, Duberry was the third central defender, after Jakob Kjeldbjerg and David Lee, to fall by the wayside so far in the season. It was also confirmed around this time that another long-term casualty, Dmitri Kharine, would definitely not play again this season. Further surgery had been required on the Russian goalkeeper's knee, which he had damaged at Sheffield Wednesday in September, and this had revealed that his cruciate ligament had been ruptured, the second time in his career that Kharine had suffered such a debilitating injury. 'I feel much better than after my last operation,' he said. 'I can bend my knee now, I can walk, I can do exercises. I didn't do anything for three months last time.' It hardly seemed like a consolation. Kharine was encouraged in his recuperation by Chelsea's goalkeeping coach, Eddie Niedzwiecki, whose own career had been ended by the same injury. 'I was amazed last year how advanced the surgery has become since my first injury in the 1980s,' he said. 'If they had had this technology then my surgeon told me I might still be playing.'

The losses of Kharine and Duberry were serious blows in key areas to the prospects of the team, though not so serious as to bother the bookmakers, who before the tricky fifth-round tie at Leicester, had installed Chelsea as favourites to win the FA Cup. With Liverpool, Newcastle, Arsenal, Everton and, after a fourth-round replay, Manchester United, all out of the Cup, it was easy to understand why. Yet here was a club that has had more false dawns than an Arctic winter.

Not that Franco Zola had endeared himself to the whole of the English public when he scored the only goal for Italy in the World Cup qualifying match at Wembley in the Wednesday before the Cup game. While Zola, di Matteo and the other internationals in Chelsea's squad had gone off to play their parts in the World Cup, Gullit and his coaching staff took the remainder of the Chelsea first-team squad off to Cyprus for some winter sun, golf and training.

It was all part of the bonding process that Gullit was keen to instil, with the aim of creating 'a family'. It did not stop Gullit, Graham Rix and the other coaches sloping off to the pub one night in the week, although this was rationalised as a vital scouting mission – the bar was the only place that they could find with live coverage of the Wimbledon *v* Manchester United Cup replay, which the south Londoners won.

A week later, and Rix was watching another game, this time from the stands at Wembley. 'It was one of the most difficult games I've watched at Wembley,' Rix said. 'Being an Englishman, I wanted England to win. Glenn's a mate of mine and I wanted him to win and do well. But I also wanted Franco and Robbie to give a good account of themselves and come through unscathed. At least that happened.'

Di Matteo and Zola turned up at Harlington the following morning for training with their club. Even though they arrived wearing Italian, rather than Chelsea, blue, both were still mobbed by autograph hunters and hero-worshipping children, indicating, perhaps, that the internationalisation of the English Premiership was meeting with the approval of the next generation of football supporters, as well as the present one.

From one international cup competition to the next domestic knock-out, each game was now taking on increased importance. 'Every game is a final,' Gullit became fond of incanting to his players. Nothing could be given away, no one could afford to lose a tackle or make a poor pass. Yet Chelsea were about to show that Liverpool were not the only team capable of squandering a two-goal lead.

Chapter 15

The book of football clichés would be a long but essentially dull volume. Soccerspeak is such a repetitive language, you will have heard it all before. Not just the obvious ones, like 'Over the moon', or 'Sick as a parrot', but even the more inane offerings of pundits, managers and managers-turned-pundits, such as 'Early doors', and 'We're just taking each match as it comes . . .'

The post-match ritual at English football grounds early on Saturday evenings in the winter is one of the most keenly observed, and completely futile, exercises in a sports reporter's existence. It takes two distinct forms, dependent on whether the reporter is working for a Sunday or a daily paper (some hard-pressed scribes work for both, in which case they cover both scenarios). The ritual begins with the daily newspapermen hurrying from their seats in the press box directly the referee blows his whistle for full-time, making immediately for the warmth of the press lounge, where they will often take a drink (courtesy of their hosts), and proceed to eat most of the inadequate supply of sandwiches provided by the club. It would be wrong to underestimate the importance of such meagre victuals to reporters, who have been frozen to the bone for two hours, watching a performance that numbs the brain, while trying to shout their carefully-crafted copy down a crackling telephone line to a copy-taker who is apparently deaf. 'It's very noisy where you are,' one copytaker once complained. 'I'm at a football match,' came the short-tempered reply, since this had evidently slipped her mind.

But some clubs – often the smaller ones, those with the better organised press steward, those possessing a more accommodating entertainment budget, or simply those with fewer press attending – do manage to lay on a good spread, and have enough food to go around. Wolves, during a particularly sticky spell in Graham Taylor's management there, even provided cream cakes after the game, perhaps as some sort of culinary comment on the manager's tribulations.

The Sunday reporters usually have to stay on at their phone in the press box in order to file the final elements of their reports, and so will emerge into the press lounge to discover two or three sandwich trays devoid of sandwiches. Taking consolation in a drink, they then wait . . . They might gather around a TV set to find out other results, perhaps (if they are lucky) catching replays of the goals in the game they have just been reporting on (offering a good opportunity to 'tweak' their first edition piece when they re-write). And they wait . . .

Eventually, both managers, and sometimes a player, will come through separately and proceed to give their views on the day's match. Some managers prefer to take a shower and get changed after the game. Some have been known to spend upwards of an hour in the changing room berating their players for a dire performance. Yet once they emerge before the press, the same sorry clichés will be trotted out. To some extent, this is the reporters' faults, because they tend to ask only the same questions (or variations thereon), though that may be forgiven because it is borne out of experience – they already know what answers they are going to get.

After the general press conference, the managers or players will go off into a separate huddle with the daily newspaper reporters. This is exclusive territory for the 'Mondays', in the hope that it will reveal something fresh and interesting. It rarely does. A look at a notebook after one of these sessions will offer little to cast light on the outcome of the game, nothing that had not been witnessed during the 90 minutes of football that the reporters have just witnessed.

There are no courses, no special training, it is just something which somehow players and managers learn to do instinctively: they learn to say nothing, offer no insight, they hide behind the clichés. They offer nothing but formula interviews, indentikit quotes for set circumstances. Some managers have got the empty comment technique off to a fine art: the often guttural Kenny Dalglish being as skilled in this verbal sidestep as ever he was on the pitch. Few are prepared, as were the Cloughs and Shanklys of 20 years ago, to risk anything in the public domain by daring to express an original opinion on some aspect of the game, whether it be their own players' performances, a controversial refereeing decision, or even their own fear that, by this time next week, they might be on the dole.

Of course, there are exceptions to this gross generality – Dave Bassett is worth listening to in an entertaining way; Ron Atkinson always had a one-liner to offer, like some old-style comedian working the northern clubs; and Ruud Gullit, at his first games, was unique in his frankness and openness. As his first season at Chelsea drew on, though, even Gullit developed a verbal defence, a facade of openness behind which he could hide his real thoughts and views. You decide if there is any difference between: 'We take every game as it comes', and one of the *bon mots* offered by the Chelsea player-manager: 'I do not think about the end of the season and about what we might have won or what we might not have won.' Tough to call?

Gullit, too, was finding some difficulties in his new job. 'The hard part of life for me is not to tell lies. Every day there is one decision, then another decision about other people's lives. Honesty is important. That is what I try to live by. Sometimes now I'm learning that you have to not tell the truth to protect people. That's different to telling a lie. That is also sometimes good, to protect other people from being unhappy.' Gullit had also learned that it was good to protect himself, because anything he said might be taken down and used as evidence against him later.

It is not just because of some sort of professional paranoia that people in football are so coy. Obviously, Gullit is a rarity, being as articulate with words as he is with a football. But the reluctance to speak among football people generally is due to more than simple distrust of the press. Despite the massive public interest in professional football as we approach the millennium, the sport in England is still Victorian in its approach to public relations when compared to the access provided to the sports media in Europe and the United States. On top of that, the authorities still operate a disciplinary system that punishes any comment which they may adjudge to 'bring the game into disrepute'. In football, there is no defence of 'fair comment', managers are not entitled to their own point of view. The FA's thought police are always watching. So when Martin O'Neill decried the refereeing error that might have cost his Leicester City side a place in the quarter-finals of the FA Cup, his outspokenness was immediately threatened with disciplinary action.

Leicester, despite fielding a virtual reserve side, had fought back from 2–0 down at half-time in their fifth-round tie with Chelsea at Filbert Street, and had earned a replay at Stamford Bridge. Chelsea were as dominant in the first-half of this game as Liverpool had been in the previous round, and but for some excellent goalkeeping by Kasey Keller, might have scored more. Like Chelsea in the previous round, an experienced, tough old pro, Steve Walsh, got a goal back just after half-time, and changed the tenor of the game. With Zola and di Matteo, their influential Italians who had played significant parts in the World Cup defeat of England in midweek, tiring in the second half, Chelsea had to hang on, tough it out. They very nearly did, until a free-kick was conceded outside their penalty area with three minutes of the match remaining.

As Garry Parker's kick floated towards the goal, all Chelsea's defensive vulnerabilities and self-doubts re-emerged and Eddie Newton dived in for the ball ahead of his own keeper and turn the ball inside the post.

Even Mark Hughes, who nearly scored with a diving header in the last minute, could not retrieve this situation for Chelsea. It was a match Chelsea ought to have won, and perhaps because of the ersatz nature of the Leicester play, Gullit afterwards described them as 'lucky'. There can be a fine line between confidence and arrogance, honesty and diplomacy, but this was a post-match quote which would come back to haunt Gullit. O'Neill, proud and pleased that his scratch squad had fought back so well, when presented with his counterpart's remark by an enterprising reporter, reacted with customary brio. 'It may well have been that we did not use intricate passing moves and little bits of skill like Chelsea,' O'Neill said. 'But I've got news for him: this was a Cup tie and you get through it any way you can with the resources available to you, and that's what we did.'

What Gullit had also done was to provide the Leicester underdogs with a bone to gnaw on over the next ten days until the replay. In the meantime, Chelsea were more than fully occupied with a significant league fixture and a friendly. Somehow, someone had managed to arrange a friendly with Milan. A match at the San Siro against Gullit's former masters of Europe would seem a great opportunity, but at this stage of the season, it could perhaps only serve as an unwanted diversion. After all, Chelsea's swelling band of international players had just spent more than a week away from the club, playing in World Cup fixtures. Now, the following week's training sessions would also be disrupted by a couple of flights, the hassle of airport check-ins, even the loss of rest. And it was coming just three days before Chelsea were due to face league leaders Manchester United in a match which could very well determine whether Chelsea would continue to have any interest in the outcome of the Premiership.

Craig Burley, for one, was unconvinced of the need for another game in an already hectic season. 'I think it was a financial thing,' he said. 'It's probably not even up to Ruud.' As the squad made their way through Gatwick airport, though, the anticipation of playing in one of the world's great stadiums against the likes of Baggio, Davids and Maldini could not fail to excite even the older players. 'Perhaps we could have done without the trip, with our not beating Leicester first time round in the cup,' Steve Clarke said, 'but I've never played in the San Siro . . .'

A deal's a deal, and the arrangement that was to see Gullit playing at the San Siro once more, along with Italian heroes Zola and di Matteo, was reputed to be worth anything up to £1 million. According to Ken

Bates, the Chelsea chairman, the important thing about the game was the experience of playing in Europe. Others, like Burley, suggested otherwise. 'I think it was a shopping trip,' he said. Indeed, there had been talk of Gullit putting in a bid for Paolo Maldini, the Italian captain, or Paul Ince, the England midfielder also based in Milan, with Internazionale. Was this what Burley meant? 'Nah, the lads were all following the Italians about and getting 30 or 40 per cent off clothes. That's what it was all about.'

Bates, too, benefited from a little local knowledge about one of Europe's most fashionable cities. 'Ruud recommended the best shopping street (via Monte Napoleone) and the best restaurant (Al Girorosto) on Corse Venetia. Unfortunately we went shopping first, so I was lucky to have enough money to pay for lunch.' Gullit was at pains to dismiss speculation about his shopping for anything other than clothes. 'What do I want Paul Ince for when I already have Eddie Newton?' he said.

The match was considered important enough to attract five pages of previews in *La Gazzetta dello Sport*, and about 15,000 spectators. Milan may have been enduring one of their worst seasons for more than a decade, languishing in mid-table of *Serie A* and ruled out of a place in Europe the following season, but their international superstars were still able to despatch Chelsea 2–0, although after the first half, Gullit rested most of his first-choice players and made eight changes, giving the likes of Chris McCann, Neil Clement and Jody Morris – youngsters who not long before had been on the club's £37-a-week YTS scheme – a chance to play against one of the giants of football. 'It was better to play there than at Kingstonian,' Gullit said of the alternative, conveniently overlooking the differing travel arrangements.

The following Saturday, against one of the giants of English football, there could be no experimentation nor any chances to blood youngsters. If Chelsea were still to have any chance of outdoing Milan and qualifying for European competition the next season through their league placing, they needed to beat the champions. Before the game, Chelsea were sixth in the table, 12 points behind United, but with two games in hand.

A second league victory over United seemed a distinct possibility when, within five minutes of kick-off, Dan Petrescu took a cross-field pass from Dennis Wise on his chest, carried the ball briefly forward while United stood off, and then slid it outside Denis Irwin to Gianfranco Zola. The little Italian danced beyond Irwin and cut inside, turning Gary Pallister quite beautifully before lashing a low shot home between the static Schmeichel and the near post. It was another Zola classic, to match his effort against Dicks before Christmas. The difference here was that he had managed single-handedly to dissect an entire defensive unit.

Chelsea might have extended their lead, had Mark Hughes managed to bury a couple of gilt-edged chances against his former club. But with David Beckham switched to a more central midfield role in the second half, Chelsea's one-goal lead never looked to be enough as United came back into the game. It was after a poor clearance that Beckham hit a volley that was to extend his side's unbeaten streak to 15. For Chelsea, any hopes of leap-frogging up the league table were dashed, although they had managed to take four points off the champions-elect during the season. From now on, though, Chelsea's season would be all about the FA Cup. Their fourth game in ten days the following Wednesday was now crucial.

There is another well-used footballing cliché, that 'our name's on the cup this year'. It seems to be an uncannily successful, fateful remark, as the team whose name is supposed to have been pre-ordained to be on the trophy by The Great Engraver In The Sky always seems to win it. This, of course, is so much nonsense: it only seems to happen because we only remember the successful our-name's-on-the-cup-this-year sides, conveniently forgetting about those who made similar claims but got knocked out in the third round by Worksop Town.

Yet fate did seem to have a hand in Chelsea's progress in the FA Cup this season. Some suggested that there was some sort of heavenly intervention as Matthew Harding looked down on his favourite team; others, more pragmatically, thought that Harding's death had in some way galvanised the squad to produce a more earthly spirit, but one that was similarly inspired and indefatigible. Martin O'Neill, after the fifth-round replay, felt that there was only one hand involved in Chelsea's march towards Wembley, and that was the one in which referee Mike Reed held his whistle.

After 206 minutes of football, deep into extra time, there was still no separating the two teams, as Leicester, determined to make Gullit and his team regret the 'lucky' comment from the previous week, fought an inspired battle. Keller, their American goalkeeper, had once before helped to knock Chelsea out of the Cup at Stamford Bridge, when a game against Millwall a couple of years earlier had eventually gone to penalties. Now, Keller, after another inspired performance, was within three minutes of pitting his goalkeeping skills against Chelsea penalty-takers in the ultimate footballing test of nerve.

Then Erland Johnsen, brought on as a fresh pair of legs by Gullit just ten minutes earlier, picked up the ball in his own half. Although Vikings were once renowned for their daring, marauding raids into enemy territory, it was not something the big Norwegian centre-back had done much of during his time at Chelsea. Now, though, with the midfield runners of both sides slacking in their pace with sheer fatigue, gaps opened up in front of him, and he kept going onwards towards the Leicester goal. On the edge of the Leicester box, Johnsen played a quick exchange pass, the return going up in the air. Johnsen's momentum carried him forward at pace, where he seemed to collide with one, perhaps two Leicester defenders, and went down. Referee Reed blew his whistle. He pointed to the spot. Leboeuf ended the agony.

Martin O'Neill is possibly one of the best young managers in the Premiership. A Northern Ireland international midfielder in his own time, he had learned his trade under Brian Clough and Billy Bingham, and owns a European champions' medal to prove it. As a former law student, O'Neill also possesses a sharp intellect and willingness to speak his mind so often lacking elsewhere. When Reed blew his whistle again, this time to end the match, a combination of disappointment at the result and outrage at the injustice of what he called the referee's 'unbelievable decision' saw O'Neill launch into a tirade.

'Managers and players look over videos of games to analyse where we have gone wrong, what has gone right and where we might have done better,' O'Neill said. 'I think the referee should maybe take a long, hard look at his performance in this game and maybe it could do some good. It is scandalous that a team should be put out of such an important competition in this way, because of a totally wrong decision, and the frustrating thing is that we can do nothing about it.

'Chelsea are now going to Portsmouth in the sixth round and good luck to them. It's all over for us. In a few weeks time, all people will remember is not how we went out but just that we lost the game. I am not saying we would have won the tie. I consider penalty shoot-outs to be a bit of a lottery, but I think we deserved a chance to at least be in one.

'I would rather have gone out to Southend in the third round than suffer this sort of thing. My players had battled very well against a very good team and simply did not deserve to lose like this.'

Gullit, for his part, had learned the craft of saying something, and nothing. 'I didn't see the penalty, so I'm not going to comment. I understand that Leicester were angry, but my only concern is for my team.'

Referee Reed had been just yards away from the incident, with Johnsen the other side of a Leicester player, who was perhaps blocking his view. 'The penalty that never was' became a talking point on television and radio for the rest of the week, the incident replayed endlessly. Eventually, Reed himself admitted he had made a bad decision. 'The TV cameras showed from a different angle there wasn't any contact. But, from where I was, there was. I gave a correct and honest decision, made honestly from what I saw.' It was no consolation for Leicester, but perhaps Reed's remarks managed to get O'Neill off the hook with the FA over his comments.

Ken Bates's comments about the incident in his programme notes for Chelsea's next home game summarised the situation rather well. 'There is no doubt that Mr Reed had a bad game, that was evidenced by yellow cards distributed like confetti in what was not a dirty match. One thing, however, is clear: Erland did not cheat. The Viking is an honourable man and would like to discuss the incident on a one-to-one basis with those cowards in the media who said or implied otherwise. He was going too fast – he had already run some 40 yards with the ball and was still accelerating when he went down. Fall, perhaps, nudge – perhaps – but dive never and in my opinion, the more you watch the video, the more debatable it becomes.

'Anyway, the fact of the matter is that it was the right result. Leicester should never have got a replay because the free-kick which led to their equaliser wasn't . . . it was no foul in the first place. Did we make a fuss about it? Did we heck, we just got on with it because that is Chelsea's way. Over the 117 minutes of the tie we outclassed them in style, territorial possession, shots and corners, so even if it was rough justice – justice prevailed . . .

'Clubs never complain when they get the benefit of dodgy lucky decisions – only if they suffer from them.'

There was a second casualty of that penalty award, too, radio presenter and professional Millwall supporter Danny Baker. Hosting a BBC phone-in show on the night of the game, Baker used the airwaves as an opportunity to vent his spleen over the incident. At the calmest of times, Baker attempts to be a sporting shock-jock, provocative and outrageous. This night, Baker was far from calm. 'Something important has happened in football tonight and, as usual, the BBC and Radio Five want to suck up so that they can keep their licence.'

Baker, who in the past had called on Spurs fans to protest by chucking their programmes on the White Hart Lane pitch, and invited others to send rotting vegetables to Gillingham, this time called on those who disagreed with Reed's decision to go round to his house and let him know what they thought of him. 'I'm not interested in having some kind of balanced argument,' he said, apparently fulminating against his producer for letting on the air callers who disagreed with his own views. Baker later claimed it was all a stunt, a bit of fun, an argument which held up, since at no time did he mention Reed's home address.

Yet some wondered whether he needed to, whether this was a prank too far. When he was manager at Southampton, Ian Branfoot had been subjected to all sorts of abuse, not only at The Dell, but also at his home. Determined football fans had a way of finding out where he lived, just as Manchester City supporters did with Peter Swales, the chairman they wanted off the board. Danny Baker, the BBC decided, had gone too far, and the day after transmission, he was sacked. Former Tory MP David Mellor was their preferred version of the radio football pundit.

If Reed bore the brunt of the attacks over the penalty incident, Johnsen also came in for criticism, with some accusing him of taking a dive. Approaching his 30th birthday, the Norwegian was also coming to the end of a stay of more than seven years at Stamford Bridge. With his contract up for renewal in the summer, Johnsen had opted to return to part-time Norwegian football, where he could start training for an alternative career, working in a bank.

It may all seem something of a come-down for a former Chelsea player of the year, but with Susunne, the eldest of his two children, approaching school age, now was the time to move his family home, and back to the sort of lifestyle he had when he started out as a footballer, earning £5,000, with local team Moss. Johnsen had won a *Bundesliga* champions' medal playing alongside Stefan Reuter and Jürgen Kohler at Bayern Munich in 1989 before joining Chelsea, and had played for Norway in the 1994 World Cup, but he could no longer guarantee his place in the Chelsea line-up. Besides, he thought there were too many foreigners in English football.

'All these foreigners coming into the Premiership,' Johnsen said, 'it cannot be good for the future of the national team, however much the clubs and spectators may benefit from their presence.' When he voiced these opinions in Norway, a rich source of low-cost imports for the English game, Johnsen was flamed by his own countrymen. It had not been so long ago that Norwegians had been in awe of English football ('Norwegian players would take their autograph books with them when they played England,' according to Johnsen), and now he was arguing against them having the chance to earn a tremendous living in England. 'People think I should keep quiet and hope that more of my countrymen can come over to earn a living.'

Johnsen was signed from Bayern for just over £300,000 – probably about half the cost of an equivalent English centre-half at the time. What was more, there was less risk than with other foreign players that he might not have settled into the English way of life. 'Most Scandinavians you've had seem to settle in OK in England. We know the language and the way of living is much the same. The style of play in Germany didn't suit me as well as it does here. I prefer a more physical game. They played man-to-man marking, which I didn't like. The Norwegian game is more similar to the English, although it has changed here since I came. Most teams try to play more football now.'

In some respects, Johnsen had been a victim of those changes at Chelsea, unsuited to playing on the left side of a back three, uncomfortable at playing in the reserves. He had once before nearly left the club, after making just 14 first-team appearances in two seasons. David Webb's short-term stay in the Stamford Bridge manager's office, though, had seen Johnsen's Chelsea career revived – one bucaneering old centre-half obviously liking what he saw in the Norwegian.

Webb's sides, though, played with a back four. Glenn Hoddle, and then Gullit, tended to go for just three defenders. By the spring of 1997, Johnsen was a square peg in a total football hole. He remained unconvinced that the wholesale import of foreign players – at least partly to blame for his own marginalisation at Chelsea – was a Good Thing for English football. 'It's good for the fans because they can watch some really good players and the clubs will have a better chance of doing well in Europe, but it just makes it even more difficult for young home-grown talent to come through.

'They end up, in some instances, having to move down two divisions, because there are foreigners in the first division now. On the other hand, the young players can learn technique from the foreigners, and how to play the European way. But in the long term, I don't think it's good. We'll see in about ten years' time if I'm right.'

It would be a lot sooner than that for Johnsen to make his point in Chelsea's 1997 FA Cup run.

Chapter 16

Derby County were playing their final season at the Baseball Ground. The legend that the site had been cursed by gypsies, moved on to make way for the stadium builders, had not stopped the club winning the Football League title in Brian Clough's time there as manager, but it might have had something to do with the cursedly rutted and bumpy pitch which Chelsea were expected to perform on three days after knocking Leicester out of the Cup. There would have been a few oaths cast in the direction of the Derby ground by the Chelsea side as their team coach pulled away after another game where points have been lost after conceding a late goal.

Eddie Newton will have cursed Derby, as he tore some fibrocartilage in his knee during the pre-match warm-up, an injury which would see him sidelined for nearly six weeks. Frank Leboeuf will have cursed Derby, as his handball on the line saw him sent off and suspended. And Ruud Gullit will have cursed Derby, not just because of lost points, but because, within ten minutes of bringing himself on as a substitute, he was forced to leave the field.

Hospital X-rays two days later revealed a chipped bone in the player-manager's lower leg, while Newton required arthroscopy – the so-called 'key-hole surgery' which reduces the size of the surgical insertion and thus speeds the pace of recovery. Best estimates suggested Newton would be out for a month.

'A lot of strange things happened to us,' Gullit said of the Derby game. It was as if, in adversity, a fighting spirit was welling up inside the Dutchman. 'Things are going well, then strange things happen. There's a feeling around you, you have to be aware. It can be anything, an accident, the people around you, jealousy. I'm a patient and tolerant person, but now I feel like a beast is coming out. A fiery spirit is rising out of me, an extra force, giving me more energy.' Here he was, on the verge of a decisive few weeks in his first season as a manager, and Gullit was forced to watch from the sidelines. Perhaps there was another force at work.

Certainly, any suggestion that refereeing decisions, good or bad, balance themselves out over the course of a season was borne out by events at Derby. Gullit had only come on to the field to try to add balance to the remaining ten-man line-up after Leboeuf's dismissal, and according to skipper Dennis Wise, the move that led to Leboeuf's deliberate handball should never have been allowed.

According to Wise, Derby's Ashley Ward handled the ball, which should have given Chelsea a free-kick and chance to clear their lines. 'I said, "I saw it, you must have, ref?"' Wise said. 'But he didn't. They won a corner from that, from which they got a goal and Frank sent off.'

The injury list at Stamford Bridge had grown so long, it was beginning to resemble a waiting list at an NHS hospital. Recent casualties included Craig Burley, hobbled by an injured ankle, Dan Petrescu carrying a knock that finally saw him sidelined at the Baseball Ground, and Kevin Hitchcock ruled out by the injured shoulder he sustained in the first half of the match against Manchester United. The addition of Newton and Gullit brought to ten the number of first-team players put out of consideration for selection. It was considerations such as that which rendered Ward's late, deciding fifth goal of the game relatively unimportant. The game also showed quite how dependent Chelsea had become on the talents of Gianfranco Zola. With the Italian rested for the match, Luca Vialli got a rare chance to start a game, yet he was the attacking player 'sacrificed' after Leboeuf's dismissal, when Gullit brought himself on to shore up the team's defence.

So it was with some relief the following Sunday that Chelsea lined up against only First Division opposition at Portsmouth in the next round of the FA Cup. Once again, Chelsea had been chosen for a televised match, on a Sunday, just another sign of the growing fashionability of the club. Gullit's and Hughes's signings by Hoddle, Gullit's appointment as player-manager, and his foreign signings, had put Chelsea up among the most talked about and most written about clubs in the country. The demands of the manager's and the players' time – for interviews, presentations, public appearances for their individual sponsors – was mounting all the time.

Widely acknowledged as a stylist in the clothes he wears off the pitch, as well as in the manner he fashions his football team, Gullit was voted Britain's best dressed man in 1996. The plaudit led to him, for a six-figure fee plus a commission, putting his name to a range of designer 'urban streetwear' – 'Ruud', manufactured by Hay and Robertson, the new owners of the Admiral brand. Although golfers, such as Greg Norman, and tennis players, like Bjorn Borg, have had their own-label clothing deals before, footballers had been avoided by clothes merchandisers, in all probability because of the poor image of the game. Gullit was seen as above all that. 'I get a lot of offers commercial-wise, and this sounded just the sort of thing I would like to get involved with,' Gullit said.

'I will design some things myself, I have a lot of ideas about what clothes should look like, but that doesn't mean everything in the range will be the sort of thing I would wear. Life always is an adventure, and if you have a good feeling about something, you must just do it.' Gullit had already had good feelings about being in a reggae band in Holland in the 1980s, where 'Revelation Two' had had two top ten hits (although this was in the country that gave the world The Smurfs), and had more recently made an acting debut (of sorts) in a commercial for M&M sweets. Instantly recognisable because of his dreads, articulate, handsome and streetwise, he was an ad man's dream.

His celebrity reached far and wide, even seeing him take time out in the midst of the busy season – just two days before Chelsea's game at White Hart Lane – to go across to Dublin to front the launch of a £180 million deal which saw Telia, of Sweden, and Holland's KPN, buy a 20 per cent stake in the Irish telecommunications firm. Ulrika Johnsen was there in the restaurant on St Stephen's Green, too, representing the Swedish influence on the deal, mingling among the wine-drinkers and hors d'oeuvres-eaters, the PR people and the journalists, those satellites of celebrity. But the couple of hundred football fans who turned up outside that morning were there not because Johnsen sometimes fronts a TV programme with a former Wimbledon striker. Nor did they care a jot about the long-term employment prospects in the Irish telecommunications industry as a result of the foreign investment. It was Gullit who had pulled in the crowds.

'He's gorgeous,' sighed one woman, still a little unsteady on her feet after getting the man's autograph. That was the odd thing about this horde of football fans – there were as many shrieking girlies as there were hard-faced lads. Just as he had attracted mini-bus-loads of Dutch teenagers to Stamford Bridge the previous season, now Gullit's magic had taken effect on another audience.

Tom Humphries, the excellent sportswriter with the *Irish Times*, sought an interview with the man: 'We are ushered into his radiant presence by the PR woman who has solemnly warned us that the footballer wishes not to speak about football today. Yikes!

'"So Ruud, you don't want to talk about football?"

'He shrugs his shoulders. "If you want we can. It's just that football isn't all that I talk about or think about."

'Indeed it is a waste to talk about football to Ruud Gullit when he can speak so fluently about so many other subjects in so many other languages. Footballers holding forth about politics or philosophy are rather like dogs on bicycles: you don't expect it to be done well, you are fascinated rather by the fact that it is done at all. Gullit does it and he does it well.'

It had just been announced that Gullit was to receive from President Nelson Mandela of South Africa a special medal, the Order of Good Hope, South Africa's highest honour for foreigners, for the stance the footballer had taken against apartheid. Effectively, this acknowledged Gullit's own gesture when he had dedicated his 1987 European Footballer of the Year award to Mandela. It also reminded people once again of Colin Hutchinson's joke about the option the club had had two years earlier, of signing either Gullit or Paul Gascoigne, and the unthinkable prospect of having Gazza now as player-manager at the Bridge. It was no more possible to consider 99 per cent of English pro footballers ever making a public declaration against social injustices in another country than it was to consider Gazza setting up a refuge for battered women.

But with the adulation also comes the attention, so close as to be positively claustrophobic at times. With two daughters by his first wife, Yvonne de Vries, living in Holland, and two more children with his estranged second wife, Christina Pensa, living in Italy, Gullit's private life was already a complex tangle of international relations. It became fair game for the tabloids in March when he began court proceedings to gain greater access to his Italian children, Quincy, aged five, and three-year-old Cheyenne. The court case provided the perfect excuse, if any were needed, for the tabloids to focus on his latest relationship, with Estelle Cruyff, the 19-year-old niece of Gullit's footballing mentor, Johan.

Those who had been unfortunate enough to get the wrong side of Gullit during his oftentimes tempestuous playing career also now found themselves a new, and intrigued, audience bearing cheque books as well as notebooks. Gullit had become big news, and the media's appetite for stories about him insatiable.

The situation with Vialli had caused some to think that, just maybe, Gullit was not the perfect man-manager behind the scenes as the smiling face beneath a curtain of tassled hair suggested. The rapid departures of John Spencer, Gavin Peacock and Terry Phelan reinforced the view that with Gullit there would only be two ways – with him or against him, and if you were against him, you would be out. As Spencer looked on from afar as his former club enjoyed their march towards Wembley, he said, 'I don't want to talk about his man-management. I was really glad to leave Chelsea. I have a lot of mates there, and I hope they go on and win the Cup. But I don't want to talk about Gullit. Better speak to someone who likes him, if you can find anyone.'

Thys Libregts does not like Ruud Gullit. 'He is Dr Jekyll and Mr Hyde,' said Libregts, the former Dutch national team manager. 'I have seen much more Mr Hyde.'

Libregts, of course, had good cause to admit, 'I do not like Gullit.' For Libregts was forced out of the Holland job by a player-power revolt led by Gullit. Libregts had been coach at Feyenoord in 1984, when Gullit was playing there, and the two men had a falling out over a racist remark, which Libregts said had been misrepresented in the press. Gullit, evidently, had never forgiven his former club coach, so that when he was appointed to the national job, the two men were set on a collision course.

'We had a big fight,' Libregts remembered. 'Holland had just won the European championship and everyone expected us to go on and take the 1990 World Cup. Gullit, van Basten and Rijkaard wanted to decide everything. They did not need a coach. The other players were afraid of them. Gullit was the leader. He always has to be.'

For Gullit's coach at Sampdoria, Sven Goran Eriksson, Gullit's leadership qualities were something to encourage. 'Ruud is a born leader. As long as he loves the work and finds it interesting, he will do a great job at Chelsea.'

When Gullit again tried to exercise influence over the national team four years later, refusing to go to the World Cup in the United States, he came off worse. This time, he was vilified in his own country, decried as a coward and traitor when he returned to Amsterdam with Milan. 'Ruud has a story about missing the World Cup,' said Dick Advocaat, the Dutch boss left to pick up the pieces in America. 'He said it was something to do with tactics, but I do not think so.' Advocaat and Gullit had not spoken in the three years since.

In any situation of confrontation between a player and manager, Advocaat said, 'the coach must always win . . . but it depends how important the player is.' After what happened to Advocaat in 1994, Libregts, the coach who lost out to the most important player in his squad in 1990, somehow felt vindicated. 'Of course, Gullit was a great player,' Libregts said, 'but he has a bad character.'

Libregts pondered whether a man who could twice walk out on his national team might yet walk out on a club if things did not go as he wished. 'Most of the time he was only interested in himself. When you become a coach of any side, like Chelsea, you have to think about how to deal with lots of different personalities. I do not think at the moment he is ready for that.'

Gullit had said that none of the pressure of the job would ever get to him, that he thrived on pressure. 'What would really upset me,' he told a Dutch magazine, 'is if I read something in the tabloids which was really very private. I would think that there was someone in my surroundings who was gossiping.'

Until he had his leg put in plaster after the Derby game, Gullit had, in any case, contrived a method of escaping from all pressures for an hour a day after training, seeking the solitude and sanctuary of an hour in the massage room. The aches and pains that he had not felt in his younger days needed some heavy kneading from the physio, every extra minute he was on the table acting as a reminder that his playing days were numbered.

Stiffness after training would affect the way he walked, stiff-legged, perhaps accentuated by Gullit as a joke: no longer The Man, now he was The Old Man. He did not feel pressure of nerves during games, either, he said. 'I do not watch as a supporter, I watch how our players behave during the game. I don't follow the ball, I follow their movements, I look to see if the team is in the right shape.'

At the much diminished Fratton Park, Gullit would have liked what he saw. Portsmouth's ground, which had once held more than 50,000 in their post-war, halcyon years, had a capacity of just 15,000 for this FA Cup quarter-final, woefully inadequate for the event. Chelsea's meagre allocation of 2,000 tickets had sold out in less than 90 minutes, and the pressure on space in Fratton Park that Sunday afternoon was such that Peter Osgood, 'The King', mixed with his subjects – like all the other Chelsea fans, he had to be accommodated in the away supporters' enclosure, there being no VIP seat for him in the directors' box alongside another former 1960s star of Stamford Bridge, Terry Venables, now the owner of the south coast side.

If their ground was unable to cope with the event, so Portsmouth's team, too, proved to have serious short-comings. Only a mist which rolled in off the Solent in the second half presented anything like a threat to Chelsea – that poor visibility might see a game all but won abandoned before the 90 minutes had been played. Chelsea showed the difference in class between a Premiership side and a First Division team which had been enjoying recent good form, being unbeaten in nine games. Chelsea ended the sequence.

After the expected, early onslaught of blood and guts from the home side, Chelsea started to weave together their passes. The first goal came when a 30-yard through ball from Frank Leboeuf found Mark Hughes on the edge of the area. He let it bounce up and then hit a thumping, dipping volley into the far corner. It was such a copybook strike that one of the television football shows soon adopted pictures of it, from behind the goal with the ball curving and swerving towards the camera, in their opening credits.

From then on, it was not a question of whether Chelsea would win, but by how many. Even Steve Clarke, who had not scored for Chelsea in five years, nearly got in on the act, his header from a Zola free-kick just before the interval being only half-stopped by Alan Knight, the Portsmouth goalkeeper. Clarke had managed to steal in, unmarked, as the Portsmouth defence prepared themselves for a Zola shot. But it was Dennis Wise who ultimately denied Clarke the score, because he leapt in to get the final touch on the ball.

The second half often saw Portsmouth over-committed to attack, and ten minutes in, a slip by a Portsmouth defender on the half way line allowed Hughes to break free down the left. He squared it to the edge of the box to di Matteo, who in turn pushed it to an unmarked Zola around the penalty spot. Game over.

It was in the 70th minute that Frode Grodas made his first save of the game, but as Chelsea eased up somewhat, so Portsmouth produced a couple of chances, one resulting in a goal with seven minutes left to play. Chelsea upped their tempo once more, and Knight came to Portsmouth's rescue more than once, as Burley and Paul Hughes came close and Zola hit a post. It was Wise who scored the final, fourth goal. Chelsea were through to their third FA Cup semi-final in four years.

Chapter 17

'This has got 0–0 written all over it,' said one would-be pundit in the stands after 30 minutes of the game. As the possibility of a Wembley final had begun to hove into view, so Chelsea's league form had become less inspired, almost noticeably distracted. The quarter-final victory had been followed by a midweek defeat at West Ham, the odd goal in five being conceded (again) in the final moments of the match. Now, after half-an-hour at Stamford Bridge, it was Sunderland who looked to be getting on top.

One sporting truism is that football is a game of opinions. What happened in the next hour's play, though, ought to have been enough to convince the opinionated supporter who had given up hope of any goals that in future, he should keep his opinions to himself.

First, he was silenced by Dan Petrescu, as the Romanian got into the Sunderland area, stepped over the ball to create some space, turned, crossed and Zola hit the volley where it would hurt most – the back of the net. Two minutes later, and Zola provided the cross for Frank Sinclair to score. With a third goal coming from Petrescu, after Lionel Perez in the Sunderland goal had failed to hold on to a shot from Zola, within ten minutes of the re-start, and Chelsea seemed to be cruising.

But being Chelsea, ever the enigmas, there is always scope for defensive disarray. 'We're totally in control one moment,' Gullit acknowledged, 'and then we're even. It's the way we give goals away.' Sunderland, from being out of the game at 3–0, were back fighting after half-time, at 3–2.

Mark Hughes, though, was the man to put a steady hand on the tiller, as he got Chelsea's fourth. Sunderland were routed with another two goals in the closing minutes, Vialli, the substitute, helping with both. But Chelsea, without Leboeuf at the back, had again looked vulnerable, and the prospect of another aerial bombardment from Wimbledon, Chelsea's FA Cup semi-final opponents, did not inspire confidence.

Off the field, there was also cause for concern, as the situation with

Vialli appeared to be worsening. Nothing, it appeared, could he do to regain a regular starting place in the Chelsea line-up. The man who had scored the winner at Old Trafford, who had scored two of the goals to knock Liverpool out of the Cup, seemed to be an unwanted adjunct to Gullit's squad.

He scored in the defeat at West Ham, yet was dropped to the bench again for the game against Sunderland. There, he came on with six minutes of the game remaining, and helped to create two goals, one an unselfish lay-off for Hughes, just when one might have considered that his own professional self-preservation might have demanded that the Italian would go for goal himself. The following Wednesday, at a somewhat dull, workmanlike home win over Southampton, and the biggest cheers of the night seemed to be reserved for the supersub as he warmed up along the touchline – 'Vi-alli! Vi-alli! Vi-alli!' Again, he was denied even the chance of a late call-up, to charge at the tremulous Southampton defence. Still, thousands lingered behind in the stands after the game, just to watch Vialli, as the Italian put himself through his paces, sprinting across the pitch, working up sufficient sweat to at least make it worth his while getting in the shower after another game where he had been surplus to Gullit's requirements.

All the time this went on, and Vialli the supersub risked becoming regarded as a superflop, the player on £20,000-plus a week wages who only ever sat on the bench. Even Gullit let slip that he regarded his star signing as a 'jinx', that the side was unable to win with him in the starting XI. 'Sometimes,' Vialli said, trying his best to disguise his obvious frustrations, 'I don't know what's happening between me and the manager. Gullit doesn't speak to the players very much. I know as a professional player I must work hard in training and then the manager makes his decision.

'I'm trying my best to remain calm and then at the end of the season I'll decide what to do. Gullit has called me a loser and a jinx. I cannot have lack of respect from a manager to a player. But even after the way I have been treated by Gullit, I could not walk out. I couldn't do that. The fans have been great to me and the other players love me.'

Such statements had all the appearances of irreconcilable differences between Vialli and Gullit, and in any struggle with the player-manager, there seemed likely to be only one winner, and it would not be the Italian. Perhaps it was because Vialli was still unsure of his command of English, which had improved rapidly thanks to ten hours of lessons every week, but his soft-spokenness and politeness was at odds with the usual behaviour of a professional footballer, and certainly one with the superstar reputation that he had arrived with in London. Vialli had none of the brashness or shallowness associated with so many of his fellow professionals; if anything, he came over as gentle, even shy, certainly reluctant to force his case.

It was around this time that reports started appearing about Vialli having breakfast meetings with Graeme Souness, the manager at Southampton. In his playing days at Sampdoria in the early 1980s, Souness used to have his boots cleaned for him by a young Italian pro called Gianluca. The breakfast report was denied, the asking price for 32-year-old Vialli – around £3 million – in any case well out of the reach of struggling Southampton. It also seemed unlikely that Vialli would accept a drop in wages with the drop in status that such a move would entail, for his salary at Chelsea was more than double that of Southampton's highest-paid player, Matthew Le Tissier.

Football insiders who knew both Gullit and Vialli sensed that there was something wrong between the two men. When Chelsea had played against Manchester United in February, the match had been beamed around Europe, and watching the game in Madrid was Fabio Capello, one of Gullit's former managers at Milan (although by no means a bosom pal), who was now in charge of Spain's champions-elect, Real Madrid. As United got the upper hand in the second half, Capello could hardly believe what he was witnessing when Gullit brought himself on as substitute, while Vialli sat, stock still, a sad figure on the bench. 'How arrogant of Gullit to put himself on up front and leave Vialli on the bench when everyone knows he's finished as a player. He didn't get anywhere near the ball.'

Increasingly, Gullit's press conferences, before and after every game, were becoming dominated by talk of Vialli – Would he play? Why would he not start? Would he be sold? Had there been a row? Rarely were the answers enlightening, Gullit seemingly bored with the entire topic, always sticking to his line that all the players in the squad had been asked what playing formation they preferred, that they had opted for two up front, and that therefore he could only accommodate Zola and Hughes at the beginning of each game. 'I cannot talk of Vialli all the time,' Gullit uttered, his impatience with the constant probing beginning to show.

Some suggested that Gullit's treatment of Vialli was something of a reaction to earlier observations that he favoured foreign players ahead of Britons. By sidelining such a star, Gullit was demonstrating his international even-handedness. Another (outlandish) suggestion was that, in some way, Gullit was envious of Vialli's popularity with the crowd, worried by sales reports from Chelsea Sportsland that Vialli's Number 9 shirt was out-selling his own Number 4. The most obvious explanation, though, was out there on the pitch every time Chelsea played: the Zola–Hughes combination was as delightful and as potent as you could wish to see, contributing more than a goal a game since they first played alongside one another in December. If it ain't broke . . .

Gullit would say later that his jinx jibe had been a deliberate attempt to get his player wound-up. 'Sometimes you have to try confrontation,' Gullit explained. 'The good players always react in the way you want them to. They get angry because they are proud, and they want to show everything they have.' Which would have been fine in Vialli's case, except he never seemed to get a chance to vent his anger, to show what he could do. The club sought to dismiss the speculation by going to the extraordinary lengths of publishing a prominent statement in one of the match programmes. The article stressed that Vialli had just moved into his new London home, a £100,000-a-year flat in elegant and exclusive Eaton Square, one of the flashiest addresses in the capital. Just up the road from Buckingham Palace, Vialli could number former prime minister, Margaret Thatcher, or Britain's richest man, the Duke of Westminster, among his neighbours. 'I want to stay here,' Vialli told the official Chelsea programme, denouncing the press reports as 'rubbish'. 'I want to win something with Chelsea and become a Chelsea legend.'

Yet the only thing Vialli was becoming legendary for was the expense of his goals – 11 at a rough cost of £90,000 each. It was all enough to prompt further questioning – was there really some personal animus between player and manager?

After the Southampton match, Vialli was given his chance, at Middlesbrough, while Mark Hughes rested a strained groin muscle, at least for half the match. One piece of brilliance from 'Boro's Brazilian midfielder, Juninho, settled that game, and Chelsea dropped out of the top five in the Premiership. Vialli had appeared out of touch, perhaps what you might expect of a man who had started just two games in the previous four months. Vialli may still have been Chelsea's leading goalscorer, but the man once described as *l'uomo simbolo del calcio Italiano*' – the living embodiment of Italian football – and a man who was used to wearing the very best designer-label fashions, was fast tiring of wearing his new label, that of failure and scapegoat.

In the previous six weeks, Chelsea had played midweek as well as on weekends. It had taken its toll in the Chelsea dressing room. The club's physio team was working overtime just to patch up players and send them back out into the fray. Battered, bruised and tired, the players would line up on Monday mornings in the corridor outside the massage room at Harlington, waiting for treatment or a rub down. Four of the Chelsea back-room staff having been trained as masseurs usually meant that most players could get treated quickly enough, but such was the demand for treatment by the middle of March that, at four o'clock on the Monday after the Sunderland match, Kevin Hitchcock was still there, having his shoulder manipulated by Mike Banks.

Such a crowded programme of matches also meant that the opportunity for full squad training sessions were becoming limited. Fitness now depended as much on getting sufficient rest as on exercise. Some players had enforced rest periods, though, as they were suspended after accumulating too many disciplinary points. The nadir came with the much-awaited visit to Stamford Bridge of Arsenal. In addition to the long sick list, Chelsea had di Matteo, Mark Hughes, Sinclair and Wise all suspended. At least it meant that Vialli got a game, and there would be a Chelsea debut for Paul Parker. The former England, Queens Park Rangers and Manchester United defender had been without a regular job since being released from Old Trafford, and had been playing on weekly contracts at a series of clubs. With Chelsea's squad stretched beyond its reach, it seemed Parker might offer an experienced stop-gap until the end of the season.

The Arsenal game had an 11.15 a.m. kick-off, to enable Sky to televise the match ahead of that afternoon's Grand National at Aintree. By the end of the match, most of the Chelsea players probably wished they could have rolled over in bed that morning and given it a miss altogether.

Gullit could field only a makeshift team. Craig Burley, only just back from injury, and youngsters Paul Hughes and Jody Morris formed an untried partnership in the centre of midfield. On the bench were four other youth team products – Andy Myers the most experienced at 23, having made his first-team debut seven years before. But alongside him that day were two teenagers, Mark Nicholls and Neil Clement, both of whom had played in the first team already this season, but never before in a side so inexperienced as this. The fourth outfield substitute was 22-year-old defender Danny Granville, signed from Cambridge in March for £300,000, and yet to venture into the Premiership.

Graham Rix, the coach who had guided the youngsters through the youth team in previous seasons, must have felt some pride and trepidation as he saw them take the field that day against his old club. All of them had been great players for their school, county and district sides, but their apprenticeship at Chelsea had been tough. Rix had made sure it was tough. On the training pitch, he would strike a chord somewhere between an army sergeant major and Brian Clough.

In the old National Service days, Britain's youth were introduced to rifles, and told to love them and cherish them like their closest friend. Clough was notorious for the brevity of his pre-game pep talks: sometimes, he would place a ball in the middle of the Forest changing room and extol his players to 'Love that ball'. Rix had obviously been to the same management school: 'That ball's got to be your best mate,' he would shout across at his charges as they practised their skills. 'If it isn't, it could become your worst enemy.'

The kids would spend as much time scrubbing toilets and boots as they would practising banana-bending free-kicks. 'Every single boy who walks through that door thinks they're gonna make it,' Rix said, knowing the whole story, the hard truth. After two years of hard slog, six days a week, doing all the menial, skivvying tasks around Stamford Bridge and at the training ground, and all for £37 a week from the government's YTS scheme, of the normal annual intake of 13 youth players, only three would be offered professional terms at Chelsea. The rest would be left to fend for themselves, drifting perhaps into semi-professional football, getting a 'normal' job elsewhere, or, if they were lucky, getting a professional contract with a lower league club. Chris Waddle, famously, was rejected when he was a youngster as not being good enough, and was only 'discovered' when playing non-league football on Saturdays while working in a sausage factory Monday to Fridays. So it was possible to fight back, but rare. Very rare.

Rix knew how important 'making it' was to all his young players. That was why it was so difficult. 'It's tough. It's a man's world, a bloody tough world,' Rix said, reflecting back to his own time 20 years earlier when he was a trainee at Highbury. 'You lose a bit of your childhood.' Now, against Arsenal, the boys would be asked to do a man's job.

Jody Morris had come through all the shitty jobs of the YTS, his footballing skills setting him apart despite his small stature, and he had been signed as a professional with Chelsea. He still had to polish boots, but now there was a chance that his boots would be cleaned for him. Born and bred up the road from Stamford Bridge, in Hammersmith, Morris was as local a player as you could wish for, almost a rarity among the cosmopolitan millionaire players he now trained and played alongside. He was living out his dream.

Morris had made his debut as a substitute in the 5–0 drubbing of Middlesbrough the previous season, and had it not been for injury earlier in the new season, by March he might have been more established as part of the first-team squad than he was. Nonetheless, at 18, he had been one of the few outstanding performers for the England under-21 side that had played against Switzerland at Swindon in the week before the Arsenal league game. He was progressing. His dreams were still intact. 'I want to be the best. Captain England. Do everything you can in the game. Be a manager after. Do the lot.'

For Morris, football was an escape to a better way of life. They used to say that boxing was a way for East End boys, or boys from the Bronx, to fight their way out of the ghetto. Morris saw football as his ticket away from crime and drugs scenes of west London. 'All my mates from school were doing drugs and thieving. They're good at heart but had nothing else. My mum and dad were really worried about me.

'My mates have just gone the wrong way – who knows what could have happened to me. Instead, I've had a little taste with Chelsea. And I want more.'

Paul Hughes, meanwhile, from the same London borough but a couple of years Morris's senior, had taken a different route into the club. There is a tale of one Youth Training Scheme lad who, after his first day at Chelsea, dragged his weary body home that evening. He had been expecting to be playing football all day, knocking off at four o'clock, perhaps even earlier. But when he was eventually dismissed at six o'clock in the evening, he smelt more of Jif than embrocation. He had not even seen a football. 'What did you do today?' his mother asked. 'I've just cleaned loos all day,' came the bewildered reply. 'Son, I've been doing that for years.'

Paul Hughes had been on Chelsea's books from the age of 11. He graduated to the England schoolboy international side, all the while continuing his education to A-level standard, and so he avoided at least some of the YTS menial duties, at least some of the time, because he only had to report to Chelsea a couple of days each week. Although older than Morris, Hughes's progress into the first team, and his debut, had come much later. Persistent, inexplicable injuries, had seen him on the brink of leaving the club. But Chelsea had seen enough of a footballer in Hughes, though, to be patient. Three times, they gave him a one-year contract, ready to wait until he was fit. The management at Chelsea obviously rated his midfield talents very highly, because despite his injuries and growing pains, they kept faith with Hughes.

'When I was due to sign professional forms, I had shin splints and could not play. But Glenn Hoddle still gave me a one-year contract,' he said. A year later, and ankle ligament problems might have jeopardised Hughes's career. But again, the club stood by him, and gave him another one-year contract. 'Then came a serious pelvic problem, and they still gave me a one-year deal. That drove me on. I just got on with it because the club had faith in me.'

When, in January, he made his first-team debut when he came on in the second half of the Premier League home game against Derby, he showed exactly why Rix had had such faith in his ability, with a surging run from midfield, a sweet couple of exchange passes and a crashing shot to seal a victory. 'One minute you're on the bench, the next minute you're coming on for Wisey, and it just rolls on from there,' Hughes said.

His goal on his debut was one that he and the Stamford Bridge crowd would always remember. 'Roberto played the ball to me. I was looking to play a one-two with him. When he played the ball to me I thought he was going to run on, so I pointed to where I wanted him to go but he peeled off again. He'd knocked a good ball through to me and then Hughesy made it easy. He peeled off again and said, "One-two," so I Looked up and just played one with him, and he played another good ball. At that time I thought the keeper was going to come for it, but he seemed to stop and I just passed it into the net.'

Yet Paul Hughes's football career had been so close to being still-born, as the lad was crippled by injury. While under Hoddle, Chelsea had sometimes used a faith healer for their long-term injured; under Gullit, Hughes's back problem was solved by a Dutch sports psychiatrist who treated his jaw . . .

Ruud Gullit trusts Ted Troost so absolutely, he lets him read his private diaries. Troost had assisted Gullit for the previous 16 years of his career, ever since he had been at PSV. When Eindhoven won the European Cup in 1988, more than half their squad were being treated by Troost. When Gullit moved on to Italy, it had been Troost who had managed to keep him playing, when many experts, football and medical, said that his knee injuries were career-ending.

Trained as a masseur and physiotherapist, Troost's holistic approach saw him branch into sports psychiatry, able to work on the mind as well as the body. Above all, Troost seemed to have an ability to recognise, diagnose and treat problems which had left conventional medicine baffled. Gullit's Milan and Holland team mate, Marco van Basten, described his own relationship with Troost as like a Formula 1 car and its chief mechanic. 'Without the mechanic, the car won't drive and will not win races,' van Basten said. 'Only Ted knows how to tune the car and its engine to perfection.'

Gullit described Troost as 'more than a friend. We have more than just a bond.' So it was natural that by the end of Gullit's first season in charge at Chelsea, Troost, his *eminence gris*, would be seen seated on the bench at Stamford Bridge during practice matches. He had already been consulted to solve some of Chelsea's injury problems, Paul Hughes's pelvic injury among them. 'I'd seen every specialist in this country and they could not find a solution,' Hughes said. The player was even sent to see a specialist in Italy, but there seemed to be no cure. Hughes was in pain just when he walked. Playing seemed out of the question. Once he was called in, Troost looked the young player over, then he approached Hughes. 'He got hold of my teeth and yanked my jaw. It gave a click and after the initial shock, the pain disappeared.'

Troost had established that the pain was due to Hughes's deportment, the way he carried his head, and its effect on his spine. 'It was a real breakthrough,' Gullit said, 'because he was a good player who could not play.'

Hughes still had to win his place in the first team, though, not an easy task since Gullit, the man who picks the teams, did not watch the reserve games, relying instead on his staff's reports. When the call-up came on the day before the match against Derby, Bob Orsborn, the club's kit man, had to get a new shirt, with a new number and Hughes's name on the back, made up at late notice.

After that, Hughes became a regular bench-warmer, and even got a run where he started in five games leading up to the Arsenal match. Nothing, though, prepared him for the Grade A football lesson which title-challengers Arsenal would dish out that morning, as Ian Wright, Dennis Bergkamp and David Platt exploited the inexperience, naïvety even, of the Chelsea's kids and crocks. Zola looked below par, Vialli was never in the game. Midway through the second half and with the Chelsea crowd silenced by the lacklustre spectacle, the Arsenal supporters began mocking them, parodying *The Blue Flag* by chanting, 'No silverware/ No silverware/ You've still not won/ No silverware.' Trust Arsenal to come up with a double negative.

Gullit, normally the calm, collected manager, this time exploded in the dressing room after the game. 'Today was an opportunity for players to show themselves,' Gullit said, for once letting his anger show. 'I thought that there were players who would show some more passion, some more skills. Jody Morris and Danny Granville, at least they showed what I expected. At least if you can't cope with skill, then I want to see them battling for something. The game today was important for us to get into Europe, and I didn't see that today. The players have to be ashamed.' The defeat meant that Chelsea dropped two places down the Premier League table, to seventh, four points off the pace for a UEFA Cup place. Increasingly, it was beginning to look as if Chelsea's hopes of qualifying for Europe the following season depended entirely on the FA Cup. All or nothing.

But before the semi-final showdown, Chelsea had yet another midweek league game to endure, at Coventry. Nothing went right, from the moment in the tunnel before the game when the referee, Dermot Gallagher, delayed the kick-off by ordering Chelsea to change out of their blue shirts, which he adjudged clashed with Coventry's kit. Instead, Chelsea were forced to play in Coventry's away strip, red and black checks.

It has been suggested that, had the manager of Coventry City been hired to skipper the maiden voyage of the *Titanic*, she would not have gone down. So although Paul Hughes scored just before half-time, the home side, inspired by Gordon Strachan, battled back. Muscular, pragmatic football swept Chelsea aside, as their defence conceded another three goals. It was the third league defeat on the trot, the 11th time in the season that Chelsea had taken the lead in a game but not won it. With the brutality and aerial power of Wimbledon waiting for Chelsea at Highbury just four days away, nerves were beginning to fray.

Steve Clarke ripped into his team-mates in the dressing room. 'I got a little bit carried away,' was about as much as he would admit to. 'I said a few things, but there were a few things that had to be said.' As the senior pro, Clarke had felt that maybe his last chance of honours in the English game had passed him by when, three years earlier, Chelsea had been trounced in the final at Wembley, and then had lost again in the previous year's semi-final. Yet now, with a better team, and with a better chance of glory, he was determined that his team would not throw this chance away. 'It was another second-half collapse, it was a poor performance again, and we're now going into the semi-final on the back of a terrible run. I don't think that's good enough. With the players we've got, the performances haven't been good enough.'

The obvious fear was that Wimbledon, riding high on a successful season, would storm into Chelsea just as they had at Stamford Bridge back in October. The force and determination of Wimbledon's 'Crazy Gang' would knock the highly paid Chelsea stylists off their lofty perch. Gullit, in his first season as a manager, was staring across the precipice: what could he do to transform his side's fortunes?

Chapter 18

Kipling was writing about India, and polo. 'It was then that Powell, a quiet and level-headed man as a rule, became inspired and played a stroke that sometimes comes off successfully on a quiet afternoon of long practice. He took his stick in both hands, and standing up in his stirrups, swiped at the ball in the air, Munipore fashion. There was one second of paralysed astonishment, and then all four sides of the ground went up in a yell of applause and delight as the ball flew true.' Another time, another place: although Kipling had been writing about polo, he might have been writing about football, and little Franco Zola, and the one second of paralysed astonishment that swept about the verdant fields of Highbury as the Italian took the FA Cup semi-final game in both hands and swiped it into Chelsea's pocket.

It was almost as if he had chosen the perfect stage for the most daringly outrageous piece of skill he had contemplated all year. A bright, spring day in London, a live television audience numbering millions, and Zola chose to perform this right at the foot of the famous North Bank, the massive stand, steeply raked, full of thousands of Chelsea fans. When Zola hit the ball past Neil Sullivan into the Wimbledon goal, after a second of paralysed astonishment, the floor of the North Bank shook, such was the thunderousness of the applause and delight.

Zola's pantheon of great goals for Chelsea was already impressive: the Dicks disembowelling and making Schmeichel look like a schmuck had been the choice examples thus far. But this goal, for its significance and the pressure of the occasion as much as the sheer, unmitigated genius of its execution, was surely the pick of them all. The facts, which do the effort little justice, are as follows.

In front of 32,674 people at the neutral venue of Highbury, Chelsea were playing against Wimbledon in the semi-final of the 116th Football Association Challenge Cup competition. Kick-off was midday: high noon at Highbury. A great deal was at stake. By this stage of the season, it was all or nothing.

Accordingly, the opening exchanges, by both sides, had been a little tentative, the standard of the play somewhat subdued. But as the first-half wore on, so Chelsea began to assert themselves, their style of football. Wimbledon's sometimes direct, robust approach was being circumvented. Just before half-time, Chelsea were rewarded with a goal. Leboeuf's 50-yard crossfield ball opened up play. Zola met the pass, stunned the ball, then flicked on to Dennis Wise, who was over-lapping. Wise sent in a telling cross, which Craig Burley dived in at with total commitment. Kimble nearly cleared it, but the ball fell to Mark Hughes, who managed to control it and volleyed home from short range. But this was Chelsea, and this was the FA Cup semi-final. They say that there is nothing worse than being a runner at the Olympic Games and finishing fourth, one place out of the medals. So near, and yet so far: you never get to savour a moment of glory, standing on the podium, watching your country's flag being hoisted up the mast in front of you. For a tennis player to be knocked out in the semi-final at Wimbledon, just one match away from the Centre Court, is supposed to be the most gut-wrenchingly awful moment of a playing career. It is much the same to be on the losing side in an FA Cup semi-final. You do not even get the chance of a day in the sun at Wembley. Most of the Chelsea side knew too well what that felt like, because they had been through all that just 12 months earlier, losing to Manchester United at Villa Park. They had been ahead in that game, too.

So after 15 minutes or so of the second half, there was still a great deal of edginess about the Chelsea ranks, a fear of the known. Then Steve Clarke got the ball on the left-hand side of the Chelsea defence, passed to Wise, who found di Matteo. Di Matteo looked up, and saw Zola making a run, from right to left, across the front of Wimbledon's 18-yard area, shadowed closely by one of their best defenders, Dean Blackwell.

What happened next is difficult to describe, because no one knows, will ever know, quite what happened. It has been watched and watched again, perhaps hundreds of times, wearing the video tape of the game quite thin, but still producing nothing more than bafflement and bewilderment, rather than explanation. Like a prism which so brilliantly collects and splits up a beam of light, Zola turned the ordinary into the extraordinary, but no one quite knew how.

As the ball came in to him, Zola met it at pace, but his first contact did not seem to be as true as had come to be expected. He seemed to step over the ball, pass it by. Meanwhile, Blackwell and another Wimbledon defender, plus Sullivan, their goalkeeper, and about 5,000 Chelsea fans, rising as one from their seats in the North Bank, were still going with the initial direction of the ball across the face of the goal.

Was what followed instinct, or was it a sublimely conscious application of skill? With a conjurer's sleight of hand, Zola turned about and started going back to the right-side of the pitch, while Blackwell and the North Bank's 5,000 others continued going in the other direction. By the time the defenders had reacted and turned back, the Chelsea player had half-a-yard of space, no more. It was all he needed. Sullivan was out of position in goal, and could not reach the Italian's shot as it skidded low into the bottom corner. *That* was the moment Chelsea won the FA Cup semi-final. The statistic of a score was welcome enough, but like a bull-fighter in the ring making the final thrust with his sword, Zola, with his pivot and snapshot, had mortally wounded Wimbledon. They would charge no more that afternoon. As they stood around, waiting for the game to re-start, you could see them visibly deflating, like sad, sorry balloons three days after the party had finished.

Mark Hughes had witnessed Zola's goal at close hand, seen what his team-mate had done to Blackwell. 'He's given the lad twisted blood,' said Hughes.

Hughes was to score again, in the last minute of the game, exploiting a defender's mis-header from Frode Grodas's kick, showing that Chelsea could go down Route One when the opportunity presented itself. But they were playing against a well-beaten team by then. If anything, it may be that Wimbledon were defeated even before the game began. For before the kick-off, Ruud Gullit, the player-manager wedded to his 3-5-2 system, changed Chelsea's playing formation.

Great generals, it is said, always choose where to fight their battles. For the FA Cup semi-final, Gullit, like some latterday Napoleon, chose to call up his Old Guard. Two days before the game, Gullit had staged a secret training session, behind closed doors at Stamford Bridge. The entire first-team squad was there, with the exceptions of Dan Petrescu, Clarke and Eddie Newton, who were all receiving treatment for injuries. It was here that Gullit rehearsed his battle plan.

He organised his troops into 4-4-2, with Erland Johnsen alongside Frank Leboeuf at the heart of the first-team defence. The defeat in the league match against Wimbledon almost six months before obviously worried Gullit, and he was determined to find a way to cope with the aerial bombardment against which Chelsea had proven to be so vulnerable, and which Wimbledon were certain to launch at them on the Sunday.

In midfield, Gullit's strategy was to have a diamond formation, with one player (he hoped Newton would be fit) just in front of his defence, closing down any space, denying the likes of Vinnie Jones the chance to make surging runs from deep. Wise, if fit after a three-match absence, and Burley would offer width on either flank, and just behind his two attackers, di Matteo would be Chelsea's creative force. 'I saw them playing Newcastle, and I knew exactly where I could do the damage,' said Gullit.

By the time, barely an hour before the kick-off, Chelsea's team sheet was handed over to Joe Kinnear, it was too late for the Wimbledon manager to do anything, make any adjustments. When he looked at the team sheet, Kinnear must have asked himself what was going on: no Scott Minto, no Dan Petrescu, Gullit had clipped his own wing-backs. Whether it was the merits of Chelsea's different formation, or, more simply, the fact that it was something which Wimbledon had never anticipated, Gullit's plan worked. Wimbledon were unprepared for this, they did not know how to cope, how to break down Chelsea's more solid defence. Gullit was, outwardly, at least, relaxed about it all, watching the entire game from the dug-out with his feet up, as if he was watching a sleepy Sunday afternoon movie.

Johnsen, playing what was to be his last big match for Chelsea, was the rock. 'Erland and the lads at the back were magnificent today,' Mark Hughes said, 'Everything they threw in the box, they got their heads on it. I don't think they were expecting Erland to play, and he's come in and done a great job. We never looked in trouble.' Even Grodas, the goalkeeper criticised for his handling at high balls and crosses, had managed to snaffle the ball off the heads of Vinnie Jones and Efan Ekoku when the occasion demanded.

Gerald Ashby, the match referee, played his role, too. Perhaps he anticipated that Wimbledon would attempt the sort of physically intimidating play that had seen Chelsea crumble at the Bridge in October, because when Ardley crashed into Steve Clarke within the first ten seconds, Ashby showed a willingness to use his yellow card which was to temper the Wimbledon approach for the remaining 89 minutes and 50 seconds of the game.

When Ashby blew his whistle for the final time in that game, there came a release of tension, a display of joy, and simple triumphalism from Gullit's men. They had done it, they had not let themselves down. Chelsea, like this, were unbeatable. *We* were unbeatable. There was a sense that it had not just been the 11 on the pitch that had won this game, there was a broader feeling, complete, of togetherness. The Chelsea players did not swap their shirts with the other side, this time they swung them about their heads and launched them into the stands where their own supporters were enjoying the occasion. Everyone hugged everyone else, symbolically even Gullit and Vialli (sub, again), embraced in the middle of the Highbury pitch.

There had been a unity of purpose in Chelsea's play that had rarely been seen before, a unity that seemed to embrace the Chelsea fans. As the celebrations continued on into the changing rooms and out on to the streets of north London, Grodas managed to find a window through which he levered himself, half naked. He then sprayed a cascade of champagne over the hundreds of singing and dancing Chelsea fans outside, the liquid catching the sunlight like specks of stardust.

At the centre of it all were Clarke and Wise, the senior pros. Dennis, his team shirt discarded, wearing his 'Cheer up Luca' vest but with his captain armband still wrapped high up by his shoulder, could not contain himself. The two players had roomed together the night before, the team staying at a hotel. 'Rats are supposed to be nocturnal,' Clarke said, 'and last night every time I turned over in bed I had a rat scuttling about the room. Wisey just couldn't sleep. He must have been nervous.' In the match, Wise had been at the centre of most things, putting in an outstanding performance. 'I hadn't played for two weeks,' he said, 'and the good thing was I was fresh.'

And amid all this, the crowd had begun singing, endlessly, 'Matthew Harding's blue and white army'. Gone, but far from forgotten.

How Harding would have revelled in that day, the epitome of all that he and every other Chelsea supporter had longed for. Already, this cup run felt different from 1994, when only Luton had had to be disposed of in the semi-final. That match had been played at Wembley, accommodating the ticket demands of both clubs. Ken Bates had argued that the 1997 semi, too, ought to have been played at Wembley, such would be the demand for tickets. The FA instead opted for Highbury, a stadium with half the capacity of Wembley. Yet even then Wimbledon had failed to sell the whole of their allocation. Like Chelsea, they had been given 15,000 tickets, which may have been a little optimistic on their part, since their average home gate at Selhurst Park that season had been 12,000, a figure vastly boosted by their only capacity match on the opening day, when they had been home to Manchester United.

In fairness to Wimbledon, they had tried to return thousands of their unsold semi-final tickets, but the FA refused to re-issue these to Chelsea because it would ruin their crowd segregation plans. The net result was that thousands of Chelsea supporters had been left ticket-less for the game. Those that had been fortunate enough to be at Highbury had faced anything up to eight hours in a queue at Stamford Bridge two weeks before. Nearly 30 years after they had managed to put a man on the moon, at a time when technology had advanced so far that telephones were so small and mobile that they could fit in a pocket yet communicate with the world, and as the developed world moved ever-closer to the cash-less economy, Chelsea Football Club still required people to queue up to buy tickets.

Queuing at Chelsea is one of those things of legend which can only be believed when seen. In part, it is the result of stricter security requirements – important matches, and away games, require the submission of a voucher from a membership book, as well as cash or a cheque. Credit cards, even in 1997, and even after the club had launched its own branded credit card with the Co-operative Bank, were unacceptable for ticket purchases.

Strange things would happen in the ticket queue at Chelsea. Old friends would meet up, new friendships would be struck, life stories exchanged. A friend of mine told the tale of how, a couple of seasons before, he had turned up for a home game early, in order to buy a ticket for the next away match. The line for that day's game was already a lengthy one, so my friend, Paul, approached a steward to ask if there was a window open just for away match tickets. 'There ain't one mate. You'll have to queue with the rest of 'em,' was the reply. Nothing changed there, then.

With an hour until the kick-off, Paul was forced to stand in line with a bunch of latecomers. Forty minutes later, he neared the front to hear the box office manager announce that the only tickets left were restricted view in the lower North Stand. With that, there was a surge from the back of the queue, as those who had just spilled out of the Crossed Eyed Newt across the road began to panic. Amid this pandemonium came a voice of some salvation, as someone began offering a pair of tickets. Paul looked around, and saw what he thought was a Del Boy lookalike, a spiv in a flashy suit and dark Crombie overcoat, striding purposefully towards the front of the queue waving two tickets in the air. Somehow, this character had evaded the usually ultra-efficient stewards who patrol the ticket queue to prevent such dealings.

As the man got closer, Paul realised that, in fact, it was the socialist millionaire and philanthropist, Matthew Harding, the man who had recently come on to the board of directors at Chelsea and injected part of his massive fortune into the club. No wonder the stewards had let him pass. Now, he stopped just in front of Paul and asked two youngsters if they would like the two tickets. They answered unhesitatingly and in unison.

But, as they say on all the best television sports quiz shows, what happened next? Did Chelsea's famous benefactor say: (a) 'I know what it's like, I am a real fan just like you, I've got a couple of boys myself, the same age as you. Have these tickets on me lads and buy your mum a decent Christmas present'; or was it (b) 'Fifty quid'?

Yes, the answer was (b), leaving the two youngsters, who had come to the Bridge with a budget for much cheaper tickets, desperately trying to cobble together the required amount, which they handed over, a combination of crumpled fivers and a stack of coins. 'Thanks lads,' said Harding, 'enjoy the game.' And with that, one of Britain's richest men disappeared in the direction of the Directors' Box, leaving the two young fans wondering how they were going to get home after the match.

When tickets had gone on sale for the 1997 semi-final, the first people had started queuing at 8 a.m., when the ticket office was not due to open for another 12 hours. The Chelsea box office would work through the night, checking vouchers, passing over tickets. The queue had something of the queue for Wimbledon tennis tickets, with a smattering of the Blitz spirit, contributed to by frequent visits across the road to the Cross Eyed Newt or offerings from a local off-licence. What the atmosphere might have been like had the weather that spring evening been less kindly does not bear thinking about.

As the queue wound its way back past the East Stand and snaked around behind the Mathhew Harding Stand, building work was continuing on the three-star hotel that had risen up from where the old Shed terrace had once stood. It was all part of Ken Bates's masterplan, which had also seen the recent launch of a colour Chelsea magazine, an in-house radio station (with a signal so weak, Bates himself complained that he could not pick up the broadcast as he drove through Knightsbridge in his Bentley) and a special web site, bringing Chelsea into the computer age. Bates had been fond of saying that the hotel would guarantee the club's future financial stability. 'The club's at the heart of the West End,' Bates would say, 'just 15 minutes from Harrods'. As they stood, bored, well into their wait for tickets, one of the queuers looked up at the building work on what had inevitably been dubbed 'The Bates Motel', and wistfully announced to anyone nearby, 'I'd rather be 90 minutes from Wembley than 15 minutes from Harrods.'

On the same day that tickets for the semi-final went on sale, so a memorial service for the club's vice-chairman was held at the Queen Elizabeth II Conference Centre at Westminster. Perhaps typically of Matthew Harding, the event was organised by a public relations firm, and everyone left the event holding at least one bottle of 'Matthew Harding Celebration Ale', with a picture of Harding, smiling, raising his full pint glass in a toast, on the label.

The memorial's audience was drawn from all the aspects of Harding's life: the insurance business, politics and football. A selection of Chelsea players, past and present, were there, as were the likes of Lawrie McMenemy, Southampton's director of football, Sam Hammam, the

Wimbledon owner, commentators John Motson and Brian Moore. Even Tony Blair, the Labour party leader, managed to be at the memorial, taking time out to pay his respects to the millionaire donor to his party funds in the midst of the General Election campaign. One person who was not at the memorial, though, was Chelsea's chairman, Ken Bates.

Bates was away on business, though he later admitted that Steve Chalke, the priest who co-ordinated the service, had spent an hour with him, trying to persuade him to alter his plans. 'Why should I?' Bates reasoned, 'It would just be hypocritical.' With just one month of the season left to go, with just a month to go before the FA Cup final, old enmities within Chelsea were never far from the surface.

Chapter 19

A handful of people were milling around in the reception area, all with things to sell – leisure shirts, woolly gloves, flags. By one wall, there was even a mountain bike, decked out in Glasgow Rangers colours, but obviously another product up for offer as part of the new Chelsea range. Richard Milham, the new manager of the Chelsea Megastore due to be opened in the southern complex of Stamford Bridge later that summer, was holding court in his office with prospective suppliers.

Such work and preparations continue behind the scenes at the club regardless of what goes on out on the training pitch, or from 3 p.m. on a Saturday. Milham's business depended on the match results, for sure, but his business, and the revenue it might generate, could, would, ultimately affect the match results, too. In 1996, Manchester United's commercial operations had generated more than £18 million income for the club's coffers. Even so, in the world of football economics, the engine driving the business is always success on the pitch, and the match result at the end of this week would do a lot for the Chelsea Megastore.

For it was FA Cup final week. The league season had come to an end the previous weekend, Chelsea winning at Everton for their third victory in their last four games, enough to place sixth in the Premiership, but not enough for a place in European competition the following season. 'We have found it hard to focus on our Premiership fixtures,' Ruud Gullit would admit that the cup had become a distraction over the previous month, 'because the lads were choosing their suits and making the record. I have never known anything like it.' Now, the cup was the only possible route for Chelsea to qualify for lucrative European competitions the following season.

The night before, Newcastle United's 1997–98 new home strip was put on sale for the first time at their club shop. Geordies had queued all day ready for the store to open at midnight. The 'new' Newcastle shirts were '70s-style, round necked. They were for sale at '90s prices – £40 each – and the entire initial batch had been sold before nine o'clock that morning. Enthusiasm for such success got the merchants who had gathered in the Stamford Bridge reception area talking.

'You know what our best-selling shirt was last summer, during Euro '96? The 1966 England red shirt with the badge. Simple, classic, couldn't get enough of them,' said one, who was there to sell flags, but, sure, he could run up other products on demand. He believed in giving the punters what they want. 'The punters like the retro look – I got meself a plain blue, '70s-style shirt in the Fulham Road last week, the old Chelsea badge on it, with the FA Cup and 1997 next to it. Classic. Just a tenner, the punters were loving it.

'They never used to sell old Chelsea shirts here. At first, it was that northern firm who started selling old Chelsea shirts, but the Chelsea shop soon saw that, and now they sell them, too.'

As the conversation meandered on, one of the merchants, tired of shirt-talk, wandered over to the wall to examine more closely the polished brass plates which, like simple, cotton, round-necked blue shirts, were now just curiosities. The plaques were antiquities from another, more genteel age, earlier in the century, when members of the royal family and crowned heads of Europe used to visit Stamford Bridge to watch football, and the event was deemed sufficiently worthy of commemoration for posterity. The Duke of York, if the brass plates are anything to go by, was particularly keen on football at Chelsea.

Then, from one of the slow, cramped lifts to the side of the reception area, there emerged a kids' version of the mountain bike, closely followed by a grown man so small he might have been able to ride the bike comfortably. Terry Gibson, the former Wimbledon player, had already had his share of Milham's time. Behind the reception desk, a secretary looked up from her work – rubber-stamping autographs on to picture postcards of Dennis Wise. 'Give my best to Dennis and the lads for Saturday,' said Gibson to her as the shirt merchants took the lift for their chance to pitch.

Outside, a delivery van pulled up. It contained half-a-dozen cardboard boxes full of merchandise that was too precious to sell. These shirts would never be for sale. The Chelsea team's kit for the Cup final, different from the usual shirts in that it had a special motif commemorating Wembley 1997. 'We'll have to lay out the kit in the dressing room tonight,' said one of the staff. A vital check, to make sure everything is there, everything in order – not like the Spurs side that managed to play in the Cup final ten years earlier, all wearing different style shirts.

The Cup final shirts represented just another task for the busy front-of-office staff, alongside organising enough button-hole carnations to be delivered to the team hotel and to the club on Friday afternoon, and then making sure that the flowers would be kept in a fridge overnight. 'I'm not having just six carnations being sent over to Harlington on Saturday morning . . .' said one when told that some of the boot room staff would be travelling from the training ground. Her exasperation was beginning to show, just.

The phone rang again. It never stopped ringing all afternoon. 'How many goals has Vialli scored this season?' the receptionist repeats the question, only slightly indicating that she might just have better things to do. 'Nine in the league, two in the Cup so far. Pardon? Yes, well there is still one more game to go, you know, and we don't know what the team will be yet, do we?'

'How did you know that without looking it up?' one of her colleagues asked, surprised and a little amazed. 'Someone else asked me yesterday,' her colleague replied.

Never more than a hint of impatience crept into the voice of the receptionists. Between three of them, they changed over their tasks regularly, which probably helped. 'You want to know the date of the 1970 FA Cup final replay so you can win a bet? Just a moment, I'll look it up . . . 22 April, yeah, I thought so.'

One call was from a charity offering to give Dennis Wise a four-foot tall bear ('Yes, Dennis, four-foot tall. As big as you') for him to give to his niece, in return for a T-shirt signed by the team, which could later be auctioned. But most calls were from people who wanted to buy tickets for the FA Cup final, just four days away. It's amazing how many people believe that, for something such as the FA Cup final, you can just ring up in the week of the event and book your seat.

At least one seat in the Royal Box had been safely booked long ago. Ken Bates, after all, as well as being chairman at Chelsea, is a high-ranking Football Association official. Just after 5 p.m., he strode into the reception area, across the midnight blue carpet, towards the desk. He asked for the keys to his Bentley. It is said that, when his car was dented, Bates went to the showrooms in Mayfair and bought a new one. He paid cash. Although Bates had recently launched a Chelsea credit card, he is said never to resort to plastic himself. Now, he was concerned about his new car. 'I gave them to you this morning,' he said to the woman, who obviously had experienced this sort of post-lunch performance by the chairman before.

She said that she had returned them. 'Check in your jacket pocket,' she suggested. He did, and found the keys. Bates grinned, then turned to confront me. 'Who are you?' he demanded. He had obviously forgotten about our appointment, even though after my initial approaches, he had telephoned me personally to check out what the interview would be about, and to arrange the appointment. After an explanation from me, Bates said, 'I've just had lunch with ten of your colleagues from the press,' not so much as an apology for being late, not even offered as an explanation, more to show his disdain and dislike for journalists, and perhaps to illustrate and reinforce his own importance.

Once on the Mezzanine floor where his office is located, he turned left out of the lift, passing among a number of glass-walled cubicles that have a curious 'The Chelsea Style' logos in frosted glass sections on them, remnants from a previous attempt to launch Chelsea on the world as some sort of low-rent designer label. Colin Hutchinson occupied one of the cubicles, working quietly at his desk, not looking up, perhaps not wanting to catch the eye of the chairman.

Bates strode on purposefully to our left, pausing at desks en route to check in-trays for messages, acting all the time as if he owns the place, which, effectively, he does. 'Where's Jane?' he asked, not listening to the answer. 'Tell her I want her.'

For someone who distrusts so much of the press, Ken Bates has not been afraid of collecting his clippings and caricatures – two walls of his large working space are covered with framed cartoons and cuttings, most showing his bearded image in buccaneering mode, usually in some sort of confrontation. Looking around, the multi-million pound cheques that Bates was reputed to have framed and hung on those walls are no where to be seen. 'Harding did those,' he says when asked, 'and I got rid of 'em.' No place for sentimentality here, then.

His wide windows behind his desk look out over the building site that will soon be the South Stand. The Shed in the old days would never have afforded such a decent view. A small sideboard next to Bates's big, dark wood desk, is cluttered with a collection of what appear to be family photographs – children, grandchildren, perhaps – and one poorly photographed print (looking as if it had been taken on auntie's instamatic) of the old Chelsea offices. It seemed like an elegant, ivy-covered Edwardian building. Probably quite cramped, and certainly not in keeping with a massive, 21st century leisure and entertainment business that Chelsea had become. Noticing my interest in this photograph, Bates picked it up and said, 'That's where we used to have the offices. I had it knocked down.' Something else, like the football club, the old club badge, and any opponents, swept away by Ken Bates.

Bates sits on a dark green leather sofa, drinking weak herbal tea (no milk), which had been brought through by Jane, his assistant. She shows Bates a poster that had come free with that afternoon's *Evening Standard*, a photo-montage of a selection of Chelsea players, with Bates himself pictured at the centre of it all. 'How many have you got?' he asks. 'Three,' says Jane. 'Go out and get more,' he commands.

He did not sit back or relax for the whole of our hour-long talk. It was edge of the seat stuff, all the way, but less for what Bates had to say, more for the way he chose to tell it. Later in the week, as the journalists who had lunched with Bates had their accounts published as previews to the Cup final ('Bates building the Bridge for the Millennium', that sort of thing), it became clear that what I was getting from the chairman was a well-rehearsed version of the performance he had already given over lunch. Although the Bates interviews, mine and theirs, had been given completely separately, it was remarkable how the quotes, *bon mots* and expresssions that Bates came out with were virtually exactly the same. Clearly, the only thing Bates was really concerned with building on that afternoon was his own image.

Before I had been able to refer to my notebook for my first, tame question, a gentle loosener designed to break the ice, Bates leaned over the coffee table between us and said, commandingly pointing at my tape recorder, 'And before you start, you can turn that off, I'm not answering any questions about Harding.'

'But I'm writing a book about this season at Chelsea. Matthew Harding's death was an important event in that year, and I'm interested in your views.'

'I'm not answering any questions about Harding.' On another two occasions during the next hour, he leant across again and indicated that he wanted the tape machine switched off, before launching into an account, often colourful, never fond, of his battles with Harding; his view of Harding's morality (or lack of it); his views of Harding's finances. Unrecorded, but not unremembered. There were things that Bates said that could never be forgotten.

Clearly, he was suspicious of my motives for seeing him ('You're an opportunist, aren't you?' he said after another straight question to which he refused to give a straight answer. 'Aren't we all, Mr Bates?'). Bates was so cautious that his answers during what he considered to be the on-the-record portion of the interview – the bits when the tape recorder was whirring – were so anodyne as to be uninteresting, virtually worthless.

'Who's getting your vote for player of the year?' I asked, perfectly innocently, hoping to get Bates's impressions of the joys and successes of the team in the soon-to-be-ended season, perhaps a comment in praise of Zola, compliments about Mark Hughes, or a truly contrarian choice, justified with some insight unique to the chairman. But no. 'It's a private vote,' was Bates's less than illuminating reply.

He went on, like someone reciting the rosary, going through the chain of events that had led Chelsea all the way back down Wembley Way. Most of it had been well accounted for already. 'Glenn took us from being a traditional run-of-the-mill English club to one with a continental outlook and style . . .We are now moving towards being a world-class club. Appointing Ruud was not a risk . . .

'Manchester United have achieved their objective but at the end of the day they are still on an industrial estate in a run-down suburb. Arsenal and Tottenham are good big clubs but in suburban areas. We are in the West End . . .We should be generating enough money to enable us to research, buy and train the best players in the world . . .

'People who four years ago were telling me I was mad to think of building a hotel in a place like Stamford Bridge are now among the major investors, operators, developers and managers queuing up to try to get it off us. But they won't, because it's a goldmine. They know it, and we know it.

' . . . players are now attracted to Chelsea because they sense that the progress is real, that it is a club where ambition outstrips image . . .'

'Let's talk in hard cash – £2.5 million for Lebouef and £4.9 million for di Matteo, £4.5 million for Zola. That's £11.9 million, all paid for from the club's own resources, and that's after Petrescu, Phelan and Mark Hughes. We only ever had loans from Harding, and we've paid all those back.

'Then there's the ground development – the Southern complex is costing £13 million, the North Stand cost £12 million, and the new West Stand is a huge scheme which will cost £22 million. Harding gave us £5 million.'

Even though he had ruled Harding off limits, Bates himself could not manage not to mention the former vice-chairman. With Harding on the agenda, the chance to pose a question about Bates's relationship with him was taken. Readying myself for an eruption of volcanic proportions, expecting to be expelled from his office without notice, I looked down at my notes and stuttered into the question: 'Now some people say that if Chelsea win the Cup on Saturday, they'll be winning it for Matthew. How do you feel about that?'

Bates took it all in his stride. Calmly, he leaned back in the soft leather, smiled, and almost whispered his reply between the bristles of his beard. 'There was a turnstile operator, who'd worked here for 20 years, dropped dead three days ago. Perhaps we should be winning the Cup for him, or the 500 other Chelsea fans who die every season. I'm not getting into the thing that you're trying to get at. If we win the FA Cup, we will win it for every supporter, who's supported us through good times and bad. One individual's no more important than any other.'

'That's interesting, Mr Bates. I'll need to know the turnstile operator's name, can you tell me?' I asked. Bates did not know the man's name.

It was clear that Bates still smarted at Harding's popularity with the Chelsea fans, that he still bitterly resented the affrontery that Harding had shown in trying to unseat him from the club chairmanship. 'It wasn't the first time he'd done it. Did you hear what he did to Ted Benfield? Disgraceful . . .' But was it not a case of all being fair in business? Did not Bates himself manage to get rid of the previous chairman of Chelsea in a boardroom coup? Was it not the same? 'No, because I have moral scruples.'

Bates went on. 'Where was he in the hard times? Why did it take him so long to come forward if he loved Chelsea so much? He held us back, he held up the development of the ground. But in the end, we were going to get rid of him. We would have got him out sooner or later.' Bates said other things about Harding, airing sentiments which he had divulged to other journalists around that time. They were hurtful things. They were things I would never forget

The interview did not last very long after that. I had come expecting to get the chairman's views, Bates's insight, on a spectacularly successful season. You might have expected Bates to bask in the glories, enjoy the good times. Yet not too far beneath the surface, there was this brooding resentment that seemed to sour the whole thing. There was not much more I could say, or ask, after that outburst.

Though Bates must have been privy to business information denied to the bulk of Chelsea's lifelong fans, his view of Harding was in a minority on Cup final day. One open-top bus making its way from west to north London had a banner draped over the front – '1997 – Matthew's Final'. A sense of footballing history had offered up that slogan, harking back to the 1953 Wembley match dominated by Stanley Matthews. It was beginning to seem that, like Marilyn Monroe, John Lennon, even Bobby Moore, by dying young, Matthew Harding had ensured he would always be remembered at the peak of his popularity with his audience, the Chelsea supporters. His memorial would be how fondly people remembered him, and not the Chelsea Village balance sheet, regardless of how hard Bates tried to alter that.

The widespread hope was that the FA Cup final between Chelsea and Middlesbrough would be a 'classic', offering up free-flowing football, spectacular goals, a showpiece occasion. Wembley would be the icing on the Premiership season cake, showing off how English football had become accepted by the best players from around the world, the pitch a latterday Babel for voices from Italy, France, Brazil, Romania, Holland,

Norway and Denmark. The 116th FA Cup final would be an affirmation of the globalisation of English football.

The ingredients were there in the head-to-heads between the two sides' players – Zola and Juninho, Middlesbrough's midfield genius from Brazil; Vialli and Ravanelli, two European Champions' Cup-winners with Juventus 12 months earlier, now on opposing sides at Wembley; the midfield confrontation between Emerson and di Matteo.

Since he had seen his side trounced 5–0 at Stamford Bridge just over a year before, Bryan Robson at Middlesbrough had followed a similar course to Gullit, and recruited heavily from abroad. Now, the two teams would meet up again, this time at Wembley. Their paths to the final could not have been more different. For while Gullit's foreign legion had, in the main, settled in well, Middlesbrough's continentals had tended to drift. Branco, the Brazilian defender, had not lasted long on Teesside, and Emerson's frequent flyer points had broken all records at the turn of the year when he had shuttled backwards and forwards to Rio as if he was visiting the local cornershop.

Such obvious discontent had had a detrimental effect. Illness and injuries had deprived Middlesbrough of so many of their first-team squad for one league match before Christmas that they had simply not bothered turning up. The Premier League docked the club three league points, and the rest of their season was spent playing catch-up.

Middlesbrough had had their successes. They managed to make the final of the League Cup, for instance, but Martin O'Neill's Leicester had beaten them in a replay, which considering their plight in the league, was an extra fixture that Middlesbrough probably could have done without. And while their route to the FA Cup final had hardly been demanding – including the less-than-mighty Chester City and Hednesford Town, with Derby being their only Premiership opponents in their cup run – it had not been without its hiccups, as Chesterfield, the surprise semi-finalists, had come so close to winning their 3–3 thriller at Old Trafford.

By the time Middlesbrough arrived at Wembley in May though, their league fate was sealed – relegated and with doubts mounting about the immediate future at the club of their star international players, such as Juninho and Ravanelli. Both players had given their all in the final league fixtures, in a vain attempt to preserve Middlesbrough's Premiership status. Both had paid a price, Juninho in sheer physical and emotional exhaustion, Ravanelli with a hamstring injury which put his place in Middlesbrough's Wembley starting line-up in doubt. In truth, Middlesbrough's last four league matches had all been played with the ferocity, the freneticism, of cup-ties. Some observers wondered whether, at Wembley for Middlesbrough's first FA Cup final, their players would go back for another bucket-load of adrenalin and find that the well was empty.

Chelsea, too, had had their concerns over injuries. Steve Clarke had needed epidural pain relief on a back injury that had kept him off training for a week, and Gianfranco Zola was not used in either of Chelsea's last two league matches in an attempt to get an injured hamstring to heal. Zola had tweaked the back of his thigh when chasing a ball in the final minutes of a game at Wimbledon. He needed to be substituted again a week later, when playing for Italy. The concerns were obvious.

Less well known, but probably as vital to Chelsea's prospects, was the fitness of Dennis Wise. The party line, as announced at the club's official open day at Stamford Bridge two days before the final, was that the club captain was fit and ready for Wembley. Yet he had finished the game at Everton with a torn muscle in his stomach. In between being fitted for suits and leisurewear supplied by Yves St Laurent, recording the video for Chelsea' *Blue Day* Cup final song, starting the balls rolling for the National Lottery and being interviewed by BBC Grandstand, Wise missed the behind-closed-doors training session at Stamford Bridge, such was the pain he was suffering.

Would he be able to play on Saturday? 'I knew that it needed an operation,' Wise would admit later, 'but I had some pain killers and it was fine. It was worth the gamble to play in the Cup final.' While Wise's injury was Chelsea's Cup final secret, attention was instead focused on the health and well-being of Zola, viewed by many as the keystone of Chelsea's season.

After all, Zola had just been voted the Player of the Year, the first Chelsea player to win the honour in 50 years of the awards, and on the Thursday evening before the final, he was presented with the trophy by the first winner of the award, Sir Stanley Matthews. Yet such plaudits did not faze Zola. Not for him the great acclaim of a natural born thriller: Zola attributed his own success to hard work.

'I'm proud and honoured to be well thought of, but I try not to let it affect me too much. You're only as good as your last couple of matches. When I go out on to the pitch, I try to forget everything that's been said about me. I might have been given the best write-ups ever in the morning papers, but I always tell myself, "You've done nothing today – and today is what counts". That's the only way for me.

'You can never take anything for granted, I've always had to work hard for everything I wanted to achieve – and I still do,' he said. 'You don't just learn to play football, then think that's it, you're there. You have to keep at it all the time. You can't lie back and say, "Well, what I've got is a God-given talent, it'll always be there". You have to practice, you have to be dedicated and give 100 per cent all the time.'

Sitting next to Zola over dinner in the plush West End hotel that night was his father, Ignazio, on his first visit to England. The Football Writers' Association gala dinner was something of a surprise to Ignazio Zola, since his son had not told him about the Player of the Year awards – he had had to read about it in an Italian newspaper. 'That is typical of Franco – he is so modest,' said Zola senior. 'When I saw him I asked him why he had not told me and he simply shrugged his shoulders and said, "I forgot". He's always been the same.'

Getting interviews with the parents of players was about as close as most people could get to Chelsea during Cup final week, as the players' pool swung into operation. Supervised by an agent, Paul Stretford, anyone wanting to talk to or photograph any of the Chelsea squad had to contribute to a fund, which would be divided up between the players, with a proportion going to charity, after the match. Prices started from £12,000 for exclusives – not a bad fee for players who were already on mega-wages and bonuses.

There was no possible revenue avenue which Chelsea did not seem prepared to take. A deal was signed with the designer menswear label, Yves St Laurent, for the supply of leisurewear and the suits which the squad would wear on the day of the final, which contributed to the kitty. Other potential sources of income, however, were less lucrative. Wembley, when putting together the contents of the Cup final programme, were referred to Stretford's Pro-Active Sports Management consultancy and asked for a 'contribution' to the players' pool. Even FA Cup sponsors Littlewoods were asked for a £25,000 fee to ensure that the company would be 'branded' at the open day.

There was also controversy over the manner in which Chelsea had organised 'hospitality packages', charging £500 for a Cup final day champagne brunch at Stamford Bridge, a coach trip to Wembley and ticket for the game. The problem was that the Football Association had an exclusive deal with a commercial agency for the sale of hospitality packages for all its games at Wembley. In his last programme notes of the season, Bates went to some length to dismiss the press reports that he, an FA councillor, had broken FA rules. 'The facts are somewhat different,' Bates wrote. 'The FA sells hospitality packages for the FA Cup final, a few thousand of them. The buyers are those who don't want to travel by Underground and enjoy the pleasure of a Wembley hamburger. They are prepared to pay well for the privilege. The FA claims that the profits go to youth development and the grass roots. Mindful that the FA refused Crystal Palace the right to copy them, I cleared it with Jack Wiseman, the chairman of the FA match and grounds committee who agreed a special case for the finalists. We have sold 500 hospitality packages to our supporters and corporate partners who enjoy similar comfort on matchdays at Stamford Bridge. Like the FA we intend to devote any profits to our youth development, the grass roots. Sauce for the Gander!'

Yet still the controversy would not go away. 'I'm getting fed up with this,' Ken Bates said. 'I got FA permission to do it, and I am going to do it. I'm not cancelling it because I have done nothing wrong.

'Why should I spoil the enjoyment of a lot of Executive Club members? These Executive Club members enjoy this kind of match-day facility at every home game with Chelsea. Why shouldn't they be allowed to do the same this time? People are willing to pay and enjoy themselves.'

There were a couple of problems with Bates's version of events, however. The first was that no one at the FA could find any record of Chelsea being formally granted permission to offer hospitality packages in competition with the FA's own, official £800 deal. The second was that, before the storm broke in one Sunday newspaper, Chelsea had been selling its packages to anyone who called at the club wanting to buy their way to the front of the queue for Cup final tickets, regardless of whether they were Executive Club members or not.

There was even one queue-jumping scheme where the club offered to sell Cup final tickets to anyone willing to buy two £100 shares in the Chelsea Pitch Owners' scheme. The FA issued a simple, bland statement, 'Cup final tickets are not meant to be a vehicle for other money-raising schemes.'

For some, though, Bates's ticket schemes represented the only option to get to Wembley, short of dealing with a tout and running the risk of being caught with an illict ticket, or paying over the odds and spending two hours sitting on their hands while surrounded by Middlesbrough fans. After more than a quarter of a century, the FA Cup final was a match that no Chelsea supporter could miss.

Chapter 20

Stress can manifest itself in numerous ways in the human condition. There is pressure on a person when they are moving home. There is stress when someone has to take a penalty kick in a shoot-out to determine who goes through to a World Cup final. And then there is pressure when you are a Chelsea supporter and you are outside Wembley stadium on FA Cup final day, without a ticket for the game, with just minutes until kick-off.

Had someone like Gareth Southgate not had a ticket, they might have tried their best, but still missed the match. A Paul Ince-type might have turned his back, opting out of taking his 'shot' and walked back down Wembley Way, never to see the game. In footballing terms, my friend Kevin, outside the gates at Wembley without a ticket and able to hear *Abide With Me* being sung by 80,000 people on the inside, rose to the occasion marvellously, slotted the ball home perfectly, nervelessly. When Kevin bought his ticket, it was gone 2.45 p.m. on Saturday 17 May 1997.

We had planned to go to Wembley early on Cup final morning in a convoy of cars. There were my regular match-going friends Mike and Paul; there was Paul's brother Tom, who had flown back from Australia for this one game; there was Chris, a friend of Mike's from work, and his two kids who had seen every game in the Cup run; there was Paul's other brother, Dave, the man who works as a body double for Compo on *Last of the Summer Wine*, and who had driven down from the Yorkshire filming location in the early hours of that morning in order to add the 1997 Cup final to his experiences of seeing Chelsea at Wembley in 1967, 1970, 1972 and 1994. Then there was me. And there was Kevin.

We had met Kevin in the Pied Bull the night before the final. He was a friend of Tom's from Australia, who had decided to come home months before. Having been abroad at the start of the season, though, Kevin did not have a Chelsea season ticket or membership, and therefore had not been able to get a Cup final ticket through the regular channels. He had tried other avenues, and he had hoped. But the night before the game, he still did not have a ticket. He resolved to go up Wembley Way ahead of us, with a wad of notes in his pocket, determined not to give up, to give it one last try. We exchanged mobile telephone numbers, on the off-chance that if we found someone selling a 'spare', we might be able to call Kevin and tell him the location of this Eldorado. But we did not hold out much hope. The cars parked, we wandered through Wembley town centre, placing our bets on various combinations of a Chelsea victory (Dave, perhaps befitting a thespian, had gone a particularly dramatic combination: Chelsea to win 4–1, with Frank Sinclair to score the first goal. William Hill rated the chances of that happening at 750-to-1, which is why William Hill is one of the world's most successful bookmakers, and Dave is Compo's stunt double).

By one o'clock, as we gathered on the steps outside Wembley waiting for the gates to open, we had found no one selling 'spares', and Kevin, by now calling us every ten minutes, was sounding increasingly desperate and despondent. Any suggestion that he could have taken consolation from 'soaking up the atmosphere' would only ever come from someone who has never been in such a position – unless you can be *part* of the atmosphere before a Cup final, confident of eventually finding your way to your seat, you become oblivious to it. If anything, the high jinks and jolly japes before the game become an irritant, almost mocking the person who is there without a ticket as an outsider.

Eventually, we all took our seats. Kevin was left to fend for himself. What passes for pre-match 'entertainment' (in this instance, sky-divers, variously trailing blue or red smoke, skidding divots out of the preciously manicured pitch and then taking penalties, badly), barely served as a distraction as the clock ticked down. Cliff Richard missing the opening words of *Abide With Me* was embarrassing, although the Royal Marines unwittingly attracted the vocal accompaniment of 30,000 Chelsea fans as they struck up tunes from the Stamford Bridge songbook (though the bandsmen might have thought they were playing *Land of Hope and Glory*).

While all this was going on, the players were assembling just inside the door of their dressing room, ready to march out into the arena. Just before a steward knocked on the door of the Chelsea dressing room to call the team forward, Steve Clarke turned to Dennis Wise and said, 'This is it, this is the day we lay the ghost of the 1970s. It's about time people started talking about this team.'

Soon enough, the teams emerged from the tunnel at the opposite end of the stadium from the Chelsea contingent, at the red end. But even all that distance away, Ruud Gullit still led out the Chelsea team looking like a giant, looking as if he owned the place, cool and calm in his dark blue suit, the first foreign coach ever to lead a team to a Wembley Cup final. The Man had pride, you could see it. 'I know pressure is there all the time,' Gullit had said. 'Wherever I go, people are looking. They think you must perform as a footballer or a celebrity. There is admiration, jealousy, envy. You know it and must be sensitive to it. I keep my head the same because I believe in myself and my possibilities and my limits.' Gullit also believed in his team.

A secret training session at Stamford Bridge on the Thursday, watched over by Gullit and his mentor, Ted Troost, had convinced him of the system for the final. During the game, Gullit had made Andy Myers close-mark Zola, in an attempt to see if the young midfielder-defender might be able to cope with a similar job on the Saturday on Middlesbrough's star player, Juninho. Myers did enough to convince Gullit, who picked him among the 14 who would play or be substituted. To announce the team to his players, Gullit had walked into the room and just chalked the names on a blackboard in front of them. Myers would be a substitute, to be brought on if things were not going well and the threat of Juninho needed to be suppressed. Alongside Myers on the bench at Wembley would be Gianluca Vialli, who had pleaded with Gullit during the week – 'Please, give me just five minutes on the pitch in the Cup final –and reserve goalkeeper Kevin Hitchcock.

As Gullit marched across the Wembley turf towards the halfway line, the 11 men behind him who would start the game were Frode Grodas, the goalkeeper; Frank Sinclair, Frank Leboeuf, Steve Clarke and Scott Minto, who would form a defensive back four; four midfield players in Eddie Newton, Roberto di Matteo, Dan Petrescu and Dennis Wise, the captain who had taken pain killers in order to play; and up front would be Gianfranco Zola and Mark Hughes. The initial strategy was to use zonal marking with the midfielders to snuff out Juninho, while in order to confuse the 'Boro defence, Zola would play deeper than in previous games, leaving space for the midfielders to burst through and join Hughes in attack.

The selection meant heartbreak for some of Chelsea's squad though – Erland Johnsen, such a vital part of Chelsea's progress to the final, had played his last game for the club, and Craig Burley was omitted and could only watch from the sidelines. He, too, would never play for Chelsea again.

When the teams were lined up in front of the Royal Box before being presented to the guests of honour, the Middlesbrough half of the stadium began gesturing in such a manner that it looked like some sort of Nazi rally. In unison, around half the ground, they would thrust their right arms into the air and chant. Every one of the Middlesbrough fans was holding up three fingers, their rumbling chant being 'Three points', the target of their protest being Keith Wiseman, the FA chairman, who was leading the royal party up and down the lines of players, though you could see that the Duchess of Kent was made a little edgy by it all. It would do no good: Middlesbrough never did get the points back, all their appeals against relegation came to nothing.

Now, it was all about the 116th FA Cup. Middlesbrough and Chelsea were the last two teams left in a competition in which 574 had started, all the way back in another summer, another year, the previous August. Twelve rounds later, the 572nd match in the competition would decide it all, winner-takes-all. In more than a century of footballing history, eight clubs had enjoyed greater influence than most, winning the oldest soccer competition in the world more than 52 times. Yet none of these eight clubs – Manchester United, Tottenham, Aston Villa, Arsenal, Blackburn, Newcastle, Everton and Liverpool – had managed to make it past the fourth round in 1997. This time, the FA Cup could be won by Middlesbrough for the first time; it could be won by a relegated side for the first time; or it could be won at Wembley for the first time by Chelsea. As well as Gullit being the first foreign manager, the 1997 final was the most international ever, with players from ten countries in the sides. A Welshman, Chelsea's Mark Hughes, stood to collect his fourth winners' medal.

The bright sunshine, the colours and flags, balloons and ticker-tape, all contributed to an atmosphere of friendly rivalry, not dissimilar to that which had thrived at Wembley during Euro '96, which was recalled as the public address played *Three Lions* and the whole stadium joined in.

It was about this time that my friend Kevin made his decisive move. Outside, on the Wembley stadium concourse, he could hear the chants and cheers. He was so near, yet so far. Suddenly, he bounded over one of the barriers into the stadium, only to be caught immediately by a couple of waiting policemen, who exercised their discretion by only feeling his collar in order to expel him through the nearest exit gate, rather than press any charges. Yet as they did so, another Chelsea fan, watching nearby, went after Kevin and called to him through the grille. 'I've got a spare ticket if you want it,' the good Samaritan said.

'How much?' Kevin asked.

'It's a 30 quid ticket,' said the man on the inside.

'Yeah, but how much do you want for it?'

'Thirty quid.' He could not believe his luck. Kevin's patience and boldness had, at the last, been rewarded. The deal done, he now entered Wembley stadium through a proper turnstile, and took to his seat.

Would Chelsea's 26 years of hurt finally come to an end? The Chelsea fans were as determined as Steve Clarke that it would. The presentations and the National Anthem over, the Chelsea supporters struck up their theme song – *Ten Men Went to Mow* – its relevance to football, even to Chelsea, inexplicable, but as closely associated with them as *My Way* is with Sinatra. As the game kicked off, everyone wearing blue that day had associated themselves with the song, as they rose as one man to sing the last chorus. Just as they were taking their seats again, the whole Chelsea end was propelled back on its feet, yelling in delight and disbelief as Roberto di Matteo sent the ball screaming over the head of Ben Roberts and into the Middlesbrough goal.

Barely 42 seconds had passed in the match when the referee, Steven Lodge, blew his whistle to signal the goal and the need for a re-start. It was the fastest Cup final goal at Wembley, the fastest Cup final goal this century. Indeed, the only time anyone had scored a quicker goal in the FA Cup final was in 1895, when Bob Chatt hit the net after 40 seconds for Villa against West Bromwich Albion, although in those days, the referees were still using sun dials for their time-keeping.

The move that had led to the goal had been clean, simple and swift. Dennis Wise won the ball quickly, and fed it to di Matteo in the middle and in his own half. The Italian midfielder then went on and on. No Middlesbrough players attempted to close him down in midfield, while up ahead of him, Mark Hughes set off on a run that opened up the Middlesbrough defence like Moses and the Red Sea. As Hignett and Emerson lazily lumbered towards di Matteo, his socks pulled up over his knees, he swung his right leg and sent the ball flying goalwards from 30 yards out.

Earlier in the season, the Italian had scored a couple of screamers – once against 'Boro in the league at Stamford Bridge, and memorably at Tottenham, too. But lately, he had been more reluctant to shoot from afar. As the ball curved downwards near the Middlesbrough goal, closing in on the bar, there were several in the Chelsea crowd who suffered flashbacks three years, to the time in the first-half of the final against Manchester United when Gavin Peacock could have put Chelsea ahead but for the cross-bar. This time, though, the bar seemed to help the ball into the goal. For the first time in FA Cup history, Chelsea were in front in the final. As the 'Boro players trudged back to their positions for the re-start, it seemed unlikely that this was a lead that Chelsea might ever yield.

It had been a month since the semi-final, and the build-up to the game at Wembley had gathered momentum ever since, the hopes and fears for the match having been discussed endlessly in pubs up and down the land. And now, after 43 seconds, all discussion seemed to have been rendered pointless. Yet, this was Chelsea. The Chelsea of old might have squandered the one-goal lead, perhaps making a foolish mistake, conceding a penalty, even, as had happened three years earlier when the initiative was handed to Manchester United. But the Chelsea of Ruud Gullit would prove itself to be different. The players would have had Gullit's own words ringing in their minds: 'I make mistakes. But I don't make the same mistakes all the time. I make a lot of mistakes and I hope that I learn from them. I give everyone a chance to make mistakes, but I don't expect them to make the same mistakes all the time. When they do that, then I get angry with the players.' Chelsea, a side which had conceded so many late goals in the league season that it had cost them a chance of the championship, never mind a place in Europe, would not make that mistake again at Wembley.

In fact, Chelsea nearly extended their lead in the next ten minutes, as first Minto – playing his last and possibly best game for Chelsea – and then Petrescu went close. As the game drew on, so Middlesbrough looked increasingly disjointed, disaffected, even. Ravanelli, who had been hamstrung in recent weeks, gambled by declaring himself fit to play, yet within 20 minutes had to leave the field. Mustoe, too, had to be substituted before the half-hour. Middlesbrough were in disarray. The difference between the sides was glaringly clear: while Bryan Robson had fielded a fine collection of international players at Wembley, Ruud Gullit fielded a *team*. And this was very much a team game.

For while Zola, in his withdrawn role, hardly figured in the first-half, it did not seem to matter. Di Matteo was masterful in midfield, and only Pearson, it seemed, could prevent Hughes from running amok. Juninho, meanwhile, ran himself weary in the clammy heat, yet constantly found his path blocked by Wise, Newton or Petrescu. Once, when he did break through, Juninho was brought down by di Matteo, but since the Italian was not the last line of defence, he was shown only a yellow card.

Despite Chelsea's dominance, Festa managed to get the ball in the back of the Londoners' goal, although the linesman's flag had been raised for offside some time before. It was a warning, though, which found Gullit on his feet, uncharacteristically yelling at his players. 'They were playing the ball backwards. I wanted them to control the game by going forwards. It was a matter of attitude,' Gullit said. When he sat down on the bench again, Toost, his trusted friend, was there at his side, offering advice, calming things down.

The second half was, in many ways, disappointingly disjointed. Ravanelli's replacement, Mikkel Beck, had obviously never bothered to learn the offside rule, as he constantly caused the game to be stopped and re-started. Chelsea, it seemed, could comfortably deal with anything 'Boro had to offer, their one shot on target being well saved by Grodas. As the game wore on, so Zola's influence became more noticeable. He even produced one run, beating four players and shooting at the near post, which, had he succeeded, might have surpassed all his other scoring efforts of the season. As it was, in this game Zola would only provide the telling final pass for a goal. As if to prove Chelsea's multi-national team work, their Cup final victory would be secured by goals from one Italian international and a Hammersmith boy who had worked his way through from the youth team.

There were less than ten minutes of the match remaining. Newton brought the ball out from his own half and passed the ball to Petrescu wide on the right, but kept his run going. Petrescu sent a cross over to the far post, where Zola had to leap athletically to get the outside of his boot on to the ball and send it back towards the six-yard box, where Newton had arrived, breathless but still able to hit the ball home against the wrong-footed Middlesbrough defence. End of argument.

With the game won, Gullit made his only substitution of the match, bringing off Zola for Vialli, a gesture of reconciliation which somehow signalled that the match, the season, could now end.

Having gone up the steps to the Royal Box to collect the trophy and their medals, Wise led his side on the longest lap of honour after a Wembley final, the players, backroom staff and even Ken Bates savouring every moment for nearly an hour in the arena. *Blue Day*, Chelsea's new song, was sung lustily. But for many, it was when it seemed that the entire stadium was singing *Blue Is The Colour* that the tears started to flow: the old song, for so long the club's anthem, had been recorded in 1972, just before Chelsea lost in that year's League Cup final. It had taken all this time for the old song to be sung so well, so loud, so proud after a great victory. One wondered whether now, like the fading posters of the team of the 1970s, the scratchy old 45 could also be put away for the last time, a treasure of times past. Certainly, Steve Clarke thought so.

Clarke wanted the Chelsea team of 1997 to be talked of for years to come. 'It was great for the guys who did so well for the club in 1970,' Clarke said after he had put in an outstanding performance at the heart of the defence which was a big factor in Chelsea's dominance of the match, 'but it had gone on far too long. It became like a huge weight on our shoulders, but we've finally laid the ghost once and for all. When I came here ten years ago, we were just playing at being a big club. The change has happened quickly this season.

'Now, with the quality we've got in the team, it's important that we go on from here to win things. We don't want to wait another 27 years for our next trophy.'

Wise, Clarke's room-mate and buddy who had also played such an important role in the Wembley success, was of like mind. 'We have messed up so many times, got close and then failed. We had to get over that first hurdle and this is it.' As he waited to collect his fourth FA Cup-winner's medal, Mark Hughes was already looking forward to even more honours. 'We have to grab this now, we must not let the opportunity go. Chelsea are set up to be a major club. Last season, we were a good side, not a great one. The players Ruud brought in added the quality we needed.

'The win was so important – it broke through a barrier. When United won their first championship for a long time, you could sense the relief. That title win was the catalyst for everything that has happened since, and Chelsea can do the same.'

The day before the final, Mark Hughes had signed an extension to his contract, such was his confidence that he was with a winning club. Gullit, too, is a natural-born winner, even if this time he needed a prod to go up the Wembley steps to collect the medal he deserved as the winning manager. Could Gullit lead his side to the title? 'I certainly want to do better. I'm a little bit more proud as a coach than maybe I have been as a player, because I had a hand in the tactics that shaped the team. I'm really proud of this day. I feel I've grown up as a person.'

The celebrations would go on well into the night. Chelsea's victory banquet was to be at the Waldorf in London's Aldwych, where the guest of honour was Pele, and where Gullit announced to the world that his girlfriend, Estelle, was pregnant. A few miles to the west, the King's Road was blocked as Chelsea revellers danced and sang, drank and cheered outside the pubs and restaurants on a two-mile stretch of central London. There was not just a mood of jubilation, there was a sense of liberation, as if these Chelsea fans had been the citizens of some long-besieged city, and that, finally, a relief column had arrived on the horizon. Gullit had taught his team, and now his fans, what it feels like to be winners.

As if he could not bring himself to leave the stage of his first great success as a coach, it was Gullit who had been the last to leave the pitch at Wembley that afternoon, still holding the precious silverware. He took the FA Cup with him into the Chelsea dressing room, where the champagne had already been flowing for some time. In one corner, loudly, Mark Hughes had taken the liberty of sending a crate of beer to the 'Boro dressing room, 'We won't need it,' he announced with confidence, 'and they won't be drinking champagne.'

As Gullit entered the room, a cheer went up as Wise shouted, 'Here's the yeti.' His manager held the cup aloft and then launched it towards his players, who caught it safely. Chelsea, at last, had their hands on a trophy, and they were not going to let it slip anymore. Gullit had taught them what it is like to be winners, and like him, they had developed an appetite for more.

Chelsea's 1996–97 Season

FA PREMIERSHIP

Date	Opposition	H/A	Result	F – A	(HT)	Attendance	Chelsea Goal Scorers
Aug 18	Southampton	A	D	0 – 0	(0–0)	15,106	–
Aug 21	Middlesbrough	H	W	1 – 0	(0–0)	28,272	Di Matteo
Aug 24	Coventry	H	W	2 – 0	(1–0)	25,024	Leboeuf, Vialli
Sep 3	Arsenal	A	D	3 – 3	(2–1)	38,132	Leboeuf, Vialli, Wise
Sep 7	Sheff Wed	A	W	2 – 0	(1–0)	30,983	Burley, Myers
Sep 15	Aston Villa	H	D	1 – 1	(1–1)	27,729	Leboeuf
Sep 21	Liverpool	A	L	1 – 5	(0–3)	40,739	Leboeuf
Sep 28	Nottm Forest	H	D	1 – 1	(0–0)	27,673	Vialli
Oct 12	Leicester	A	W	3 – 1	(0–1)	20,766	Vialli, di Matteo, M. Hughes
Oct 19	Wimbledon	H	L	2 – 4	(1–2)	28,002	Minto, Vialli(pen)
Oct 26	Tottenham	H	W	3 – 1	(1–1)	28,373	Gullit, Lee (pen), di Matteo
Nov 2	Man Utd	A	W	2 – 1	(1–0)	55,198	Duberry, Vialli
Nov 18	Blackburn	A	D	1 – 1	(0–0)	27,229	Petrescu
Nov 23	Newcastle	H	D	1 – 1	(1–1)	28,401	Vialli
Dec 1	Leeds	A	L	0 – 2	(0–2)	32,671	
Dec 7	Everton	H	D	2 – 2	(1–2)	28,418	Zola, Vialli
Dec 15	Sunderland	A	L	0 – 3	(0–1)	19,683	
Dec 21	West Ham	H	W	3 – 1	(3–1)	28,315	M. Hughes(2), Zola
Dec 26	Aston Villa	A	W	2 – 0	(2–0)	39,339	Zola(2)
Dec 28	Sheff Wed	H	D	2 – 2	(2–2)	27,467	Zola, M. Hughes
Jan 1	Liverpool	H	W	1 – 0	(1–0)	28,329	di Matteo
Jan 11	Nottm Forest	A	L	0 – 2	(0–1)	28,358	

205

Jan 18	Derby	H	W	3 – 1	(2–1)	28,293	Wise, Leboeuf, P Hughes
Feb 1	Tottenham	A	W	2 – 1	(1–0)	33,027	Cambell o.g., di Matteo
Feb 22	Man Utd	H	D	1 – 1	(1–0)	28,336	Zola
Mar 1	Derby	A	L	2 – 3	(1–0)	18,039	Minto, Leboeuf
Mar 5	Blackburn	H	D	1 – 1	(0–0)	25,784	Minto
Mar 12	West Ham	A	L	2 – 3	(1–0)	24,502	Vialli, M. Hughes
Mar 16	Sunderland	H	W	6 – 2	(2–0)	24,027	Zola, Sinclair, Petrescu, M Hughes(2), di Matteo
Mar 19	Southampton	H	W	1 – 0	(1–0)	28,079	Zola
Mar 22	Middlesbrough	A	L	0 – 1	(0–0)	29,811	
Apr 5	Arsenal	H	L	0 – 3	(0–1)	28,182	
Apr 9	Coventry	A	L	1 – 3	(1–0)	19,917	P Hughes
Apr 16	Newcastle	A	L	1 – 3	(0–3)	36,320	Burley
Apr 19	Leicester	H	W	2 – 1	(1–0)	27,723	Minto, M Hughes
Apr 22	Wimbledon	A	W	0 – 1	(1–0)	14,601	Petrescu
May 3	Leeds	H	D	0 – 0	(0–0)	28,277	
May 11	Everton	A	W	2 – 1	(2–0)	38,321	Wise, di Matteo

FA CUP

Round	Date	Opposition	H/A	F – A	Attendance	Chelsea Scorers
3rd round	4 Jan	WBA	H	3 – 0	27,446	Wise, Burley, Zola
4th round	26 Jan	Liverpool	H	4 – 2	27,950	M. Hughes, Zola, Vialli(2)
5th round	15 Feb	Leicester	A	2 – 2	19,125	di Matteo, M Hughes
5th replay	26 Feb	Leicester	H	1 – 0	26,053	Leboeuf
6th round	9 Mar	Portsmouth	A	4 – 1	15,701	M. Hughes, Wise(2), Zola
Semi–Final	13 Apr	Wimbledon	* *Highbury	3 – 0	32,674	M. Hughes(2), Zola
Final	17 May	Middlesbrough	** **Wembley	2 – 0	79,160	di Matteo, Newton

COCA–COLA CUP

Round	Date	Opposition	H/A	F – A	Attendance	Chelsea Scorers
2nd rnd, 1st leg	18 Sep	Blackpool	H	4 – 1	9,666	Morris, Petrescu, M. Hughes, Spencer
2nd rnd, 2nd leg	25 Sep	Blackpool	H	1 – 3	11,732	Spencer
3rd rnd	22 Oct	Bolton	A	1 – 2	16,867	Minto